The New Project Management

J. Davidson Frame

—ⵔ— The New Project Management

Second Edition

Tools for an Age of Rapid Change, Complexity, and Other Business Realities

JOSSEY-BASS
A Wiley Company
www.josseybass.com

Published by

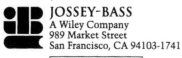
JOSSEY-BASS
A Wiley Company
989 Market Street
San Francisco, CA 94103-1741

www.josseybass.com

Jossey-Bass books and products are available through most bookstores. To contact Jossey-Bass directly, call (888) 378-2537, fax to (800) 605-2665, or visit our website at www.josseybass.com.

Substantial discounts on bulk quantities of Jossey-Bass books are available to corporations, professional associations, and other organizations. For details and discount information, contact the special sales department at Jossey-Bass.

We at Jossey-Bass strive to use the most environmentally sensitive paper stocks available to us. Our publications are printed on acid-free recycled stock whenever possible, and our paper always meets or exceeds minimum GPO and EPA requirements.

Jossey-Bass also publishes its books in a variety of electronic formats. Some content that appears in print may not be available in electronic books.

Library of Congress Cataloging-in-Publication Data

Frame, J. Davidson.
   The new project management : tools for an age of rapid change,
complexity, and other business realities / by J. Davidson
Frame.—2nd ed.
      p. cm.—(The Jossey-Bass business & management series)
   Includes bibliographical references and index.
   ISBN 0-7879-5892-1
   1. Project management. 2. Reengineering (Management)
I. Title. II. Series.
HD69.P75 F73   2002
658.4'04—dc21

2002001909

SECOND EDITION
HB Printing   10 9 8 7 6 5 4 3 2 1

The Jossey-Bass

Business & Management Series

⟶ᴠᴠ⟶ Contents

~~ Preface

The New Project Management was written for men and women working in a broad range of fields who find themselves struggling to manage projects in a chaotic world. Whether undertaking conventional projects in construction or the defense industry or pursuing Information Age projects in such areas as information systems, finance, research and development, marketing, pharmaceuticals, or insurance, many of these men and women have discovered that conventional wisdom about project management is only marginally relevant to them in these turbulent times. They know that there is more to project management than mastering scheduling techniques (such as PERT), budgeting techniques (such as S-curves), or resource allocation techniques (such as resource histograms).

I wrote this book to explore concepts and techniques that are not generally covered in conventional project management texts. When I began, the book carried the working title *Beyond PERT.* I came up with that title in a frivolous moment. It has long bothered me that project management is so closely associated with a set of standard tools developed decades ago—PERT/CPM networks go back as far as 1957, and Gantt charts were first used during World War I! It has reached the point that when people ask, "Do you know project management?" what they mean is "Do you know how to calculate the critical path on a PERT chart?" When I reflect on my own project management experiences, I sense that what is taught in conventional project management texts played a fairly small role in determining whether my projects succeeded or failed.

The New Project Management focuses on the key concerns project professionals face today. These men and women operate in an environment dominated by chaos and uncertainty. Their jobs are undergoing tremendous transformation as their employers undertake radical efforts at corporate reengineering. They can no longer function as mere *implementers* of projects but must assume the role of *initiators*. To help project managers function effectively in the new environment, this book examines such key issues as ensuring customer satisfaction, managing complexity, accelerating schedules, coping with empowerment, managing contractors, managing managers, and dealing with risk. Readers interested in acquiring more traditional project management insights can get these from a large number of basic project management books, including my own *Managing Projects in Organizations* (1995). Readers who already possess a copy of that book should view *The New Project Management* as a companion piece that fleshes out some of the ideas hinted at in the first work.

The content of this book is strongly influenced by recent experiences I have had. Since *Managing Projects in Organizations* was first published, three experiences have dramatically affected my outlook on project management. One is the immense increase in the volume of training and consulting I have conducted in recent years. Since 1987, I have trained some thirty thousand managers throughout the world on project management topics. Some of this training has occurred in large corporations, such as AT&T, Morgan Stanley, and Sprint; some in highly dynamic mid-sized companies, such as Freddie Mac, Fannie Mae, SITA, and CUNA Mutual; and some in government agencies, such as the Defense Information Systems Agency, the Internal Revenue Service, the Smithsonian's National Museum of American History, the Beijing Institute of Chemical Engineering Management, and the China State Shipbuilding Corporation.

The point is that I have had an opportunity to meet large numbers of people working on projects in a wide range of environments. Some of them are in growing industries; others, in declining industries. Some build highways; others write software; still others process mortgages. To many of these people, downsizing, organizational flattening, outsourcing, and empowerment are not abstract concepts but facts of life. From these people I learned about organizational experiments with total quality management, self-managed teams, time-boxed scheduling, economic value added (EVA), and reengineering, long before they were discussed in the press and grew into fads. Most of the ideas I deal with in this book were stimulated by my interaction with these diligent, earnest project workers.

A second experience that has colored my outlook on project management has been my volunteer work with the Project Management Institute (PMI), the world's largest society of project management professionals (more than eighty-five thousand members in 2002). As director of certification at PMI from 1990 to 1996 and PMI's director of educational service from 1996 to 1998, I dealt with issues of project management competence on a daily basis. I came to appreciate the work of scores of PMI members who over a number of years have devised and revised *A Guide to the Project Management Body of Knowledge* (PMI, 2000), a document that is the acknowledged world standard of project management knowledge. The *PMBOK Guide,* as it is known, attempts to define the core competencies of effective project professionals. It identifies nine areas of project management competence. The first four are obvious: project management professionals should be competent in the areas of scope management, time management, cost management, and human resource management. No surprises here.

The second five areas of competence—risk management, quality management, procurement management, communication management, and integration management—are more surprising. They reveal that project management has moved beyond its traditional concern with the famous triple constraints of time, budget, and specifications and that the skills and insights required of effective project personnel are far broader today than in the past. Personnel must know how to assess risk, produce quality goods and services, operate in a contracting environment, and communicate competently with their managers, customers, vendors, and staff. Any project management text that purports to be relevant to the needs of project workers should give serious treatment to these new additions to project management wisdom. For more information on project management competence at the level of individuals, teams, and organizations, see my book *Project Management Competence* (1999).

The third recent experience that has colored my outlook on project management has been my extensive exposure to project management practices throughout the world. Over the last few years, I have had a chance to spend about a month a year engaged in project management work in Australia and a month a year in China. Beyond this, I have had a chance to work in Singapore, Taiwan, Hong Kong, South Korea, New Zealand, South Africa, India, Argentina, Brazil, Canada, France, Germany, and England. I have also worked closely with project managers from Russia, Colombia, Mexico, the Netherlands, Japan, Denmark, New Zealand, Malaysia, Ghana, Nigeria, Bangladesh, India, and Egypt. I have seen firsthand that project managers worldwide experience identical challenges. My travels have confirmed my belief that the majority of the problems faced by project staff are universal and totally predictable.

AUDIENCE

A number of audiences will find this book useful. Certainly individual managers who want to acquire knowledge of current key practices not generally treated in standard project management texts will find the book edifying. They can quickly get up to speed on important topics—such as configuration management, critical chain scheduling, integrated cost and schedule control, contracting principles, project metrics, and risk management—that are normally discussed only in hard-to-find and hard-to-comprehend literature.

Project management trainers interested in teaching advanced topics will also find the book useful. The material contained in it can serve as the core of a course that goes beyond teaching the basics of budgeting and scheduling. The book will also work well in university-level project management courses. It can be used to supplement standard texts or as a stand-alone text in a second-level course.

OVERVIEW

The book's first chapter describes the business environment in which project workers currently function. It demonstrates that the traditional approach to managing projects does not work effectively in the new environment, which is characterized by complexity, chaos, and uncertainty. It describes what new project managers should be like if they want to survive and thrive in such a messy environment.

The book is then organized into two parts. Part One deals with new project management realities. It contains five chapters. Chapter Two points out that an important characteristic of today's business world is *complexity*. People face a bewildering array of options even when making the simplest decisions. The systems they work with lie beyond the ken of even the smartest individuals. Even when people achieve mastery of some aspects of their work, rapid change makes their hard-earned knowledge obsolete. The chapter presents several ways to cope with project complexity.

Chapter Three deals with the constancy of change. Technology is changing, people are changing, budgets are changing, resource scarcities suddenly appear, new regulations invalidate old practices overnight, and so on. Project personnel must become, in the words of Rosabeth Moss Kanter (1983), *change masters*. They should develop an appreciation of the inevitability of change. They must learn when to resist it (for example, through configuration management) and when to go with the flow (for example, through rapid prototyping).

Chapter Four deals with one of the hottest of the hot buttons in today's project management: the management of risk. It describes the role that risk plays in projects and outlines a risk management process that can be employed. It also highlights some risk management techniques, such as Monte Carlo simulation, that are being used with increasing frequency and success.

Chapter Five examines the enormously important role that customers now play in project management. It addresses the important issue of learning how to identify exactly who the customers are. It offers strategies for minimizing problems in dealing with customers and maximizing customer satisfaction (for example, through customer partnering arrangements).

Chapter Six focuses on bridging the gap between business customers whose needs must be satisfied and the technical team charged with delivering technical solutions to address these needs. The problem is that business people seldom understand technology and technical team members have little understanding of the business.

Part Two reviews the new project management skill sets. Chapter Seven looks at people management skills that project personnel should develop. In particular, it deals with the development of the political skills that project professionals need to survive and thrive in a typical project environment. It also looks at techniques for building authority and managing managers.

Chapter Eight offers practical advice on how to build team spirit in the matrix environment. Matrix management entails the employment of borrowed human resources. The problem with this is that project workers find they have little or no authority in their dealings with these people. The chapter includes a checklist of things to do to build team spirit even when the resources are borrowed.

Chapter Nine looks at decision making on projects. Rational decision making is fundamentally a process of creating priorities. This chapter reviews various techniques for making rational decisions, ranging from benefit-cost analysis to the murder board. These techniques have particular relevance for the selection of projects. They can also be used to select project personnel and vendors.

Chapter Ten focuses on improving the quality of estimates made by project staff in the areas of costs, schedules, and resource requirements. Too often schedule slippages and cost overruns are not caused by poor project execution but are rather the consequences of excessively optimistic time and cost estimates made at the outset. This chapter presents techniques for improving the quality of project estimates, thereby lowering the likelihood of schedule slippages and cost overruns.

Chapter Eleven takes a look at two of the hottest scheduling techniques around: time-boxed scheduling and critical chain scheduling. By adopting these techniques, most projects will be able to deliver their products faster than ever.

Chapter Twelve examines a rapidly growing phenomenon in today's business environment. Increasingly, work is being handled by outsiders— contractors over whom the project organization has marginal authority. The chapter examines some principles of contracting as they relate to projects and offers suggestions for operating effectively in an outsource environment.

Chapter Thirteen draws attention to the fact that effective project control requires simultaneous review of both cost and schedule performance. A simple graphical approach to integrated cost and schedule control is provided, followed by a treatment of the sophisticated earned-value cost-accounting technique. The earned-value methodology is rightfully one of the major growth areas of contemporary project management.

Chapter Fourteen examines how accountability can be increased on projects. A major shortcoming of managing with borrowed resources is that accountability becomes diffuse. The constructive use of evaluation allows for the sharpening of accountability. This chapter discusses some of the pitfalls inherent in evaluation and describes an example of a user-friendly evaluation methodology—IBM's structured walk-through.

For evaluation to be effective, organizations must develop meaningful metrics of performance. Chapter Fifteen describes how this can be done.

Chapter Sixteen offers conclusions about the evolving direction of project management and changes in the project manager's role.

Finally, Chapter Seventeen reviews how the establishment and maintenance of project support offices can help organizations improve their project efforts dramatically. These offices remove much of the administrative burden from the shoulders of project team members. In addition, they provide organizations with the project management expertise they need to sustain their growing project efforts.

ACKNOWLEDGMENTS

This second edition of *The New Project Management* contains three new chapters: Chapter Six on bridging the business-technology gap when defining requirements, Chapter Eleven on time-boxed scheduling and critical chain scheduling, and Chapter Sixteen on establishing and maintaining a project support office. These chapters would not have been written without substantial input from colleagues at Crédit Suisse First Boston and Morgan Stanley.

First, I need to thank the Management Services folks at Pershing, the IT arm of Crédit Suisse First Boston. In particular, the head of Management Services, Bill Jacobs, provided me with valuable leads and insights that enabled me to explore advances in time-boxed scheduling and bridging the business-technology gap. Bill and his team continually reviewed my work in these areas and helped me solidify my thinking. They are obsessed with driving project management into the organization, and their efforts are paying off with major improvements in project management processes.

I also need to thank the program management group at Morgan Stanley, especially the head of the program management initiative, Thomas Tarnow. The project office operation the group has established at Morgan Stanley is the exemplar of how to do things right. Although I have been working in the project office area since the mid-1990s, my two years' experience with the Morgan Stanley team gave me firsthand evidence that smart, dedicated people working in a project support office can make an enormous difference in helping organizations run large numbers of projects effectively.

Over the past two years, I have been fortunate to work with the project management leaders at Westinghouse's Washington Government Services Group (WGSG), particularly Richard Humphrey and Gerald Ostrander. A major theme of this book is that a characteristic of the new project management is the need to manage complexity. In its projects to clean up nuclear waste, WGSG deals with levels of complexity that tax the imagination of even experienced project workers. My work with WGSG has helped me refine my thinking on the role of complexity in project management.

I received great support from Julianna Gustafson, my editor at Jossey-Bass. People who have not written a book probably have difficulty understanding the importance of having a good editor. Good editors are a writer's dream. Thank you, Julianna, for your patience and your help.

I must also thank my immediate family, because they bore the brunt of my antisocial behavior as I tried to meet publisher deadlines. My wife, Yanping, provided a great sounding board to test out ideas. Daughter Lele maintained a good sense of humor even when I was scowling.

Finally, I would like to continue the tradition of thanking my daughter Katherine Adele Frame for being such a great person. She is twenty-one now and finishing her studies at Barnard College. When I began acknowledging my debt to her in my books, she was just two years old. I suppose in future acknowledgments, I had better stop mentioning her age. She's not a kid anymore.

Arlington, Virginia   J. Davidson Frame
March 2002

—⁓— **The Author**

J. DAVIDSON FRAME is academic dean at the University of Management and Technology (www.umtweb.edu), where he runs graduate programs in project management. Prior to joining the UMT faculty in 1998, he was on the faculty of the George Washington University, where he established the university's project management program and served as chairman of the Management Science Department and director of the Program on Science, Technology, and Innovation. Since 1990, he has also served as director of the Project Management Certification Program and director of Educational Services at the Project Management Institute. Before entering academia, he was vice president of Computer Horizons, Inc., and manager of its Washington office. While there, he managed more than two dozen Information Age projects. Since 1983, he has conducted project management seminars throughout the United States and abroad. About thirty thousand project professionals have attended these seminars.

Frame earned his bachelor of arts degree (1967) in history at the College of Wooster and his master of arts (1969) and doctor of philosophy degrees (1976) in international relations at the American University, focusing primarily on econometrics and economic development. In recent years, Frame's research has concentrated on the effective specification of needs and requirements. He has written more than forty articles and five books, including *Project Management Competence* (Jossey-Bass, 1999) and *Managing Projects in Organizations* (second edition, Jossey-Bass, 1995).

To Katherine and Lele

The New Project Management

CHAPTER ONE

The New Business Environment and the Need for a New Project Management

P eople have been conducting projects for millennia. The pyramids, the Great Wall of China, and the Roman aqueducts bear witness to the sophistication of some of these projects. For the most part, the method of carrying them out entailed more art than science. It was not until recent times that we began to approach the project management effort systematically and to tip the scales in favor of science over art.

Project management as it is practiced today came into being in the post–World War II era. It was the product of a number of forces at work at the time. The development of operations research brought with it the realization that decision tools could be fashioned to allow humans to conduct their affairs in optimal ways. The growth of systems analysis led to an appreciation of the interconnectedness of events and the inherent complexity of modern systems. Its focus on flowcharts also presaged PERT/CPM scheduling techniques. The Cold War led to the support of mammoth projects of unprecedented size and complexity, projects that needed new management tools if they were to be carried out effectively. The burgeoning global economy, with its emphasis on large infrastructure projects, led to a similar search for new management tools.

Together these forces shaped project management for the next four decades. The principal instigators of developments in project management during that time were people in the construction and defense industries. They tended to work on large, complex, capital-intensive projects. They held an engineering perspective and gave project management the look and feel of an engineering discipline. Project management knowledge focused on core skills in the areas of budgeting, scheduling, and resource allocation. To a large extent, project management became inextricably linked to its key tools, such as Gantt charts, scheduling networks, and resource-loading charts.

THE NEW BUSINESS ENVIRONMENT

New forces have arisen on the world scene in recent times. During the 1980s there was a major realigning of global business forces. The economic position of the Pacific Rim countries strengthened dramatically. They became fearsome competitors and challenged the hegemony of the traditional Western players. Their competitiveness was not simply based on their traditional advantage of cheap labor. It was also rooted in their ability to embed high levels of quality into their products. To put it simply, they produced cheaper and better products than their Western counterparts.

During that time, global markets and production capabilities opened up, and the concept of national economies began to wane. Strange business anomalies arose, such as the discovery that Honda cars manufactured in the United States had more American-made parts than Chrysler products or that telephone products produced by Northern Telecom, a Canadian company, had more U.S.-made content than telephones manufactured by Lucent Technologies, an American company.

The collapse of communism added to the globalization of the world economy. Suddenly, major new markets of more than three hundred million people were opened to world business transactions. Global competition increased owing to the fact that the formerly communist countries of eastern Europe possessed large quantities of low-wage workers who were highly skilled and well educated. Globalization and competition received a further boost in western Europe with the creation of the European Union and the acceptance of a single currency by its members.

The realignment of global business forces was accompanied by advances in technology that had enormous impact on how business is done. Most significant were advances in telecommunications and computing and the intersection of these two technologies in the Internet. With the Internet, national boundaries became nearly irrelevant in the business arena: owners of a small consulting practice in Buenos Aires had access to the same information channels as giant consulting practices, such as Accenture and Booz Allen Hamilton. Project teams suddenly became heavily *virtual,* with the project manager located in Paris, a sales component in Atlanta, a design group in San Diego, and manufacturing experts in Singapore.

This new business environment forced corporations to rethink how they should do business. Competition became the new watchword. For companies to be competitive, they had to reduce their costs, accelerate product development, and focus on satisfying their customers. A key to customer satisfaction lay in quality improvements and an increased emphasis on customer service.

The look of companies changed dramatically at this time. To be competitive, they instituted radical transformations in their modes of operation. Such transformations are still being undertaken under the rubric of "business process reengineering." They include such actions as downsizing, flattening, employing team-based solutions, empowering employees, adopting e-commerce perspectives, and outsourcing.

Downsizing

For companies to be competitive, they must be lean and mean. Large payrolls, which once reflected the power and success of corporations, have now become a liability. Consequently, the 1980s and 1990s experienced major shrinkages in the workforces of big companies. New hiring was frozen, early retirements were encouraged, entire operations were shut down, and personnel were selectively fired. Middle managers became particularly vulnerable, since they were perceived to add little value to operations and to contribute to the swelling of bureaucracy.

Flattening

In order to be quick on their feet, companies began restructuring their workforces to eliminate the many levels of bureaucracy that separate the CEO from the floor sweeper. In such flattened organizations, chains of command often disappear. Increasingly, employees find themselves dealing less with clearly defined bosses and subordinates and more with colleagues over whom they have no direct control. Decisions typically have to be achieved through consensus rather than by fiat.

Employing Team-Based Solutions

Owing to the increased complexity of business problems and the need for speed, enterprises began adopting a team-based approach to solving most business problems. What distinguished these teams from traditional teams was their cross-functionality. For example, companies no longer put technical projects completely in the hands of their engineers. The project team would be required to have key members from other areas as well, such as finance, marketing, operations, and information technology. Business solutions would need to accommodate a whole range of issues beyond the narrow technical ones that were the traditional focus of project efforts.

Empowering Employees

The simultaneous need for speedy decision making and customer satisfaction has led to the empowerment of employees who have not traditionally had much clout. Empowerment has taken many forms. One key approach has been to provide employees with decision-making authority in their dealings with customers. For example, if a customer wants to change the configuration of a piece of equipment, the employee is given authority to grant the change if it appears to be reasonable. Previously, the employee would have had to get permission from higher levels.

An interesting outcome of employee empowerment has been the change in the role of "manager" from that of *director* of activities to one of *support.* That is, the role of managers is to do what is necessary to enable their employees to operate as effectively as possible. This situation is called the *inverted pyramid,* a 180-degree reversal of the traditional relationship where employees served their managers.

Adopting E-Commerce Perspectives

The business process reengineering movement forced businesses and governments to rethink how they carry out their business transactions. One consequence of this was recognition that great efficiencies and improved operations could be achieved by employing intranets and the

Internet to support basic business activities, such as processing orders, managing customer accounts, and integrating all internal business activities. This led to the adoption of e-commerce tools and perspectives in the form of supply chain management (SCM) systems, enterprise resource planning (ERP) systems, and customer relationship management (CRM) systems.

Outsourcing

The drive for cost saving has led companies to depend more heavily on outsiders to help them in their work. Even as companies downsize, they may increase their business activity. This apparent contradiction is made possible by the outsourcing of services and production. The benefits of outsourcing are reduced cost of investment in new equipment and facilities, lowered pension and health insurance burdens, and a declining need to hire and fire employees in response to business cycles. Thus outsourcing has shifted many of the burdens of doing business from companies onto their contractors.

Interestingly, project management is ideally matched to the new business environment. Project managers are experienced in "thriving on chaos" (Peters, 1987), "managing in turbulent times" (Drucker, 1980), "white water rafting" (Vaill, 1989), "upside-down thinking" (Handy, 1989), and "influence without authority" (Cohen and Bradford, 1990). They are accustomed to working in organizationally flat environments, where bosses do not have direct control over human and material resources but rather are influencers. Outsourcing is not new to them. For decades they have used it as an important mechanism for acquiring products and services on projects.

Still, even though project management is well suited to helping organizations manage their efforts in these dynamic times, it too must undergo radical change. The relevance of project management to the needs of our changing world will rapidly disappear without major changes in how we look at and carry out our projects.

THE PROBLEM WITH THE TRADITIONAL APPROACH TO PROJECT MANAGEMENT

Traditional project management has enabled humans to do some incredible things. For example, it provided the U.S. National Aeronautics and Space Administration (NASA) with the management capability to put men on the moon. It makes possible the construction of oil-drilling platforms in the North Sea. It provides airplane manufacturers with the discipline to design and build complex commercial aircraft. Traditional project management has served us well, so why talk about changing it? If something isn't broken, why fix it?

The problem is that traditional project management *is* broken. One deficiency is its inattention to the importance of customers. Customer satisfaction is often treated as an afterthought. Most energy is directed toward satisfying the famous triple constraints of time, budget, and specifications. Success and failure are typically assessed against meeting schedules, budgets, and specifications, *not* against achieving full customer satisfaction.

One might argue that a focus on the triple constraints is fully consistent with customer satisfaction since the third constraint—specifications—should have customer needs and wants embedded in it. In theory, this is a correct assessment. In practice, however, the specifications often do not take adequate account of customer needs and wants because they are created by "experts" who lack the skills and training to work with customers, who don't understand the customers' business, and who design and build products that are of personal interest to them. They are often driven to build things that will gain them the admiration of their fellow experts. With such an approach, customer satisfaction is a secondary consideration.

Another problem with the traditional approach to project management is its single-minded focus on a fixed set of tools for dealing with scheduling, budgeting, and resource allocation. These tools are well known. In scheduling, they are, chiefly, Gantt charts and PERT/CPM networks. In budgeting, they are S-shaped budget curves. In resource allocation, they are responsibility matrixes, loading charts, and resource Gantts. Countless additional subsidiary tools and concepts fill the project manager's tool box. As noted in the Preface, project management is so closely tied to this set of tools that when people ask, "Do you know project management?" they are really asking whether you know how to do such things as create PERT/CPM networks and S-curves.

There is nothing inherently wrong with tool mastery. All of us can benefit by increasing our skills in using tools. A problem arises, however, when an excessive concern with tools diverts attention from other important matters, such as managing and satisfying customer needs and wants, motivating employees, and acquiring political skills.

A reality of project management is that projects seldom fail because a PERT/CPM system crashes. However, they frequently fail for non-technical reasons such as lack of commitment on the part of staff, political gaffes, and the inability to communicate ideas effectively.

A final problem with traditional project management is its narrow definition of what it should be concerned with. This is seen in two areas. First, traditional project management often limits the project life cycle to a narrow range of activity, from launching a project to closing it out. This is captured in the perspective promoted by the world's principal project standards body, the Project Management Institute, which in its standards-setting document, *A Guide to the Project Management Body of Knowledge* (2000), identifies five basic processes that all projects address: initiating, planning, controlling, executing, and closeout processes. This seems to be a reasonable arrangement on the surface. However, in the new competitive global environment, where customer satisfaction is paramount, such a restrictive definition of what project management should address is deficient. With such an approach, which ignores life after the project (operations and maintenance processes), the project team members can wash their hands of the deliverable after it is turned over to the customer. They are given an opportunity to bail out at the moment of truth. If problems arise in the postproject phase, they can take the attitude, "That's not my problem—see the maintenance people."

For customer satisfaction to be achieved, the life cycle must be extended to encompass one more phase: operations and maintenance. The project team members must be made to realize that their job is not simply to build something but also to ensure that it works in a satisfactory way after it is delivered.

Traditional project management also takes a narrow view of its domain in a second sense: it holds a constricted view of what project managers should be able to do. It sees them primarily as implementers. Someone makes decisions about which projects should be supported. After the nature of the work has been scoped out, it is handed over to the project manager, whose charge is to do the job within scope. A survey I once conducted of 113 project managers showed that only 29 percent of them played a direct role in choosing the projects on which they worked. The survey revealed other deficiencies in the power of project managers: less than a third reported having profit-and-loss responsibilities. Indeed, most reported that they did not even have adequate budget data to take on meaningful cost responsibilities. A majority also indicated that they worked on only a portion of the project life cycle—no cradle-to-grave responsibility here!

This book argues that such a limited view of what lies in the project manager's domain creates an environment in which it is difficult for project managers to serve their customers effectively. If customer satisfaction is an important ultimate goal of project management, the project manager's role must be redefined to allow it to be achieved.

Over the years, traditional project management has served us well. The time has come, however, for it to change some of its ways in order to adjust to powerful global competitive forces. Specifically, it must adapt to the new conditions organizations face today: customer satisfaction, downsizing, flattening, empowerment, and outsourcing.

THE NEW PROJECT MANAGEMENT

This book examines how project management can most effectively be employed in the new business environment. Its purpose is not to reject traditional project management. It recognizes that most of the features of traditional project management are still relevant today. Rather, it aims to enhance the traditional approach by bringing it more into line with the new business realities.

Three arguments are central to the new project management: (1) project management must become more customer-focused, (2) it must explore the use of new management tools, and (3) it must redefine the role of project managers. Each of these arguments will be discussed in turn.

Customer Focus

Project managers traditionally measure success and failure in the context of the triple constraints. Failure occurs when a project encounters schedule slippages or cost overruns or produces deliverables that do not meet the specs. This traditional outlook is undergoing rapid adjustment. Increasingly, professionals involved with project management recognize that the worst kind of failure you can have is carrying out projects that do not satisfy the customers.

This point is clearly illustrated if we consider the project to build the opera house in Sydney, Australia. This project encountered horrific schedule slippages and cost overruns. By the traditional yardstick of the triple constraints, it was a failed project. However, once built, the opera house became Australia's number one object of civic pride. It is hard to find an Australian tourist poster that does not have a photo of the opera house somewhere on it. Soon after its construction, the citizens of Australia considered it a rousing success. What we see here is success rooted in customer satisfaction, even when the triple constraints are not met.

Customer satisfaction, then, is the key. Ultimately, satisfaction is defined by whether customers actually use the deliverables emerging from projects.

Why should we worry about a customer focus? There are a number of compelling answers to this question.

First, in recent times, customers have come to expect good products and services. This expectation is a legacy of the total quality management (TQM) movement of the late 1980s and early 1990s. TQM recognized that as customers become increasingly sophisticated in their buying habits and as they gain better access to information, they can demand first-rate performance. If they do not receive it from one supplier, they can readily turn to another. TQM helped companies and government agencies orient their efforts to meeting customer needs and wants in an explicit and consistent way.

Second, a strong customer focus increases the likelihood of repeat business. If the project staff do all they can to achieve customer satisfaction, their efforts will be appreciated by customers, who may well repay the attention by doing repeat business with the project team.

Third, customer satisfaction means we can wrap up our projects more rapidly. Anyone who has had project experience has encountered the situation where customers refuse to sign off on the deliverable because they believe something is amiss. For example, they may feel that the deliverable does not contain all its promised features or that it has deficiencies in quality. The result of this impasse is an extension of the project. Final payments are delayed, and extra expenses are incurred. Greater attentiveness to customer sensibilities decreases the frequency of such occurrences.

New Tools and Nontraditional Skills

Traditional project management emphasizes acquiring basic skills in scheduling, budgeting, and allocating human and material resources. These are the primary tools of project managers who are mere implementers. They are essentially the tools of technicians.

In their expanded role, project managers need a different set of skills to be effective. Project staff should be proficient in such "hard" skills as the basics of contracting, business finance, integrated cost and schedule control, measuring work performance, monitoring quality, and conducting risk analyses. They should also be adept at such "soft" skills as negotiating, managing change, being politically astute, and understanding the needs and wants of the people they deal with (including customers, peers, staff, and their own managers).

A Redefined Role

As stated earlier, in traditional project management, project managers are seen primarily as *implementers*. Their job is to make things happen. Projects are selected—frequently with no input from project managers, who are then assigned to run them. Plans are developed—sometimes with input from project managers, sometimes without—and then project managers are charged to execute them. Project managers are very much like noncommissioned military officers. The general develops the grand strategies, the major works out the mid-range strategies, the captain develops the tactics, and the sergeants are responsible for executing the tactics on the field.

This approach works well in a stable environment where goals can be clearly defined and there is little competitive pressure. Today's business environment, however, is neither stable nor free from competitive pressure. Old assumptions no longer hold true. A new paradigm must emerge that provides guidance on the roles and responsibilities of the new project managers.

PROJECT MANAGERS MUST BECOME CUSTOMER FOCUSED. To the extent that project managers are mere implementers of established plans, they do not have much reason to worry about customer satisfaction. Presumably, the people who sold the system, working with those who authorized and designed it, have taken into account customer needs and wants. In such an environment, project managers behave like good soldiers. "Just point me in the right direction," they say, "and I'll march."

In today's dynamic and competitive business world, this approach no longer works. Consider, for example, projects that are funded through contracts with customers. With such projects, it is not clear that the salespeople, authorizing managers, and designers are doing their jobs properly. A constant complaint heard by project staff is that salespeople, eager to make a sale, are promising customers systems that project staff cannot build, at least not within the constraints of time and budget that all organizations face. Managers are authorizing these commitments because they are anxious to increase business. Unfortunately, they often do not fully understand the project implications of such commitments. Designers, who in most organizations are several steps removed from customers, find themselves trying to design systems that will meet promises made to the customers. In doing so, they frequently interpret customer requirements to match their own design proclivities, which may or may not reflect true customer needs and wants. Clearly, customer satisfaction will not be achieved readily in this all-too-common situation. Today's dynamic business environment requires project managers to be strongly customer-focused.

PROJECT MANAGERS MUST BE EMPOWERED TO OPERATE EFFECTIVELY. We hear much talk these days about empowering the workforce. Unfortunately, it is not always clear what is meant by the term *empowerment*. In this book, employees are viewed as empowered when they possess the following characteristics:

• *The majority of their decisions can be made independently without having to pass through the chain of command.* A key component of customer satisfaction is quick response time. When customers ask a question or suggest a change, they want to see results quickly. They do not want to sit around waiting while a trivial change request has to get approval from five levels of management. One way to speed response time is to give project workers the power to respond directly and meaningfully to customer inquiries and requests.

• *They possess substantial profit-and-loss responsibilities.* In modern business activity, the ultimate arbiter of effectiveness is the bottom line. Business operations that lose money are undesirable, whereas those that make money are attractive. This is an obvious truth. In addition, experience shows that people who are held financially accountable for their actions consistently outperform those who are not. Given these truths, it seems logical to insist that project employees be given profit-and-loss responsibilities for their projects. We are a long way from this situation today. The survey of 113 project managers I mentioned earlier suggests that *fewer than a third of them even have reliable basic cost data to enable them to make rational decisions!*

• *They see themselves largely as entrepreneurs running their own businesses.* One of the most effective projects in modern business history, the project to build the IBM personal computer in 1980 and 1981, was carried out as an independent business entity. The project manager was, in effect, the CEO of a small company. He had the same decision-making authority as an independent businessperson. This means that he had the authority to hire and fire. In addition, his decisions were not constantly monitored by a higher power. In the final analysis, his performance was to be measured by the bottom line. IBM's experience with the PC has been repeated many times in organizations throughout the world. The new business environment demands that project managers see themselves as more than mere technical implementers. They are, first and foremost, businesspeople whose job is to satisfy their customers while conducting a profitable operation.

• *They possess the business skills and knowledge needed to operate effectively in the new business environment.* Empowerment is very much rooted in competence. Managers who lack basic business and technical skills are not truly empowered to be effective. Traditionally, project management stressed the need to nurture technical skills. As mere implementers of solutions, project staff did not need to possess business knowledge. Today, their role has expanded beyond that of implementer. Customers are demanding that managers help them in developing business solutions as well, and this requires that they possess the business skills to meet this demand. The increased range of skills and insights project professionals need to possess are covered in detail in my book *Project Management Competence* (1999).

TRAITS OF THE NEW PROJECT MANAGER

Over the years, I have conducted an informal survey of hundreds of project managers, asking them to identify what they perceive to be the traits of an ideal project manager. The following list enumerates general traits that emerged from this survey.

The ideal project manager should

• Have a thorough understanding of the project goals
• Be capable of understanding staff needs
• Have a good head for details

- Have a strong commitment to the project—that is, be willing to put in long hours on the project

- Be able to cope with setbacks and disappointments—any discipline whose guiding principles are governed by Murphy's Law is going to be anxiety-ridden!

- Possess good negotiation skills, since a large part of project life will be spent trying to acquire resources

- Be results-oriented and practical

- Be cost-conscious and possess basic business skills

- Be politically savvy, aware of what *not to do* as well as what *to do*

- Have a high tolerance for ambiguity—little is clear on most projects

This last point is particularly important. Project managers should have an appreciation for what the Chinese call *yin* and *yang,* a perception that addresses the inherent duality of life and nature: hot versus cold, light versus dark, good versus bad, male versus female, young versus old. Projects are filled with *yin-yang* duality. Following are some common dualities project managers face.

- *Seeing the big picture versus paying attention to the details.* Project managers must constantly balance the big picture against the details. They need to have a grasp of the whole project: Why is the project being carried out? What are its most fundamental goals? Are they being achieved? Thus project managers must be able to see the forest. At the same time, they cannot ignore the details. Deadlines have to be met, specifications achieved, resources allocated, expenditures tracked. In short, they must also see the trees. In Jungian terms, they must possess sensation and intuition capabilities simultaneously (Keirsey and Bates, 1978).

- *Maintaining firmness versus being flexible.* Projects operate according to firm deadline dates, fixed budgets, and carefully conceived specifications. These things cannot be taken lightly. A major goal of project managers is to get the job done on time, within budget, and according to specs. Any forces that cause the project to drift from the achievement of this goal are strongly resisted. Yet projects are filled with uncertainty. For example, new developments arise that cannot be ignored: competitors produce products that make our goods obsolete, a key customer changes, budget cutbacks occur. Given the inevitability of these changes, project managers must know when and how to behave flexibly.

• *Being hard versus being soft in dealing with people.* A highly successful project manager once told me that a key to his good performance was his ability to wield a "velvet-covered brick." Project environments often seem to be Darwinian laboratories, where only the fittest survive. In such environments, project managers must encase themselves in the toughest armor, like armadillos, in order to endure. At the same time, they need to be responsive to people's needs and wants. They must possess a strong measure of sensitivity. A good example of the velvet-covered brick in action is a project manager's turning down a request from a supplicant in such a way that the supplicant feels good about the rejection.

• *Possessing analytical skills versus trusting one's instincts.* Projects can be complex business undertakings. I argue strongly in this book that effective project managers must possess good analytical skills in order to understand what is happening on their projects. They should know how to schedule their efforts, using such tools as PERT/CPM, Gantt charts, and earned value; how to develop and track budgets, employing standard financial tools such as present value, internal rate of return, and sunk costs; how to allocate resources with resource histograms, responsibility charts, and resource Gantt charts; and so on. But there are also times when the analytical tools are insufficient. Accomplished project managers learn to pay attention to their gut feeling. This feeling is an outcome of absorbing good and bad experiences over a period of years.

THE INCREASED VALUE
OF PROJECT MANAGERS

A review of the traits of the ideal project manager demonstrates that great demands are placed on project managers. In fact, they are traits that we do not even expect the CEOs of our great corporations to possess! Of course, no project manager scores strongly on all the desirable traits listed here. I suspect that the great majority of them are quite weak on most of these traits, and this contributes to the problems encountered on so many projects. But the more desirable traits project managers possess, the more effective the managers will be.

An interesting thing happened in the 1980s. The outside world came to realize that the key traits necessary to manage the work efforts of modern enterprises are the very ones that project managers have possessed for decades (or millennia, if you want to include the pyramids, the Great Wall of China, and Hadrian's Wall). The effective managers described in Drucker's *Managing in Turbulent Times* (1980), Peters's *Thriving on Chaos* (1987) and *Liberation Management* (1992), Vaill's *Managing as a Performing Art* (1989), Handy's *Age of Unreason* (1989), and Reich's *Work of Nations* (1991) are precisely what I describe here as project managers. These people are coming to occupy center stage in their organizations. If this is true, then the laws of economics suggest that the salaries of effective project managers should rise substantially. These are the scarce people who can *make things happen,* thereby adding tremendous value to their organizations.

To appreciate the economics of compensating effective project managers highly, consider the following scenario: Shandra Gupta is made project manager to oversee a project to gain government approval for a new drug. It is estimated that each day of delay of approval will cost the company $100,000 in lost revenue. Thus a one-month delay will cost the company some $3 million in lost revenue. Given these economic realities, it is easy to see how the company is justified in paying a project manager—in this case, Shandra—an enormous salary (coupled with a stock bonus) if by doing so it can attract an effective manager who will not encounter delays in gaining FDA approval.

What we see in project management is a large gap between "top-gun" project managers and run-of-the-mill project managers. Salaries of average project managers are not particularly elevated. They are typically in line with salaries offered to middle managers occupying responsible positions. However, salaries of high-performing project managers are generous, occasionally higher than salaries paid to company vice presidents. These top-gun project managers typically have a ten-year (or longer) track record of successful delivery of large and complex projects. What the high wages are buying is confidence that the selected project managers will carry out their chores effectively on high-value projects.

BEYOND THE PROJECT MANAGER

As projects grew more complex in the 1990s, an interesting phenomenon arose: rather than entrust the project to one person—the project manager—some organizations established coresponsibility teams. For example, in the early 1990s, the information technology branch of the Administrative Offices of the U.S. Courts began heading IT projects with two people: a development manager, who played a lead role on technical issues, and a business manager, who understood the business side of management. The question of who was "really" the project manager was irrelevant. The real question was, how can these two people, working together, carry out the project management *function*?

Many other organizations have similarly adopted two-person project leadership teams. NCR Corporation carried the concept further by creating five-person customer focus teams (CFTs) that included key business and technical people needed to deliver a project successfully (someone with marketing or sales skills, someone with manufacturing knowledge, someone with financial insights, and so on). The rationale underlying the creation of coresponsibility teams is simple: no one project manager will have a grasp of the knowledge needed to bridge the technical and business issues today's complex projects encounter.

The chief concern of adopting this approach is that it goes against the management principle that in carrying out work efforts, responsibility must reside in one person. Experience shows, however, that once the comanagers get beyond the question of who's really in charge and learn to trust each other's abilities and appreciate that they can achieve more collectively than when working alone, the coresponsibility teams work well.

Will this approach become the dominant way of doing business on larger projects? It is too early to tell. The idea that all responsibility must ultimately rest with a single individual—the "buck stops here" perspective—is one of the most cherished principles in management thinking. This is particularly true in project management, where project managers are seen as the key to delivering successful solutions. However, as organizations gain more experience using cross-functional teams to carry out projects, they may also develop skills in sharing responsibility among multiple players. If this happens, then the rise of coresponsibility teams appears inevitable.

CONCLUSIONS

The world is rapidly changing. In all areas of business, what served us well in the past is only marginally pertinent today. The area of project management is no exception. During the four decades following World War II, its outlook and required skills remained rather static. In the late 1950s, there was a flurry of creative developments that moved project management forward, but from then until the later

1980s, not much changed. One has the feeling that project managers in 1962 would have been comfortable with the project management of 1987.

The turmoil beginning in the 1980s and extending through today changed that complacency. The imperative for survival in turbulent times required that organizations do their work differently. It is this new perspective on project management and the role of project staff that is central to this book.

PART ONE

Managing in the New Business Environment

P art One of this book deals with some key issues that affect project professionals. These issues have received little attention in traditional approaches to project management. In retrospect, they have always been important, even though they have not received the interest they deserve. Today, however, they possess a compelling urgency that is forcing us to place them at the center of our management concerns.

As Chapter One suggests, a hallmark of today's business environment is its chaotic nature. This chaos is rooted in unprecedented rates of change and high levels of complexity. In turn, rapid change and complexity create an environment of high risk in which decision makers possess little certainty about what the future holds. They perceive events through opaque lenses and base their decisions on large measures of speculation and only small doses of certainty.

Complicating things further is the brutally competitive environment that has arisen with the emergence of globalization and the Internet. This competitive environment has stimulated an obsession with winning the hearts and minds of customers. In today's business climate, customer satisfaction lies at the heart of most business activity.

The chapters in Part One examine the new business realities and their implications for the management of projects. Chapter Two investigates the pervasiveness of complexity in today's world. It examines the roots of complexity, identifies its impacts on organizations, and suggests mechanisms for dealing with it.

The old maxim that "the only constant is change" is no longer a clever oxymoron but is rather a dominant reality of business life today. Unharnessed change is a leading contributor to project failure. Changes in personnel, markets, budgets, regulations, and technology stimulate changes in project needs and requirements. Project staff find themselves working with "rubber baselines." Chapter Three examines the nature and pervasiveness of change and suggests approaches to dealing with it.

Risk management is one of the fastest-growing areas of interest in project management. Projects face a plethora of risks: technological, financial, social, regulatory, market, and so on. Chapter Four looks at the increase of risk on projects in recent times and examines a number of methodologies for identifying and handling risk.

Chapter Five examines the role of customers in the new project management. It suggests that project staff must increasingly develop customer-relations skills. It also offers guidance on how to work effectively with customers.

Finally, Chapter Six examines how to take customer-focused needs and convert them into technical requirements. It examines the chasm separating business users whose needs must be satisfied and the technical team that is charged with implementing project solutions to meet the needs. The problem is that business users seldom understand the technical issues that need to be addressed to satisfy their needs, while the technical people rarely understand the users' business. For technology-intensive projects to be successful today, they must be able to close the customer-developer gap.

The sequencing of these chapters is to a certain extent arbitrary. Each has been written to stand on its own merits so that you can read them in whatever sequence is of interest to you.

CHAPTER TWO

Managing Complexity
Techniques for Fashioning Order out of Chaos

—⁓— T he level of complexity we face in our daily lives today
is overwhelming. Sometimes I wonder if life really is more complex
now than in previous times or whether the sense of complexity is an
illusion. But whenever I begin believing it is an illusion, I think back
a few decades to some mundane affairs and contrast them with comparable affairs today. Then I see how complex life is today.

For example, when I was a boy in the 1950s, the investment opportunities my father faced were limited: as a middle-class general
practitioner, he made a comfortable living in medicine and could place
his money in an interest-bearing savings account or put it into U.S.
government savings bonds. There were other investment options, of
course—for example, he could play the stock market—but these were
rather risky and would involve a nontrivial amount of his personal
attention.

Fifty years later, the investment options for risk-averse middle-class
citizens are overwhelming: tax-free municipal bonds, no-load mutual
funds, commission-based mutuals, treasury bills, savings bonds, money
market funds, and certificates of deposit are just a small sampling of
offerings that ordinary folk chat about during backyard barbecues.

Furthermore, to make wise investment decisions, middle-class investors need to be rather astute about tax laws. Beyond this, they should be conversant with the assortment of insurance options available to them (for example, term versus whole-life policies), mortgage options (fixed versus adjustable rates), and pension plan alternatives (defined-benefit versus money purchase plans). My sense is that my friends and acquaintances today are far more savvy about investment issues than professional investors were back in the 1950s.

My dad's life was simpler in many other ways as well. When he took us kids out to get a bit of ice cream, the flavors we could select were chocolate, vanilla, or strawberry. Today, my daughter must choose among thirty-one flavors when we visit the local Baskin-Robbins. If my dad wanted to purchase a writing implement in 1950, he could choose between a ballpoint pen, a fountain pen, a mechanical pencil, or a wooden pencil. Today, when I go to the stationer's, I face an overwhelming variety of choices, ranging from quality fountain pens to disposable fountain pens, ballpoints, roller-ball ink pens, vinyl-tipped pens, 0.5-mm mechanical pencils, 0.7-mm pencils, and so on.

These examples demonstrate that life today is far more complex than it was for our parents and grandparents. And it is beyond a doubt that life will be even more complex in the future.

Complexity is a fact of life we cannot escape. It overwhelms us in our personal lives. It is also an aspect of the workplace. Today's literate managers are expected to know how to use personal computers, to understand finance, to have marketing know-how, to be psychologists in their dealings with customers, and have a great many other strengths.

This chapter examines some aspects of complexity that have a bearing on project management. It first investigates the nature of complexity. Why is complexity such a dominant reality today—perhaps *the* dominant reality that organizations and individuals must cope with? It then examines the experiences of organizations that so far have managed to cope with complexity with a fair degree of success. It concludes by enumerating approaches that organizations take to dealing with complexity.

CHAOS AND COMPLEXITY

If just a few years ago you were a physics student, you would be taught that the world is an orderly place. Consider the most famous equation in science: $e = mc^2$. It contains only two variables (e, energy, and m, mass) and two constants (c, the speed of light, and the power of 2), and yet it describes one of the most fundamental physical relationships in nature.

The elegance and precision of physics have long been the envy of life scientists, social scientists, businesspeople, and ordinary, literate citizens. Physics has served as the model of how knowledge should be handled. A major goal of social scientists since World War II has been to emulate the methods of physics. This is seen most clearly in economics, where a typical research paper is so filled with mathematical symbols that in reviewing it one would think one were reading a physics paper.

Despite noble efforts to achieve the cleanliness and parsimony of physics, nonphysics disciplines have been caught up in messiness. Biologists and medical researchers find that living systems are inherently messy. Social scientists, whose attentions focus on people, find that humans defy consistently predictable behavior.

Today we recognize that even physics is far messier than popularly conceived. "Clean" physics was the product of the Newtonian era, when clockworks served as the model of physical systems. At first, the parsimonious approach to explaining physical reality worked quite well: relatively simple equations described complex phenomena such as gravitational attraction, the wave properties of light, motion, force, and the properties of heat. But as the easy problems were solved and better techniques of measurement evolved, it became evident that the physical world displayed some characteristics of messiness that were hard to explain.

Albert Einstein, the scientist who gave us the superelegant equation $e = mc^2$, won recognition for his 1906 explanation of Brownian motion. He showed that some physical processes—the messy ones—are best described statistically rather than according to tight mathematical equations. Similarly, the Heisenberg uncertainty principle in 1927 suggested that some physical processes are inherently messy. There was a hint that physics might share some things with a dice game.

More recently, physicists and mathematicians have recognized the messiness of physical processes by devising new approaches to dealing with them. In the 1970s, fuzzy set theory grew prominent. This approach suggested that in classifying things, we often do not know what group a particular item may belong to at a given point in time. We can only predict its membership in a group probabilistically. In the 1970s, the work of René Thom led to the development of catastrophe theory, which postulated that many phenomena, such as the snapping of a steel rod under pressure or the collapse of an economy, are characterized more by discontinuities than by the continuities favored in conventional physics.

The most publicized exploration of messiness is chaos theory, which emerged in the 1980s. The reading public was so fascinated by its precepts that James Gleick's book *Chaos* (1987) became a *New York Times* best-seller for months. Chaos theory emphasized the lack of predictability of basic events. A well-known example of this is what is called the butterfly effect, which holds that the flapping of the wings of a butterfly in one corner of the earth can change weather patterns in another. Thus the most simple events can, through a steady compounding process, result in highly complex consequences that defy prediction.

Concern with chaos led to a growing interest in complexity. The chaos perspective holds that many common phenomena such as weather patterns and economic activity are inherently complex and that traditional linear thinking will not help much in understanding them. In the mid-1980s, the Santa Fe Institute was established with the express purpose of understanding complexity in all of its aspects.

Consensus is emerging that complexity is closely tied to the adaptive behavior of systems. For example, a species of insect that falls prey to a certain kind of predator must either alter its physical form or its behavior (for example, by camouflage or burrowing) to avoid extinction. Through this process of adaptation, the system becomes increasingly flexible *and* complex. The rule seems to be that flexible, sophisticated systems have the edge in this competitive world. Consequently, the general drift is toward the increased complexity of systems in both the physical and social world.

In the management arena, the concept of messiness is nothing new to those who practice project management. Whereas traditional management focused on things like chains of command and tying authority to responsibility, project management has centered its attention on getting the job done in an environment where authority is lacking, goals are subject to multiple interpretations, and rules of behavior are ill-defined. In project management, Murphy's Law prevails: if things can go wrong, they will. Project management has operated in a management environment of chaos and complexity for decades.

FACETS OF COMPLEXITY

Complexity is a difficult concept to define. In dealing with it, we are tempted to say, "I know it when I see it, but don't ask me to define it." Our problems in defining it stem from its having several facets. For example, complexity is associated with size: large things with many components tend to be more complex than smaller ones with few components. It is also associated with variety: decisions entailing many options are more complex than those with few. It is further associated with difficulty: the *New York Times* crossword puzzle is more complex than the puzzles found in tabloids. Let us take a closer look at these and some additional facets of complexity.

Complexity and Size

In general, large things with many components tend to be more complex than smaller ones with few components. In software, a program containing one million lines of code is clearly more complex than one containing a thousand lines. A fighter aircraft is more complex than an automobile. A nuclear power plant is more complex than a coal-fired plant.

Volume-related complexity—what Peter Senge calls *detail complexity* in his book *The Fifth Discipline* (1990)—has two components to it. First, large things with many components have many connections that must be maintained between the components. These connections can grow explosively even as a system's components grow arithmetically. This can be seen in Figure 2.1, which shows what happens as a team gets larger. On a two-person team, only one connection must be maintained in order to coordinate the efforts of the team members. On a three-person team, the number of connections grows to three. With four people, it grows to six. With five people, it grows to ten. In general, the upper limit of the number of connections that can exist between the components of some entity is $n(n-1)/2$, or $(n^2 - n)/2$.

Second, the sheer size of something makes it difficult to comprehend. The typical human brain can handle only seven to ten pieces of information simultaneously, so as the volume of information increases, the brain's capacity to deal with it concretely grows increasingly deficient. Those who doubt this assertion can perform a small experiment on themselves. Have a friend create five "random" numbers, the first one seven digits long, the next one eight digits long, and

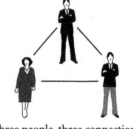
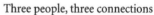
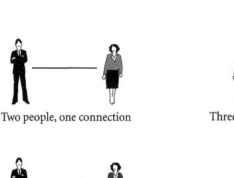

Two people, one connection   Three people, three connections

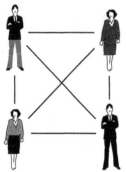
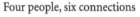

Four people, six connections   Five people, ten connections

**Figure 2.1. The Relationship Between Team Size
and Communications Channels.**

so on. Then have the friend read you the numbers, one at a time. Your
job is to write each number down after hearing it once. Most people
begin making mistakes with numbers that are nine digits long.

The projects we encounter today often entail manipulating far
larger volumes of information than in the past. This fact is obvious to
anyone who has been working with personal computers since the early
1980s. The first word processing software packages (really nothing
more than text editors) could comfortably fit onto a 360-kilobyte
floppy disk. Ten years later, standard word processing packages often
occupied 9 million bytes of hard disk space.

The larger volume of information we encounter today is a consequence of at least two factors. For one thing, knowledge is cumulative.
This was highlighted in the 1960s by Derek Price in his classic work
Little Science, Big Science (1963), which demonstrated empirically that
the growth of scientific knowledge is exponential. As a consequence,
more knowledge is generated in one year than in the previous several

years combined. Something like 90 percent of the scientists who ever lived are alive today.

For another thing, we now possess the technology to store and access huge amounts of information cheaply. Anyone with a personal computer and a link to the Internet can tie into databases containing billions upon billions of bytes of data covering every conceivable topic. Of course, this situation has led to information overload, so that even the brightest people feel overwhelmed with the amount of information they need to contend with.

Complexity and Variety

The proliferation of options we face in our lives is overwhelming. I recently encountered this fact at my university when a graduate student informed me that the number of decision support systems employed in operations research had become so large that he was in the process of creating a "meta-DSS" whose function was to offer its users guidance on what decision support systems to use on different kinds of problems. In effect, he was creating a decision support system of decision support systems. This is not a unique situation. We now have associations of associations, indexes of indexes, and search engines that search other search engines.

The plethora of options is apparent in project management as well. For example, there are scores of viable scheduling software packages being offered by vendors. How does one choose from among all the variety?

A large part of the complexity of today's projects is tied to the variety of options facing all project players, from project managers to team members to customers. These options cover all aspects of projects. For example, consider the options associated with the purchase of a single product, component, or service. Virtually any product, component, or service to be employed on a project has multiple suppliers, each with its special features. In buying a laptop computer, should I choose product A, which is exceedingly lightweight, or product B, which comes with large amounts of RAM, or product C, which has a ten-hour battery life? Decision making was a lot easier in the old days, when the range of options was limited.

The dilemma of excessive options that project managers and staff face is obvious. They must constantly make choices from among a plethora of different vendors, employees, designs, proposed solutions, promise dates, and so on. The fact that their projects tend to be unique confounds them because the lessons learned from sorting through options on a previous project are often irrelevant on the current one.

Customers are overwhelmed with options as well. In choosing a product or service, they must decide what fundamental features they want in a deliverable, what bells and whistles can be added, how much they are willing to pay, and what vendors to work with. If they grow overwhelmed by the variety of options, they may freeze up and feel incapable of making a decision (we call this "paralysis through analysis"), or they may develop cold feet once they make a decision and change their minds. Project staff should be sensitive to this dilemma. An important part of their jobs is to guide customers through the decision process, helping them navigate in unknown waters. One approach to doing this is to simplify the inherently complex decisions customers must make.

Complexity and Difficulty

Complexity is often associated with difficulty. Something that is hard to do is generally viewed as more complex than something that is easy. Integral calculus is more complex than arithmetic.

Complexity rooted in difficulty is generally handled through mastery. For someone learning how to ride a bicycle, the effort appears quite complex at first. The same holds true for someone learning how to touch-type. At the outset, the effort appears daunting. There is so much to learn. But with practice comes mastery, and with mastery what seems complex one day may seem quite simple the next.

To people who are new to a project, grasping its totality may seem impossible. Consider what they must know: the Project Management Institute's *Guide to the Project Management Body of Knowledge Guide* (2000) stipulates that the competent project manager should have some degree of mastery over time management, cost management, scope management, human resource management, risk management, quality management, procurement management, communication management, and integration management. Beyond this, project workers are expected to have the technical competence to understand the specific content of their projects. There is much to master even on relatively simple projects. Exhibit 2.1 shows some basic project management tools that competent project professionals should be able to work with.

Tool	Do We Have It?	Do We Need It?
Scope Management Tools		
Work breakdown structure (WBS)		
Benefit-cost analysis		
Configuration management		
Time Management Tools		
Gantt charts		
Milestone charts		
PERT/CPM networks		
Earned value techniques		
Cost Management Tools		
Parametric cost-estimating techniques		
Bottom-up cost-estimating techniques		
Cumulative cost curve (S-curve)		
Life cycle costing		
Capital budgeting tools (NPV, IRR, payback period)		
Earned value techniques		
Human Resource Management Tools		
Motivation and team-building techniques		
Management by objectives (MBO)		
Responsibility matrix		
Resource Gantt chart		
Resource histogram (loading chart)		
Risk Management Tools		
Risk management process		
Scenario building		
Monte Carlo simulation		
Basic statistical techniques (e.g., math expectation)		
Decision trees		

Exhibit 2.1. Some Basic Project Management Tools.

Tool	Do We Have It?	Do We Need It?
Quality Management Tools		
Standard quality control techniques		
Pareto diagrams		
Contract Management Tools		
Solid grasp of different contract modalities (CPIF, CPAF, CPFF, lump sum, time and materials)		
Communication Management Tools		
Solid grasp of basic communication principles		

Exhibit 2.1. Some Basic Project Management Tools *(continued).*

One solution to the problem of mastery is experience and education. Careful study and hands-on experiences enable project staff to function comfortably in their complex environments. Projects are seldom easy. But experienced and knowledgeable project managers learn how to cut through the complexity and to focus on the essentials.

Complexity and Change

The rapidity of change in today's world contributes measurably to complexity. One way it does this is by creating moving targets. This is seen clearly in our attempts to define needs and requirements. Even as we think we finally understand the customers' needs, they are changing. Sources of change include changing technology, the changing position of competitors, changing economic forces (for example, the growth of inflation), changing players, and changing budgets. As any duck would tell you (if only ducks could speak), it is simpler to be shot as a sitting duck than as a duck on the wing.

Change also contributes to two facets of complexity discussed earlier. First, it leads to increases in the volume of information that must be dealt with. Knowledge grows over time, and today it is growing exponentially. Second, change increases the options we face. If the product life cycle for a gizmo is five years, then over a five-year period, we encounter the one gizmo. If, however, the life cycle has shrunk to one year, then in a five-year period, we effectively encounter five separate products, contributing to a proliferation of options we face. Somehow this change must be controlled.

EXPERIENCE WITH PROJECT COMPLEXITY

Complex projects have always been with us. Many organizations routinely operate in highly complex environments. Today the greatest master of managing complex undertakings is the United States Department of Defense (DOD). Major defense programs, such as the Stealth bomber (B-2), the cruise missile, fighter aircraft, and the Strategic Defense Initiative ("Star Wars") dwarf virtually all other human activities when viewed from the perspective of complexity. Even DOD "business" activities are far more complex than what private enterprises undertake. The challenges of automating materials management, personnel assignments, and contracting procedures are overwhelming in an organization having the size and complexity of DOD.

In the private sector, complex projects are most apparent in the software industry. Software programs of over a million lines of code are no longer oddities. Consider the complexity inherent in programs where a single error in a single line of code can cause the whole program to malfunction. Today's complex software routines must function perfectly.

So how do experienced players such as DOD and software houses manage complexity?

In a nutshell, DOD manages complexity through *discipline.* It has established an elaborate set of methods and procedures for acquiring, developing, implementing, controlling, and maintaining systems. These methods and procedures have resided in documents with the titles *Military Standards* (Mil Standards), *Military Specifications* (Mil Specs), and *DOD Instructions* (DODI). They provide detailed guidance on how to buy, build, and maintain systems. In the search for management discipline, DOD has invented tools that have become project management standards. PERT, earned value analysis, and configuration management are well-known examples of DOD management innovations.

The price of this discipline has been a high level of documentation and bureaucratization. The famous Kelly Johnson, father of Lockheed's Skunkworks, conducted a study that showed that more than half the life cycle costs of major government systems were tied to chasing paper.

A study conducted by Captain Patrick O'Connell of the U.S. Navy (1990) found that 70 percent of the action items pursued on a major weapons systems program involved administrative actions rather than directly productive activities. The specifications describing something as simple as a police whistle may run sixteen pages.

DOD has been ridiculed for its labyrinthine procedures. Ultimately, such procedures lead to the purchase of $10 hammers for more than $400 each. Yet in the final analysis, DOD builds the most complex systems on earth, and its successes are tied closely to the discipline it employs. This fact is not lost on individuals who work on large, complex projects. I once encountered a group of Japanese project managers who worked on $100 million projects and who told me that they were dependent on U.S. Defense Department regulations to guide them in the building of their systems.

Whereas DOD manages complexity through brute force discipline, private sector software houses take a more subtle approach. They too see the need for discipline through documentation, but they strive to handle this through automated procedures of self-documentation. Such procedures are commonly built into computer-aided systems engineering (CASE) tools. Ideally, automated self-documentation relieves project staff of the burden of maintaining a paper trail.

Software shops also try to manage complexity by modularizing software. This tactic was employed decades ago by the use of reusable subroutines. It was supplemented by the structured programming methodology, which attempted to minimize unnecessary cross-links between different parts of a program (for example, by forbidding the use of "goto" statements). In more recent times, modularization is found in object-oriented programming and the conscious development of reusable code.

But even with their efforts to "work smart," software shops find that managing complexity entails a large amount of drudge work. For example, a key component of systems integration is testing. Scores of tests may have to be carried out to ascertain whether the different components of an integrated system function together properly. Proper testing requires the maintenance of meticulous records on test procedures and results. Another example: whereas automated self-documentation can keep track of changes to software code, changes to requirements must still be handled by labor-intensive configuration management procedures. Change requests must be screened through a change control board, approved changes lead to revisions of baselines, a configuration management library must be maintained to document the whole requirements management process, and so forth.

A review of experiences in managing complexity at DOD and in software shops leads to an unhappy conclusion: given our current capabilities in dealing with complexity, its management appears to require a high degree of drudge work. With complex projects, project staff should expect to spend a substantial portion of their time creating and maintaining an administrative infrastructure that enables complex efforts to be carried out effectively.

In his book *The Fifth Discipline* (1990), Peter Senge is critical of this approach to managing complexity, although he admits it is useful in such efforts as "mixing many ingredients in a stew" and "following a complex set of instructions to assemble a machine" (p. 71). He argues that rather than focusing on *detail complexity* (which is predictable and linear), managers should come to grips with managing *dynamic complexity* (which is nonpredictable and nonlinear). He suggests that *systems dynamics* offers the tools to handling dynamic complexity.

Senge is correct in asking us to rethink how we manage complexity. However, at present we must make do with what we've got, and what seems to work is the imposition of a high degree of discipline— an old-school approach to handling complexity.

HOW TO MANAGE COMPLEXITY

Organizations can take various steps to manage complexity. Let's examine some of the more commonly employed approaches.

Methods and Procedures

As we have seen, the implementation of rigorous methods and procedures lies at the heart of the DOD approach to managing complexity. These methods and procedures evolve over time and are fashioned from experience. Thus there is a strong trial-and-error aspect to this approach. For example, an investigation triggered by a jet fighter crash might show that the aircraft failed because a wire snapped loose from a critical circuit board. This discovery might lead to revised guidance on how to solder a wire to a circuit board. The new guidance will be issued through a new military specification. This process of experiencing, learning, revising, and promulgating is repeated countless times throughout the defense community and leads to an expanding body of knowledge on how to build and maintain complex systems (Petroski, 1985).

The key to implementing effective methods and procedures is captured in the sequence *experience, learn, revise, promulgate.* Any organization that hopes to strengthen its capabilities in managing complexity must consciously work to develop each of these steps carefully. Petroski (1985) has shown that this painstaking learning process lies behind the achievements of our greatest engineering efforts.

EXPERIENCE. People in the organization must be encouraged to recognize and report experiences that can have a measurable impact on operations. For example, a data entry clerk might notice that he is required to enter the same part number for a component in two locations on a single data form. The second entry is redundant and time-consuming and increases the likelihood of data entry error.

The data entry clerk must recognize that what he faces is not just an amusing anomaly but something that should be fixed. Procedures should exist to enable him to report this problem to someone who can initiate actions to fix it. Incentives might be established to reward suggestions that improve productivity. Quality circles and suggestion boxes are common approaches to capturing the experiences of employees.

LEARN. When a problem has been identified, an attempt should be made to understand both its immediate and its broader implications. In the data entry example, important questions that might be addressed include these: What can be done to fix the problem on this data form (immediate issue)? What are the costs of data redundancy (broader issue)? Is the problem of data redundancy a common one that exists on other forms employed by the organization (broader issue)?

REVISE. Once the full implications of the problem are understood, procedures for dealing with it now and in the future should be established. This will lead to a revision in the way business is conducted. It is important that the write-up of the new procedures be clear and easily understood. It is also important that previous procedures that are now obsolete be expunged.

PROMULGATE. If the new insights are tucked away in a dark vault out of the reach of project staff, they are useless. Clearly, they must be promulgated so that staff are made aware of their existence. For one thing, they should be incorporated into a master methods and procedures file that captures all of the official rules governing steps that should be carried out on the project. For another, all the individuals directly affected by the rule changes should be personally notified—through fliers, e-mail, Web page postings, or meetings—of the new procedures.

The importance of well-defined methods and procedures for the management of complexity is indisputable. It is a hallmark of all the organizations that demonstrate competence in successfully conducting complex undertakings. However, methods and procedures have their downside as well. Two problems stand out: they add to bureaucracy, and they stifle creativity.

The connection between methods and procedures and bureaucracy is obvious. Rules must be documented and files maintained. Project actions must be continually checked and rechecked to ascertain whether they are in conformance with the rules. Lists of methods and procedures tend to become bloated as marginal rules are included and obsolete rules are not removed. Ultimately, the lists may become an impenetrable thicket that hampers progress rather than expedites it.

Methods and procedures stifle creative solutions in at least two ways. First, they interrupt the flow of creative ideas. More energy is spent trying to follow the rules than coming up with new ideas. Second, they reflect the accumulation of past experiences whose pertinence may no longer be relevant. Constantly focusing attention on how things have worked in the past constrains the imagination from visualizing how things might be in the future.

Accent on Simplification

An obvious approach to managing complexity is to keep things as simple as possible. Scientists do this all the time when, for example, they assume a frictionless world. Consider how complex an equation would be that attempted to define fully the action of a body falling on the earth's surface. The ideal equation would account for such factors as the effects of gravity (of both the earth and other celestial bodies), the friction generated by the body passing through air, the effects of air turbulence, the level of humidity, and so forth. In practice, the behavior of a falling body is adequately explained by a simple equation in which gravity is the key parameter: $s = gt^2/2$, where s is the distance the body falls, g is the pull of gravity (about 32 feet per second per second), and t is the amount of time that has passed.

An important way to simplify complexity on projects is through *heuristics*. Heuristics are rules of thumb that provide rough guidance on actions and their consequences. A famous example of a heuristic is Pareto's 80-20 rule. Its use can be illustrated with an example from the arena of quality control. Experience shows that roughly 80 percent of the quality problems we encounter can be attributed to 20 percent of all possible causes. Let's say that we find twenty sources of problems in a particular production process. The 80-20 rule suggests that if we direct our attention to working on the four key sources (20 percent of the total), 80 percent of our problems will be resolved.

Another way to simplify complexity on projects is to make heavy use of simple test cases. The idea here is to avoid becoming overwhelmed with all the detailed aspects of a problem and to focus on solving smaller, manageable pieces of it one at a time. This is a commonly employed technique in software development. For example, in the top-down design of a complex accounting system, data entered into early test versions of the system might be directed to "stubs" that simply indicate that the data have reached their targets. As the system evolves, the stubs gradually take on increasingly complex functionality. In the end, they evolve into fully functioning modules.

User-Friendliness: Simplicity Through Increased Complexity

One of the paradoxes of complexity is that the price we frequently pay to make something look simple is increased complexity. This is commonly seen in software applications. Using just a few lines of code, I can write a software routine that computes $2y + 6$ for different values of y. Since I wrote the routine, I personally would have no problem using it. However, if I wanted to turn the routine into a user-friendly application that any computer-literate person could employ, I would have to write hundreds—perhaps even thousands—of lines of code that would create pull-down menus, data entry forms, help functions, and mouse capabilities. If I wanted the routine to print nice-looking hard-copy output, large amounts of additional code would have to be written. Note that this additional complexity would not have the slightest impact on the core computation $2y + 6$. The sole function of the added complexity would be to increase the simplicity of using the application.

What user-friendliness does is reduce the need for the mastery of complex concepts and processes. People wishing to use my simple software routine might have to spend considerable time learning the rudiments of programming in Perl language so that they could figure out how my routine functions. With user-friendliness built into the routine, mastery of Perl is unnecessary.

We see examples of simplicity through complexity all around us. Not long ago, typical automobile mechanics had a thorough knowledge of the workings of a car engine so that when one broke down, they would be able to diagnose and fix the problem based on their own knowledge of engines. With the introduction of integrated circuitry into car engines, engines became too complex for mechanics to master fully. Problems now were diagnosed using highly sophisticated computerized engine analyzers, which are in fact expert systems. From the perspective of the mechanics, diagnosis became very simple: one merely had to hook up the computerized analyzer to the engine and read the printout.

Other examples include simplification of the cockpit panels of airplanes (pilots today complain that they have become glorified babysitters), computer-aided design (CAD), and automated medical analyzers. In each of these cases, simplification has been achieved through a significant escalation of hidden complexity.

Expert Systems and Artificial Intelligence

Much of the simplicity through complexity I have described is being achieved through expert systems. Using artificial intelligence support tools, these expert systems attempt to emulate the thinking and decision processes of experts. In theory, the computer replaces the need for an expert. Much of the early work in expert systems was carried out in medicine, where it was hoped that a medical doctor in an office could survey a patient's symptoms, feed the information into a computer (which would be tied to an enormous database covering all known physical ailments), and then read the diagnosis off a computer screen.

In practice, the achievements of expert systems have been disappointing (Devlin, 1997). Problems have arisen primarily in two areas. First, today's expert systems do not capture the subtleties of the fuzzy logic of humans. Many of the most important decisions we make in life—at work or at home—contain a large subjective component that expert systems have not yet been able to emulate. Second, many expert systems are limited by the knowledge base they access. Knowledge is enormously dynamic, changing from minute to minute. Given our resource limitations, how can we continually upgrade the knowledge base of our expert system to maintain its relevance to the real world? Even if we had substantial resources to do this, what kind of knowledge would we have to include in the knowledge base?

It is apparent that at present, expert systems are most viable in highly structured, rule-based environments. This is good news to people who are dependent on methods and procedures to assist them in managing large, complex projects. These methods and procedures are precisely the kinds of application in which expert systems are most appropriate.

In view of DOD's focus on rules, it is not surprising that it is leading attempts to apply expert systems to the management of complex projects. Expert systems already exist to do such things as process travel orders for project staff, track adherence to Mil Specs, and design and cut sheet metal parts in metal fabrication processes. Given the rule-based nature of important project management techniques such as configuration management (see Chapter Three) and cost and schedule control (see Chapter Eleven), it would seem that expert systems can allow many of the housekeeping chores of project management to be carried out in an automated fashion. If this is true, the enormous administrative costs associated with managing large, complex programs can drop far below the current rates of 50 to 65 percent of total costs.

Modularization and Reusable Components

The Industrial Revolution was pushed forward by the use of interchangeable parts. Interchangeability made mass production possible. An early leader in mass production was the armaments factory in Harpers Ferry, West Virginia. By standardizing production of rifle barrels, gun stocks, triggers, hammers, and the like, the factory was able to assemble rifles for the U.S. military at unprecedented levels of output. Prior to this focus on standardization and interchangeability, the stock of each rifle had to be custom carved to fit each unique gun barrel, a long and tedious process. These developments in Harpers Ferry in the mid-1800s ultimately had a major impact on how American companies carried out their manufacturing operations.

Today's modularization is the contemporary variation of interchangeable parts. With modularization, a system is constructed in such a way that its individual parts can stand alone. For example, the system known as a house is today made up of many distinct modularized components (for example, bath and shower units in many homes are prefabricated at the factory). In software, code is modularized by breaking into stand-alone pieces (for example, one piece may carry out sorts; another may format output).

Modularization reduces complexity in at least two ways. First, it reduces the number of links between different components of the system. Each module is relatively self-contained. Within the module, there may be a great many links holding the module together, but cross-module links are minimized. This feature has important implications for fixing problems and enhancing the system. If a part of the system breaks down, one need merely replace the module in which the break has occurred. Or one can work to repair the break without worrying about the systemwide impacts of the repair. Similarly, with modularization, a system can be upgraded one module at a time.

Modularization reduces complexity in a second way: it reduces the requirement for system mastery. If modules are designed in such a way that they can be easily fit to each other or easily swapped, then people working with a system need merely be familiar with the modules' broad capabilities rather than with their details. For example, in the old days of radio repair, electricians might have had to rewire an electrical connection to fix a problem. They had to have a mastery of the circuitry so that they would not make a change that would cause more problems than it solved. Today, electronic devices are built in such a way that repairs are made simply by swapping components. No knowledge of the workings of the components is needed.

Modeling

PERT/CPM networks are a well-known example of modeling in project management. By showing how tasks are linked together, the PERT/CPM network allows project staff to examine alternative scheduling scenarios. They can address questions such as these: What will happen to project duration if a noncritical task slips by three weeks?

How effectively will the duration be compressed if several key tasks are carried out in parallel? If task A slips, what impact will this have on the scheduling of task B? With modern PERT/CPM software, fully integrated modeling can be carried out, showing the interconnections among schedule, budget, and resource allocations.

Using a well-constructed model makes it unnecessary to understand all the details defining a process in order to appreciate the consequences of certain actions. For example, we don't need to understand the mathematics of turbulence to appreciate its effect on the performance of an aircraft. We need only create a physical model of the aircraft and examine its response to various types of airflow through simulations conducted in a wind tunnel.

Thus models contribute to the management of complexity by reducing the requirement for understanding a process in all of its details. They permit people to focus on the consequences of actions without having to understand their intricacies. (The employment of models in project management is discussed in Chapter Four.)

Systems Analysis and Cybernetics

Systems analysis emerged in the 1950s as a means to get a handle on complexity. It recognized that many objects and processes can be described as systems, where *system* can be defined as a whole made up of interrelated parts. Because of the interconnectedness of the parts, it turns out that even a system with relatively few parts can possess an enormous number of connections between them. For example, a system with 10 parts possesses up to 45 connections, a system with 20 parts up to 190 connections, and a system with 100 parts up to 4,950 connections. Thus complexity is built into all but the most trivial systems.

The early systems analysts identified a number of core concepts that will dominate systems thinking today. At the heart of their model is the *system* itself. It can be a hardware system, software system, political system, economic system, or human system. (Systems analysis poses generic precepts, so the specific nature of the system is unimportant.) Surrounding the system is its *environment*. An important issue in systems analysis is identifying the *boundary* separating the system from its environment. The system receives *inputs* from the environment, which it processes in some fashion. It then issues *outputs*, its response to the inputs. The appropriateness of the response is determined through an analysis of *feedback*. This feedback leads to the cre-

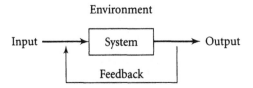

Figure 2.2. Rudiments of a System.

ation of new inputs and outputs. The purpose of feedback is to aid the system in achieving some sort of balance. The rudiments of a system are pictured in Figure 2.2.

This abstract treatment of a system is better understood through a concrete example. Consider the human body as a system. When the body enters a hot room (environment), its sensory receptors perceive an uncomfortably high temperature (input). The body reacts by instructing the eccrine glands to perspire (output). The effect of the perspiration is to cool the body. If the body continues to feel overheated (feedback), it persists in perspiring. If the evaporation of the sweat occurs very rapidly, leading to a drop of skin temperature (feedback), perspiration will cease.

Systems analysts capture the actions of the pieces of the system upon each other through diagrams. The most basic diagrams are called *flowcharts.* They detail the steps by which a sequence of actions is carried out. Very often, portraying a system by means of a flowchart is an essential action carried out in the early stages of system development. A simple flowchart is shown in Figure 2.3. By allowing us to track the details of a system, flowcharts enable us to handle what Senge (1990) calls *detail complexity,* complexity that derives from the sheer volume of things to be handled.

More sophisticated diagrams are called *systems diagrams.* They focus on how feedback (both positive and negative) affects the functioning of the system. A simple circular systems diagram is shown in Figure 2.4. Complex systems interactions can be portrayed effectively by linking together clusters of these circular diagrams. This type of diagramming allows us to capture what Senge (1990) calls *dynamic complexity.* That is, they keep us from getting bogged down in details and enable us to see high-level patterns. Various dynamic simulation tools based on these systems diagrams have emerged (Dynamo is one) that permit sophisticated modeling of complex situations.

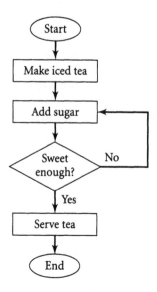

Figure 2.3. A Simple Flowchart.

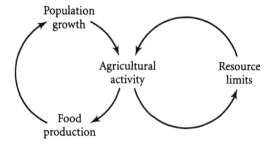

Figure 2.4. A Simple Circular Systems Diagram.

CONCLUSIONS

Complexity is a fact of modern life. Our lives today are far more complex than they were just a few years ago, and they will be more complex tomorrow than today. One of the great challenges organizations and individuals face is learning how to manage complexity. It is precisely project management's track record in successfully coping with complexity that gives it its strong appeal to contemporary management thinkers. They see in it a ready-made approach to handling the complexity that is overwhelming modern organizations. However, despite its past successes in managing complexity, project management is reaching the limits of what it can do in a cost-effective way. Unfortunately, those of us who think about how projects can best be carried out have not come up with any breakthrough ideas on how to manage complex undertakings more effectively. At present, the only guidance we can offer is to continue using the approaches that have worked in the past—to focus on maintaining rigorous project discipline through the development and maintenance of detailed methods and procedures, the development and testing of models of project activities, the close scrutiny of time and cost data, and the implementation of strong change management procedures. In the final analysis, all of these approaches amount to working hard, not working smart. As a consequence, we find ourselves in a situation where between 50 and 65 percent of our project budgets is dedicated to chasing paper.

The big question we now face is, are we willing to dedicate so many of our resources to what amounts to housekeeping chores? The increased sophistication of expert systems offers one possible resolution to some of our problems. Expert systems are most effective in dealing with housekeeping chores and might enable administrative budgets to drop dramatically. Beyond this, we must devote a substantial portion of our thinking to conceptual blockbusting so that we can develop new approaches to managing complexity.

CHAPTER THREE

Engaging Change
Knowing When to Embrace, Accept, or Challenge

During a corporate reorganization, the western region division of an industrial products company gets a new head. She sends a memo to all employees telling them of her vision of the division's future. The exciting challenge, she says, is to break out of the old mold and to blaze new trails.

After a progress review of a new control system being developed by an engineering firm, its customers are so stimulated by what they have seen that they ask the firm to add some new features to it even before the design is complete.

Owing to incompatibility of word processing software in the purchasing department of a government agency, the agency IT standards-setting manager requires that everyone use a single standard word processing system. This means that the majority of employees must be retrained to use the new software.

At the halfway point on a project, the lead contact in the customer organization moves on to another job and is replaced by someone who is lukewarm about the project and its importance. Consequently, the project is put on the back burner, and its very survival is in jeopardy.

Three months before the rollout of a new product, a company's principal competitor begins marketing its own product, which makes the new product obsolete. The company's development group scrambles to see if the new product can be resuscitated by means of some design changes. The never-launched advertising campaign for the new product is scrapped.

There is nothing extraordinary about these stories. They reflect the typical fare encountered by typical project workers in typical organizations today. The common theme of each story is, of course, *change*. In today's chaotic world, change is the one thing people can count on, leading us to quip that *the only constant is change.*

I have been so impressed by the volume of change in the workplace in recent years that I regularly conduct an informal survey of my students in executive development classes, asking them a series of questions about the change they experience in their work environments. When asked, "Have you encountered some kind of reorganization in your department during the past twelve months?" between half and three-quarters of the respondents answer yes. When asked, "Have you experienced substantive change in your own job responsibilities during the past twelve months?" about 60 to 80 percent answer yes. Over half report that a change in customer personnel in the previous year had had a measurable impact on project progress (generally a negative impact).

Consider the implications of these findings: if they reflect the experiences of typical project workers, they indicate that projects are being carried out in an environment of astounding turmoil. Such turmoil leads to fluctuating priorities, blurred visions of goals, and "rubber baselines." Ultimately, it contributes to schedule slippages, cost overruns, poorly specified requirements, and reduced customer satisfaction.

Clearly, an important management challenge for project managers is the management of change. In a stable world, change management is a nonissue: we carefully develop a plan and then stick to it. But in a chaotic world, we must come to grips with the inevitability of change. The idea of developing a plan and sticking to it is absurd in a wildly fluctuating world. Change will happen. The big question is, are we prepared to deal with it?

SOURCES OF CHANGE

Change on projects stems from a broad array of sources. Some key sources include the following.

Changing Players

A dominant feature of life today is the constant shifting of players in organizations. Much of this is a consequence of chronic institutional reorganization that began in the 1980s. Companies and government agencies are constantly adjusting their organization charts in an attempt to develop a formula that will enable them to function effectively in a chaotic world. Some do more than change organization charts and engage in radical changes to their basic business processes, an effort that carries the exotic name of business process reengineering.

A significant problem with this juggling of players is the shifting of priorities it engenders. Every time managers take over a new position, they view it as their prerogative to change the rules. Their rationale is, If I am going to be judged for my actions, then I do not want to inherit someone else's problems; I want to start with a clean slate. Although this outlook is understandable, it leads to the situation where previous commitments are abandoned each time a new manager takes over a position.

Budgetary Instability

A study conducted by the U.S. General Accounting Office (1989) found that the most frequently cited problem associated with cost and schedule overruns on major projects is "budgetary instability." Funds available to conduct project efforts at one moment are gone in the next. They may be put back into the budget a little later, only to be taken out again at some future time. Rational planning becomes problematic in such an environment. On federal government projects, the key culprit in this game is Congress, which whimsically adds and removes funds from project budgets as part of its annual budget cycle. Congressional whimsy in turn reflects institutionalized changes of players, because elections occur every two years.

Budgetary instability is not unique to government. Increases in global competition put enormous pressure on companies to watch their spending. Consequently, project workers in private companies often find that the budgets they were promised have been pared back.

Changing Technology

Technology is changing at an ever-faster pace. Such change has dramatic implications for conducting project work. In an era when the life expectancy of a new technology is extremely short, any project that has a time horizon greater than six months must grapple with changing technology. Common questions that project staff face include these: Is a particular solution that we recommend going to be relevant next year in view of changes in technology? How does technological change affect the way we conduct our operations internally? (For example, should we commit ourselves to having most of our business transactions Web-based?)

Changing Competitive Environment

In a competitive world, the actions of our competitors can have large impacts on how we do our work. If a competitor offers an attractive new product or service, we may find ourselves dropping whatever we are working on to develop a competing product or service. The sudden shift of work priorities produced by this reactive strategy is likely to disrupt ongoing work. Resources dedicated to a long-term project may be siphoned away to support our short-term response.

People Changing Their Minds

A ubiquitous source of change on projects is key people changing their minds. As projects evolve, we can count on our customers, managers, and technical staff to alter their views of what they need and want. This is a natural occurrence referred to as the *learning effect*. At the earliest stages of a project, people's vision of the deliverable is vague, and requirements are largely abstractions. As the deliverable becomes more tangible and people see what they will actually get, they ask for change. If they like what they see, they often ask for enhancements even before the deliverable is complete. If they don't like what they see, they request changes to make the deliverable more reflective of their needs and wants.

Changing Macroeconomic Forces

Changing macroeconomic forces can create enormous pressure for change on our projects. For example, a sudden surge of inflation can invalidate cost estimates for projects. This occurred on a large scale in the United States in the late 1970s when the inflation rate climbed to 17 percent per year. Economic recession can result in dramatic cutbacks in project budgets and staffing. Recession-induced layoffs of skilled workers are particularly devastating since they represent the loss of years of experience that is difficult to replace. One frustrating feature of changing macroeconomic conditions is that they lie completely out of the control of project organizations. All project staff can do is develop contingency plans to deal with these uncontrollable forces.

CHANGE MANAGEMENT STRATEGIES

This chapter offers a three-point strategy for coping with change. First, organizations and individuals must develop a pro-change mind-set. They must appreciate the inevitability of change and see it as something positive, something that offers them opportunities for growth. This is not easy to do because organizations and people naturally resist change.

Second, organizations and individuals must learn how and when to "go with the flow." There are times when resistance to change can break them, just as a dry twig can be easily snapped with little pressure. Occasionally, it is appropriate to use change's own momentum to direct it into desired channels. A promising approach to going with the flow is rapid prototyping. This methodology entails involving customers in defining requirements by having them react to tangible prototypes. The prototyping process will be outlined and its strengths and weaknesses highlighted later in this chapter.

Third, just as there are times when it is appropriate to go with the flow, there are also times when some degree of resistance to change is proper. Not all change is equally important or necessary. In some cases, it may be needed for survival. In others, it may add no value and may be unnecessarily disruptive and destructive. Configuration management, a dominant change management discipline employed heavily in technical organizations, is a methodology that puts the brakes on change. It filters out trivial or damaging change and allows meaningful change to be implemented. The basic principles of configuration management are outlined in this chapter.

Developing a Pro-Change Mind-Set

To a large extent, history can be viewed as a struggle between the forces of change and the forces of reaction. The essence of this struggle was captured by the ancient Greeks in the compelling story of Prometheus, the man who stole fire from the gods and presented it as a gift to humans. His act greatly displeased the gods because it gave humans the capacity to innovate and be rebellious, something that did not serve the interests of the gods. To show their displeasure, they punished him severely.

Punishing innovators seems to have been a favorite pastime of reactionaries throughout human history. Galileo was forced by the church to recant some of his scientific views because they challenged the status quo. In 1925, the state of Tennessee tried to stop a high school teacher from teaching Darwinian evolution because these teachings violated biblical dogma. In much of the Muslim world today, fundamentalists are attempting to turn back the clock and return to the old ways. (The irony here is that beginning in the eighth century, Islam offered a radical viewpoint that challenged traditional perspectives and led to a flowering of science, the arts, and literature.)

In the end, the forces of change consistently beat the forces of reaction. But the gains are often achieved through bitter struggle and are often short-lived because today's revolutionary becomes tomorrow's reactionary. And so the cycle goes—change begets reaction, which begets change, which begets reaction, and so on.

Most humans are not great fans of change. They tend to resist it, as individuals and at the group level. The origin of some of this resistance is psychological: results of Myers-Briggs psychological typing suggest that only 16 percent of the population is naturally "Promethean"—individuals who, following Prometheus, actively seek out new solutions. The remainder take a more traditional view of life.

Beyond psychological factors, there are external forces that encourage people to stick with the status quo. One force is captured in the expression "If it ain't broke, don't fix it." This view holds that if the current way of doing things is functioning smoothly, we should not tamper with it. At best, our fixes are unnecessary; at worst, they may create more problems than they resolve.

Another force resisting change stems from the investments we have made to maintain the status quo. When these investments are substantial, we are reluctant to walk away from them. In *Industrial Renaissance*

(1983), Abernathy, Clark, and Kantrow argue convincingly that as companies mature, their success rests increasingly on cost-saving investments in specialized equipment and processes, investments that ultimately restrict their options and their ability to support innovation.

Still another force resisting change is our reluctance to abandon formulas that have served us well in the past. Fat margins produced from the sales of mainframes made IBM blind to the precariousness of its dependence on mainframes in an era of powerful desktop computing. Consequently, IBM experienced some gut-wrenching adjustments in the 1990s to get itself back on track. Similarly, Digital Equipment's enormous success with engineering-oriented minicomputers made it reluctant to join the microcomputer revolution, much to its ultimate disadvantage. The theme of resisting change owing to comfort with the prevailing system was captured in the best-selling book by Spencer Johnson (1998), *Who Moved My Cheese?*

The problem traditionalists face in revolutionary times is that they are crushed beneath the tidal wave of change. Those resisting it are overwhelmed by the change agents. The change agents themselves derive much of their energy from the fact that they do not have a stake in the past. It has been noted many times that innovation within an industry often comes from the outside. (This is the key message of the classic work by John Jewkes, David Sawers, and Richard Stillerman, *The Sources of Invention*, 1969.) Even within a given industry, the most vigorous change agents are the desperados, those who are in bad shape and have little or nothing to lose.

Clearly, for organizations to survive and thrive in these turbulent times, they must develop a pro-change mind-set. They must alter their cultures so that change is seen as something desirable, filled with opportunity. Given people's natural resistance to change, the development of a pro-change mind-set is not easily achieved. Some steps organizations can take to create it include the following.

DEVELOP AN APPRECIATION OF CHANGE THROUGH EDUCATION AND TRAINING. Although many people pay lip service to the importance of change, few truly understand its positive nature. One way they can develop a better understanding is through education. For example, they can be taught that without a willingness to accept change, humans would still be roaming the savannas and forests, picking berries and hunting game. (A common characteristic of aboriginal societies is the total absence of change over thousands of years.) Through historical examples, they can learn that much of what makes our lives comfortable today is the consequence of change that was mightily resisted by our ancestors. Along these lines, they can also see that those who resist change are ultimately crushed by it. In the final analysis, Galileo's views prevailed, and his persecutors are vilified in today's history books. The state of Tennessee failed in its attempts to quash the teaching of evolution as a consequence of the famous Scopes trial. Although Islamic fundamentalism is a powerful force in certain nations today, it is encountering strong resistance from backers of policies that favor economic growth.

To make the educational experience meaningful in the context of change today, managers should be exposed to current management thinking and trends, which offer a perspective on the role of managers that is radically different from the traditional approach. They should see that empowerment of the workforce is not a do-good exercise but rather a requirement that must be implemented if an organization wants to remain competitive. They should understand that their role is no longer to command but rather to support their staff to do the best job possible. They should be made to appreciate that the most successful businesspeople in recent times—Wal-Mart's Sam Walton and Microsoft's Bill Gates, for example—are those who thrive on "upside-down thinking."

Although education can be used to raise people's consciousness about the benefits of change, training is required to provide them with the skills to implement it. For example, experience shows that a good way to overcome the resistance of peasants to the mechanization of agriculture is to train them to use tractors and combines. Once they have firsthand experience in using machinery, they become converts. Suddenly, those who resisted change become its foremost proponents.

Similarly, we should not expect technical project managers to become comfortable with their new role as general business managers if they lack basic business skills. To become effective general business managers, they should receive training on business fundamentals in such areas as finance, marketing, and human resource management. Further, we should not expect managers to readily accept their new role as coaches and supporters (as opposed to bosses) if they do not possess basic coaching skills to allow them to fill the new role effectively.

The chief drawback to education and training is expense. Resources must be committed to the development of curricula, the purchase of materials, the cost of travel, the salaries of trainers. Equally important, enormous costs are incurred as the trainees are taken away from their jobs to sit in the classroom. Who will do the work while they are gone? Nevertheless, despite the expense of continual education and training, successful organizations realize that it is difficult to effect the transformation of a corporate culture without it.

ENCOURAGE UPSIDE-DOWN THINKING. In *The Age of Unreason* (1989), Charles Handy argues convincingly that the individuals and organizations that thrive in turbulent times are those that are capable of upside-down thinking. They do not seize on obvious solutions. They perceive opportunity where others see threat. They also refuse to be complaisant: they are nervous with assertions like "If it ain't broke, don't fix it" and "It's worked in the past, so it's bound to work in the future."

The key features of upside-down thinking are captured in an old story in which two boys are shown a room full of manure. Upon seeing the room, the first boy, a traditionalist, says, "Ugh, that's disgusting. A room full of manure!" In contrast, the second boy, an upside-down thinker, jumps into the room and begins digging, shouting, "With all this manure, there's got to be a pony in here somewhere!"

A good example of upside-down thinking is found in the classic *Consultative Selling* (Hanon, Cribbin, and Heiser, 1970). This book introduced the idea that companies should see themselves as selling solutions rather than hardware. The authors recognized that in many industries, hardware had become a commodity, and it was difficult to distinguish one box from another. With commodities, products are distinguished primarily by price. Consequently, in a competitive market, profit margins tend to be low.

However, if salespeople see their job as helping customers solve problems, customers perceive them as offering high value. This solutions approach to making a sale makes the customer the vendor's long-term partner (another upside-down concept) and increases profit margins.

This upside-down idea runs contrary to what salespeople have been taught. Even today, salespeople earn their living through commissions and meeting sales targets, and the measure of their success is the amount of hardware they can move. A major challenge facing today's business organizations is to identify means to reward salespeople for promoting the sale of solutions rather than hardware. This is a formidable undertaking. For one thing, solutions are abstract, whereas hardware is concrete. It is always more difficult to deal with abstract things than with tangibles. In addition, the sale of solutions requires a high level of sophistication and competence in sales staff. Anyone can sell boxes; it takes savvy and perceptive people to sell solutions.

The need for upside-down thinking in project management is overwhelming. Following are some contemporary upside-down thoughts that challenge the prevailing wisdom.

• *Operations and maintenance efforts should be treated as part of the project life cycle.* The traditional project management perspective has been that the project life cycle ends once the deliverable has been handed over to the customer. This view is reflected in the position taken by the Project Management Institute (2000), which holds that all projects can be defined in accordance with five processes: initiation processes, planning processes, execution processes, controlling processes, and closeout processes. The implication is that project work is completed once the project is closed out.

The problem with this view is that it leads to short-term thinking on the part of the project team. It encourages the perspective that "our job is to get the deliverable out the door. What happens to it later is not our concern."

Of course, what happens to the deliverable after it has been delivered to the customer should be of great concern to the project team. If the deliverable is not used, is underused, or is used inappropriately, then some measure of project failure has occurred. In the final analysis, project success and failure is determined by customer satisfaction. Customer satisfaction is in turn often determined in the postproject operations and maintenance phase, at which time customers actually use what the project team has produced.

• *Technical people must be adept at understanding and offering business solutions to problems.* I once ran a seminar for thirty information systems professionals working at a large financial services firm. I asked them to identify the key problems they faced in their project work. The most frequently cited complaint was, "Our customers expect us to come up with business solutions to their problems. That isn't our job. Our job is to develop technical solutions."

These professionals were taking a traditional view of their roles. They saw themselves narrowly as technicians. Although this perspective may have worked in the old days, it does not work today. Why *not* take on the role of adviser on business solutions? In an era where few white-collar employees have a sense of job security, smart workers are those who identify their value to their customers and who work to increase it. If customers want more than technical solutions to problems, then project staff should develop the capabilities to offer expanded service. As guides to business solutions, technical people enhance their power. They should not feel threatened by the new challenges.

• *There is no such thing as "the" customer. There are always multiple customers.* The new focus on customer satisfaction on projects is healthy and gratifying. It has arisen because it works. The organizations with the greatest project successes are those that always keep one eye on customers and one on the work at hand. Organizations that treat customer needs and wants as afterthoughts get into serious trouble. Their projects are plagued with confusion and miscommunication. They have difficulty achieving customer acceptance at the end of the project. They produce deliverables that often are not utilized, are underutilized, or are employed inappropriately.

The new focus on customers is reflected in the discussions and pronouncements of project staff and management, who openly define their key objective as "satisfying the customer." This is a worthwhile sentiment. However, the way it is phrased may lead to a distorted view of what customer satisfaction entails. The problem is that *the* customer is a fiction. The phrase implies the existence of a monolithic customer perspective. This implication is picked up in such comments as "What the customer really wants is an information system that accesses data more quickly" or "The customer won't accept that modification to the design."

There is no monolithic customer perspective because all projects have multiple customers. When project staff begin to identify a single individual or group of individuals as *the* customer, they are inviting trouble. To see this, consider the case of a typical defense procurement. Let us play the role of a defense contractor working on a project to develop an upgrade to an existing fighter aircraft. We are likely to define *the* customer as a powerful general who has great decision-making authority over work on the fighter. From our perspective as a contractor, we are particularly interested in his budget powers.

Note, however, that there are other important players who are also customers. Pilots clearly fall into this category. Their chief concern is the performance of the aircraft on a mission. Maintenance crews are another set of customers. They are primarily interested in having aircraft that are easily maintainable. Purchasing personnel are also customers. They want aircraft that minimize problems in purchasing parts and services. Congress—representative of the public at large—is a customer. It pays the bills and is anxious to get value for the taxpayer dollars expended. Other actors come into play as well. The important thing to observe here is that on this project, there are multiple players who possess differing and often conflicting goals.

If the contractor defines the general as the sole customer, it is likely to produce a deliverable that leaves large numbers of other customers dissatisfied. The irony is that in the real world of defense contracting, the general will have moved on to another assignment before the project is finished, putting it at the mercy of his replacement, who has his own particular agenda. This discussion is not merely an academic exercise. In the building of Los Angeles–class nuclear submarines, General Dynamics made the mistake of defining Admiral Hyman Rickover as *the* customer. In their obsession to satisfy Rickover, General Dynamics managers caused their company to suffer one of the most notorious cost overruns in history.

• *A key function of managers is to support their workers, not to direct them.* The day of the directing boss who spews out ten orders a minute is past. A key role of managers is to create an environment that enables their team members to do the best job possible.

USE CRISES TO SHAKE UP STAGNANT ATTITUDES. Quite frequently, my students provide me with insights that dramatically affect my view of how the world functions. A good example of this occurred several years ago when four Japanese graduate students visited my office after class. We had just discussed how project managers can build authority on projects. The students approached me to say that they enjoyed the discussion and found most of the issues we covered to be pertinent to their lives in Japanese companies. They pointed out, however, that an important approach to building authority was not discussed.

"In Japanese organizations, we often create authority by announcing a crisis," said the chief spokesperson of the four students. "When a crisis is identified, we have an obligation to do our best to resolve it."

"You read in the newspapers that Japanese workers routinely put in sixty-hour workweeks," offered another student. "We spend so much time at work in order to deal with crises. You don't think we enjoy ignoring our families, do you?"

During a half-hour period, the four students described how the work life of a Japanese manager is filled with never-ending crises. Although these crises motivate Japanese workers to work long weeks, they grow a bit tiring after a while. Each student expressed distaste for this pressure-cooker environment.

Over the years, I have reflected on what these students told me. I have shared their comments with Japanese colleagues as well as with hundreds of students who have attended my seminars. My colleagues confirm that the experiences of the four students are quite typical. They point out that life in Japan has always been precarious (earthquakes, tsunamis, famine, political chaos, no natural resources), leading the population to view life as a series of never-ending crises that must be dealt with one at a time.

Interestingly, the *kanji* characters for the Japanese word for *crisis* (which is pronounced *kiki*) are comprised of two parts, the first of which indicates *danger,* the second *opportunity.* Thus in Japan, the word *crisis* implies *dangerous opportunities.* Crises are not inherently bad.

In thinking about the role of crises in Japanese management, I have been mulling over an intriguing question: Would this approach work in the United States and other Western countries, which have cultures that differ from Japan's in many respects? My conclusion is a qualified yes. In today's fiercely competitive environment, the crises organizations throughout the world face are real. In Western countries, cost pressures have resulted in unprecedented payroll cuts as companies seek to do more with less. The workforce is very sensitive to the large number of layoffs occurring across a broad range of industries. People also realize that even the best companies are only marginally competitive and must keep a tight lid on escalating costs. Consequently, Western workers are beginning to look more like their Japanese counterparts. Increasingly, they view the world as an unstable and insecure place. They recognize that they may be called on to work long weeks to help maintain their company's competitive position. They don't balk at the demands being placed on them, because to do so might jeopardize their jobs and their company's well-being.

The implications for project managers of the crisis-filled work environment are clear: it is acceptable today to use crises to direct the attention of project workers and upper management to key issues. Specifically, crises can be used to change traditional attitudes and to focus people on new ways of doing things. For example, a common problem that project organizations face is that the sales staff give away business in order to make a sale. They either offer project services for less than cost or promise to include features in the deliverable that project staff cannot produce. If this behavior leads to a number of clearly defined disasters, project managers can use the emerging crisis to revamp the way sales staff do business. "Look at the mess the old approach to doing business has created," they can argue. "We must revamp our approach to selling our project services if we want to stay viable."

Here is another example that I have encountered. I was asked by the training director of a Fortune 50 company to carry out a management seminar at a large factory in the Southwest. "I have one peculiar request to make, however," said the training director. "Is it possible to conduct the class from 7 A.M. to 1 P.M. with no lunch break?" I responded that I saw no problem with such a time frame.

I was curious about these hours, so I asked the training director why he was requesting them. He explained that headquarters was debating whether to close down the factory. During the past two years, half the employees had been laid off. The factory workers were gravely concerned that soon they would all be out of a job. They felt that to function more productively, they needed management training. Yet they didn't dare take too much time off from their work to obtain training in view of the precarious state of their operation. So they decided to do a double job: they would receive management training from 7 A.M. until 1 P.M. Then they would go to their jobs on the factory floor from 1 P.M. until 6 P.M. This made for a long day. Since such a long workday violated union work rules, they voted to suspend the work rules temporarily. Such an action would have been unthinkable a decade earlier. The point here is that crisis can be employed as a vehicle to initiate radical change.

Although I haven't conducted a scientific study of the employment of crisis management in Western organizations, my impression—based on working with many project workers throughout the world—is that it is growing. Workers are being asked to work longer days and over weekends in order to respond to crises that arise with increasing frequency. The 1970s dream of thirty-hour workweeks and two-month vacations is a thing of the past.

The dangers of reliance on crises to motivate the workforce are plain. Most obvious is the danger of burnout. How energetic and creative can we expect our workforce to be if workers spend sixty hours a week on the job and eschew vacations? What impact does this have on their family lives?

Another danger is that the continual announcements of crises can wear thin. In the West, crisis management has traditionally been associated with loss of control. The crisis manager is regarded as a re-active "firefighter" who responds to events rather than initiates them. Western workers may ultimately reject the precept that perpetual crisis is a natural state of affairs.

GOING WITH THE FLOW
OF RAPID PROTOTYPING

One way to manage change is to harness its momentum and direct it in desired directions. An appropriate analogy is a canoeist trying to negotiate his or her canoe down rapids. Ninety-five percent of the canoe's downstream progress is determined by the force of water rushing around boulders and over falls. Perhaps 5 percent is directed by the canoeist, who by means of controlled paddling can move the canoe laterally, allowing it to proceed along one channel rather than another and enabling it to avoid collisions with rocks. Attempts to go against the powerful current lead to frustration and failure. Success is based on going with the flow in a controlled manner.

Rapid prototyping is a methodology that arose in the 1980s to manage change by going with the flow. Its origins lie in software development, but today its applications extend across a broad range of activities. Its basic premise is that in a rapidly changing world, it is often impossible to prespecify requirements precisely. Even when possible, it may be undesirable to do so.

Proponents of rapid prototyping recognize that a major problem project staff have in specifying requirements is that the customers they attempt to serve don't know their needs or wants. Furthermore, customers are incapable of determining whether the requirements presented to them by project staff early in the project life cycle truly represent their interests because at this stage these interests are rather abstract and difficult to visualize. Consequently, as a deliverable gradually emerges and they see what they are actually getting, they begin demanding changes to the requirements. If they like what they see, they may very well request enhancements to the evolving deliverable. ("What you're producing is fantastic! Now can you add the following bells and whistles to make it superlative?") If they don't like what they see, they will request changes to make it right. The point is, there *will* be change, no matter what.

The rapid-prototyping perspective sees this phenomenon not as a problem but as an opportunity. Why not obtain customers' involvement in developing requirements by having them react to prototypes that are presented to them from time to time? Because the prototypes represent a tangible deliverable, customers can respond to them more meaningfully than they can to abstract statements. Rapid prototyping then becomes a customer-partnering methodology.

The Rapid-Prototyping Procedure

The rapid-prototyping methodology is summarized in Figure 3.1. The first steps in the process represent classic systems analysis. Project staff interview customers to identify their needs and wants. They then try to determine whether these needs and wants can be satisfied in view of budget, schedule, and technical constraints. They also review how these needs and wants are being addressed by current procedures. On the basis of this information, they formulate their view of what the customer requirements should be.

With classic systems development, these requirements serve as the basis for developing a new system. The requirements are used to formulate a design. Then the design is employed to actually build a deliverable. For this approach to result in a deliverable that meets customer needs and wants, the original requirements must be on target. The problem is that often they are not.

With rapid prototyping, the requirements emerging from systems analysis are viewed as just the first step in the development of customer-focused requirements. They are used to build a prototype so that customers can see what they will get. In software development, the prototype vehicle is computer screen images. For example, in a

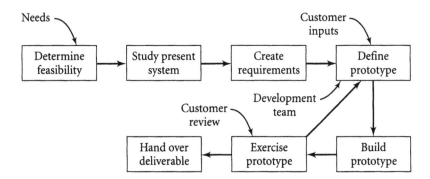

Figure 3.1. The Rapid-Prototyping Life Cycle.

project to develop a simple management information system (MIS), three sets of prototypes might be used. One would be screen images illustrating data entry forms. Another would be screen images of data retrieval forms. The third would be help menus.

When the first prototype is ready, the development team arranges to meet with a panel of customers. The composition of this panel is crucial to the success of the project. Panel members must accurately reflect the interests of the full range of customers. In our MIS example, the panel should reflect the perspective of data entry clerks, data retrieval personnel, and a set of the people who use the data to help them in their decision making. If the wrong panel members are chosen, the resulting requirements will not be relevant to customer needs and wants.

The first meeting between customers and developers is a classic kickoff meeting. Developers introduce themselves and the prototyping process. They show the customer panel the prototype they have developed. At this point, the prototype is nothing more than screen images. There is no depth. Still, the prototype images serve a valuable function because customers see what they will get. At this kickoff meeting, customers are generally delighted to find that they are working with something that has the "look and feel" of the final product. They may immediately begin offering suggestions for improving the prototype.

After the first meeting, developers go off for several weeks and begin adding muscle and sinew to the prototype skeleton. They are careful not to add too much detail. (This process is referred to as top-down design.) Their objective at this point is to produce as quickly as possible a prototype that customers can work with and that gives them an accurate sense of what they are getting. Once this revised prototype is ready, the developers hand it to the panel of customers for review. The panel then "exercises" the prototype. For example, if it is well developed, panel members may be able to enter sample data into the data entry forms. Because the prototype is just a shell at this point, it is incapable of doing anything meaningful with the entered data. Nonetheless, this data entry exercise is important because it may bring to the surface issues that might otherwise be ignored ("Look, the employee identification number is too short. Two more digits should be added to it").

On small systems, the prototype-exercising process can be undertaken quickly—in a matter of hours. On larger systems, it will consume substantially more time.

As a consequence of hands-on experience with the emerging product, the customer panel is prepared to offer useful guidance to the development team on further development of the product. Once the prototype-exercising process is complete, the customer panel meets with the developers to present reactions. In our MIS example, the panel members may find that the design of the data retrieval forms is a bit cumbersome. Some data fields can be eliminated and others added. They may also complain that the help menus use arcane terminology that they do not understand. The development team assesses these comments and determines which improvements can be accommodated and which cannot. It then goes off to add more detail to the still skimpy prototype.

The whole process is repeated over and over again until a satisfactory product emerges.

In the early days of prototyping, there was a great deal of concern that refinements of the prototype could go on indefinitely. Experience with prototyping suggests that this is not really a problem. In fact, the real problem is that customers are impatient for the deliverable and may insist that the prototype be handed over to them before the prototyping process is complete.

Three simple rules have emerged for stopping the process. First, the process can cease when a target date has been reached. Second, it can stop when the budget has been fully expended. Third, it can stop when there is general agreement between the customer panel and developers that enough has been done. Actually, with prototyping, you can stop the process at almost any time and still have viable requirements. (Remember that the process *began* with a set of requirements established through conventional systems analysis.)

At this point in the cycle, rapid prototyping can travel down one of two roads. With small, simple projects, it is possible that the prototype has gradually evolved into a usable product. If this is the case, the development team may hand over the prototype to the customers and end the whole process. Rapid-prototyping purists do not like this approach. They argue that the product that emerges through the prototyping process is poorly designed since it was put together in a piecemeal fashion. The chief problem with poorly designed systems is that they are difficult to maintain. When they break, they are hard to fix. When enhancements are desired, they may be impossible to develop.

The second road that rapid prototyping can take is called the "throwaway model" approach. With this approach, the prototype that emerges from the process is given to the development group's requirement experts. They study it to see what features the customers find valuable. As a consequence of this study, they write up detailed requirements that are ultimately used as the core of a highly disciplined development process. Once the detailed requirements have been created, the prototype is thrown away.

Strengths of Rapid Prototyping

A key advantage of rapid prototyping is that it leads to unprecedented levels of customer acceptance of deliverables. High customer acceptance occurs because customers are actively and meaningfully involved in defining their requirements. The serious problem of setting unrealistic customer expectations—a common problem in project management—disappears with rapid prototyping since customers see exactly what they will get. Another familiar difficulty—developers who ignore customer sensibilities—fades away because developers are forced to listen to what customers have to say.

Some of the greatest benefits of rapid prototyping are tied to the customers' exercising of the prototype. This effort has a number of salubrious effects. First, it entails constant testing of the evolving product. It exposes bugs early and offers developers an opportunity to deal with them while they are still manageable.

Second, it gets customers actively involved in developing requirements. They now become part of the development team. As mentioned earlier, rapid prototyping is a customer-partnering methodology. To the extent that their suggestions are incorporated into the final requirements, customers are committed to living with the solutions the developer-customer team offers.

Third, exercising the prototype is a form of training. In order to exercise the prototype, customers must learn how to work the system. The more they exercise the prototype, the more comfortable and qualified they will be in using the final product.

Pitfalls of Rapid Prototyping

Although rapid prototyping has led to astonishing levels of customer satisfaction, it is not a panacea. Over the years, I have interviewed customers and developers associated with many prototyped projects in order to learn of their experiences. The people I interviewed—both customers and developers—overwhelmingly supported the proto-typing process. However, they also warned me of some of the pitfalls they encountered. Following are the pitfalls they described.

• *The development team is not equipped to deal with customers effectively.* The most serious complaints I have heard about rapid proto-typing center on the toll it takes on the development team. "It's killing my technical people," complained the director of data processing of a large international organization. He explained that his technical staff possessed neither the training nor the inclination to deal effectively with customers. They did not become programmers and analysts because they enjoyed dealing with people. So when they were directly exposed to customers, they encountered a number of frustrations. For example, their customers had difficulty distinguishing between proto-types and the real thing. As the prototype became more sophisticated, customers didn't understand why the developers didn't simply turn it over to them as the final product. They did not fully appreciate that the prototypes they were exercising had no real depth.

A number of approaches have been implemented to deal with this problem. One is to appoint someone to the development team who has both people skills and knowledge of the technology. This individual serves as the main point of contact between the customer panel and the development team, playing the role of buffer. The problem inherent in this solution is that an additional communication layer has been placed between customers and developers, increasing the likelihood of some measure of miscommunication. Experience shows, however, that this problem is usually more than offset by the benefit of reducing stress levels on the technical team.

A second approach is to put one or two educated customers on the development team. If they grasp the technological issues involved in the development process, they can interact productively with the development team members. Two potential problems can arise with this approach: (1) the customers on the development team can start changing requirements at whim, aggravating difficulties of rubber baselines—I call this the Trojan Horse effect—and (2) the customers can become captivated by the technology and lose touch with their customer base so that after a while they no longer represent customer interests.

A third approach is to improve the human relations skills of the members of the development team through training.

• *The prototype platform is different from the platform on which the system will actually run.* The single most frequent piece of advice I received from system developers during my interviews was never to prototype a system on a platform that is different from the platform on which the built system will function. I heard many horror stories of teams that developed prototypes of mainframe systems on personal computers or high-performing workstations. Customers became accustomed to working with prototypes that were flexible, colorful, and easy to adjust. Upon delivery of the real system, customers were horrified to see that it had the cumbersomeness of a mainframe system and used monochrome monitors. Even the keyboard was different from what they used in exercising the prototypes. Needless to say, they vented their frustrations on the development team.

• *The prototyping process lacks discipline.* A key goal of prototyping is customer involvement in developing requirements in a dynamic environment. For this to work properly, prototypes must be built as quickly as possible. Creative perspectives are emphasized. In all the excitement, it is not surprising that rapid prototyping efforts frequently lack the discipline of documentation and effective change control. I sometimes quip that rapid prototyping is all heart and no discipline.

Discipline must be built into the prototyping effort. Rules must be established that each round of the prototyping process be fully documented. Key decisions and actions should be written down. In addition, changes should not be made in a haphazard, free-flow fashion. A change control board made up of representatives of key stakeholders might be established to review change requests that have a measurable impact on schedule, budget, and specifications.

Rapid Prototyping on Nonsoftware Projects

It might seem that rapid prototyping's usefulness is limited to software projects. Actually, it can be employed effectively on a wide range of projects. Two examples of its use on nonsoftware projects are offered here.

THE SMITHSONIAN INSTITUTION'S NATURAL HISTORY MUSEUM. One evening, after I presented a lecture on rapid prototyping to my graduate project management students, a student who worked at the Smithsonian Institution approached me. She was a curator at the Natural History Museum.

"The prototyping process you described is precisely what I employ when I create a new display at the Natural History Museum," she said. She went on to describe how a display is created at the museum. First, a number of drawings of a possible new display are created. Then a group of people representing the public are brought together and shown the drawings. They are asked to respond to the different drawings and to identify the features that they find most appealing. A handful of drawings are singled out as possible prospects for the display. The ideas represented in these drawings are then embodied in three-dimensional models of the displays.

The public representatives are then reassembled, shown the physical models, and asked to respond. Consideration is given to their responses, and one model is selected as the one that will serve as the actual display. This model is rebuilt and refined. The public representatives are assembled for a final time to review and respond to this last model. Their comments are solicited, and based on these comments along with other considerations, the actual display is built.

SEATTLE'S WOODLAND PARK ZOO. The designers of recent improvements to Seattle's Woodland Park Zoo used computer-aided design software to create three-dimensional images of animal habitats and landscapes that they proposed to build. These images allowed the viewer to "stroll" through the zoo and to see different displays from different angles. The designers showed these images to key zoo personnel to get their responses to the proposed habitats. These reviews resulted in important insights that led to significant alterations in the proposed designs. For example, some reviewers pointed out that various obstructions, such as tree branches and shrubs, would block a clear view of the animals in their habitats.

RESISTING CHANGE WITH CONFIGURATION MANAGEMENT

Just as rapid prototyping is all heart and no discipline, configuration management (CM) is all discipline and no heart. CM is a methodology whose chief tenet is to treat specifications like a contract. Customers should get nothing more or less than a deliverable that meets the specs. No deviations from the specs are accepted unless changes to the specs have gone through a rigorous screening process and have been approved by the proper authorities. Such a contractual approach protects customers from developers' and implementers' digressing from the specs. It also protects project staff from whimsical customer changes to the requirements.

Note that the underlying philosophy of such an approach is to satisfy the specifications (that is, the contract), not to satisfy the customer. This may seem out of touch with the current focus on customer satisfaction, but it really is not. The key to making CM customer-focused is to make sure that the specifications truly respond to customer needs and wants.

CM's origins date to the U.S. defense contracting community in the 1950s. At that time, it became obvious that building weapons systems had become too complex to be done in a traditional ad hoc fashion. In particular, a consensus emerged that all changes to a complex system should be fully documented and tracked by a sophisticated tracking system. Without proper documentation of changes, it becomes nearly impossible to fix or enhance complex systems. CM was the proposed solution to this problem. Beginning in the mid-1950s, builders of complex defense systems were required to employ CM to document and track changes on all their larger projects. Today, employment of CM has gone beyond hardware development to software projects as well. A well-known software variant of CM is called *version control.*

BASIC STEPS IN DEVELOPING A SYSTEM WITH CONFIGURATION MANAGEMENT

In developing or modifying a system with CM, every attempt is made to resist incidental change. What customers sign off on is what customers get—not an iota more or an iota less. The following development process allows CM to minimize specious change.

Step 1: Develop Detailed Specifications

With CM, the development process begins with the creation of detailed specifications. Traditionally, these specifications would be generated through classic systems analytical procedures. That is, systems analysts would go out with clipboard in hand, review existing technologies and procedures, interview key people, identify future needs, and then develop system specifications. The problem with this approach is that it often leads to the generation of specifications that are not truly responsive to customer needs and wants. Today, customer-focused specifications are increasingly being generated by means of rapid prototyping.

Once the detailed specifications have been created, they must be approved by pertinent authorities in both the customer and developer organizations. After these organizations have signed off on the specs, the specs become a *baseline.*

Step 2: Develop a General Design

Guidance on developing the general design comes from the baseline (the specifications) and only the baseline. As the general design takes form, it is frequently tested against the baseline for *traceability.* That is, every element of the general design must be tied to a specification. A *forward trace* starts with a specification and attempts to find a corresponding general design element. If no such element exists, it must be added. A *backward trace* starts with a general design element and attempts to find a corresponding specification. If none is found, the general design element is eliminated, since it represents an addition to the design that is out of line with the specifications.

After a satisfactory general design has been developed and approved by pertinent authorities in both the customer and developer organizations, it becomes the new baseline. The specifications can be put away for a while. This is not a problem since they are actually embedded in the general design.

Step 3: Develop a Detailed Design

The detailed design is built according to the new baseline (the general design) and only the baseline. As in step 2, care is taken to maintain traceability. When the detailed design is nearly finished, it may be subjected to a *functional configuration audit.* That is, independent experts may be asked to review the design and to offer their opinion as to whether the system that emerges from it will function in the prescribed fashion. After the detailed design has been approved by pertinent authorities in both the customer and developer organizations, it becomes the new baseline.

Step 4: Build and Test the System

The system is built in accordance with the last baseline (the detailed design). As it takes form, it should be tested periodically against the latest version of approved specifications. When the system is fully built, it may be subjected to a *physical configuration audit,* a full-scale test to ascertain whether the system behaves properly in accordance with the specifications. At the end of this step, the development effort is complete.

CHANGE CONTROL

Change on projects is inevitable. Even as the development process proceeds in a disciplined way, change will occur, and configuration management must be prepared to deal with it. For example, during the general design stage, it may become obvious that some of the specifications defined earlier are not realistic and must be modified. Or during the building stage, the project team may find that an important component needed in the emerging deliverable is no longer produced and that a substitute must be found.

Configuration management deals with change through careful screening of change requests, meticulous documentation, and controlled updates incorporating changes. Each of these elements of change control in CM will be discussed briefly.

Screening of Change Requests

Screening of change requests focuses on determining which change requests have merit and which do not. The process generally begins when someone (for example, a customer, a manager, or a member of the technical staff) submits a change request to the project manager on a form. Different organizations have different names for these forms: *request-for-change forms, mods* (modification requests), or *engineering change proposals* (the term commonly used on defense projects).

Upon receiving the change request, the project manager must make an important classification decision. Is this a category A change (one with a major impact on schedule, budget, or quality) or a category B change (a low-impact change)? If it is a category B change, the project manager may make a decision on the spot as to whether the change should be effected. If it is a category A change, the screening process will be more deliberate. The change request will be turned over to a change control board (CCB) for careful review.

Note that on really large projects, there will be additional categories of changes, reflecting different levels of impact that a change request can have. For example, on the F-16 jet fighter program, category A changes are major changes that take from one to five years to process. Clearly, it does not make sense to treat a trivial change request as a category A change in this case, so additional categories are created to handle smaller impact changes.

The CCB is primarily interested in the management impacts of a change. In reviewing a change request, the board members want to know its effect on the project budget, schedule, and specifications. Only after conducting a managerial review of this sort is the CCB prepared to weigh the costs against the benefits of a change.

The CCB is typically made up of a small number of people representing different stakeholders in the organization. Ideally, representation comes from technical, financial, marketing, and production groups. Thanks to its interdisciplinary composition, the team is unlikely to view change requests from an overly narrow perspective.

Many organizations subject change requests to technical scrutiny as well as managerial scrutiny. To do this, they establish an engineering review board (ERB) that operates in parallel with the CCB. The chief objective of the ERB is to determine whether change requests have technical merit. In organizations that have both a CCB and an ERB, if both boards approve a change, it will be granted. If both disapprove of a change, it will be denied. If there is a mixed verdict, the two groups will work together to establish a consensus about future action.

The principal strength of this rigorous screening process is that it discourages trivial change. "Scope creep" is not likely to occur if individual change requests are subjected to rigorous scrutiny. Another strength is that the CCB can act collectively to resist harmful change requests from powerful players inside or outside the organization. A properly constituted CCB—operating as a collective unit representing a broad range of organizational interests—is empowered to say no to even the most commanding individuals. As such, CCBs can serve as project managers' friends, enabling them to say no to unreasonable change requests through indirect means.

An obvious problem with the CCB is its potential as a bottleneck. If the CCB spends too much time reviewing change requests, progress on the project may grind to a halt. Effective employment of the CCB entails a balancing act: on the one hand, scrutiny of change requests must be rigorous; on the other, the best interests of the project require that the review process occur as quickly as possible.

Documenting Change

Very small projects do not need elaborate documentation. When you change the washer of a leaky faucet, it doesn't make sense to document the process in detail. However, as projects become larger and more complex, documentation takes on increasing importance. Following are some functions of documentation:

- It enables the project team to maintain an audit trail of their actions. If at some point, a customer complains that the team did not undertake certain crucial steps on the project, the team can pull out the pertinent documentation to support its position.

- It records information that is beyond the capability of people to retain in their heads.

- It serves as a tool for coordinating the actions of different sets of team players. When someone new arrives on the scene, the quickest way he or she can get up to speed is to review documentation on what has transpired on the project so far.

- It is necessary for debugging and enhancing systems. For example, if a building experiences an electrical problem, the first step taken to fix the problem should be to acquire a wiring diagram. Without such a diagram, the repair job will be heavily dependent on trial-and-error fixes.

In CM, careful documentation of change requests and actions is important. Effective CM systems have CM databases, libraries, and librarians to maintain the documentation. This of course means that CM systems involve a large amount of paperwork.

The CM process is heavily bureaucratic. Today, the term *bureaucracy* has negative connotations. This was not always so. As Max Weber (1964) showed, bureaucracies arise for a purpose. They are natural organizational responses to dealing with complexity. It is a fundamental premise of CM that bureaucracy is the price we must be willing to pay in order to manage complexity.

Updating Change

As changes are accepted and incorporated, the project must be revised to reflect their presence. Baselines must be revised. People downstream must be warned, "Change is on the way!" A key component of CM is updating change in an orderly fashion. The updating process is closely tied to the documentation effort since a major element of updating is revision of the documentation.

CONCLUSIONS

One of the great frustrations project staff face on their projects is constant change. The people they deal with change constantly. New bosses, new customers, new vendors, and new technical staff must be dealt with. Each time new people come on the scene, they bring a set of priorities different from their predecessors'. Hence priorities are always changing. Other common sources of change include technology, budgets, regulations, and resources.

It is easy to view change as an impediment to progress on projects. When change occurs unchecked, it is indeed a hindrance. However, change is inevitable. Ranting against it is as ineffective as King Canute's imprecations against the ocean's incoming tide. To deal with change constructively, project staff must accept its inevitability. Then they must begin developing strategies to deal with it. A good first step is to recognize that change is not inherently bad—in fact, it creates opportunity.

Strategies for dealing with change basically fall into two categories. One is to go with the flow. This approach recognizes that change can be constructive. It is particularly effective in dealing with high-flux situations, such as defining customer needs and requirements.

A second strategy is to resist change. Not all change is good. Whimsical change that reflects capricious fluctuations in mood is an example. Such change leads to cost and schedule overruns and possibly degraded product quality without adding anything to the project effort.

Effective project management requires that project staff be able to distinguish between good and detrimental change. It also demands that project staff be prepared to deal with change in the most effective manner possible.

Managing Risk
Identifying, Analyzing, and Planning Responses

—◁◁◁▷— From the beginnings of human existence, life has been chancy. During the days of hunting and gathering, humans never knew for sure whether a hunting expedition would end successfully. In order to increase the likelihood of success, they would act out the hunt through paintings on the walls of their caves. Today we see the beautiful results of their efforts in the caves of Lascaux in the Périgord region of France.

As humans settled on the land and shifted their focus from hunting to cultivation, the production of food stabilized. Still, some years were better than others; drought, floods, and pestilence could drastically lower the food supply. Some people believed that these disasters were inflicted by angry gods and therefore made various offerings to appease them—including human sacrifice. The Egyptians took a more effective approach to managing the swings of nature. As the biblical story of Joseph tells us, they developed an inventory management system for grain production, using stores of grain accrued during the fat years to cover the shortages of the lean years.

What the experience of our forebears teaches us is that humans have been engaged in the management of risk for millennia. Some of their approaches were more efficacious than others. The Egyptian case tells us that a fundamental cornerstone of risk management—contingency planning—was being employed on a large scale four thousand years ago.

In recent years, there has been a growing awareness of the presence of risk on projects and the need to manage it consciously. The existence of risk is reflected in the fundamental law of project management, Murphy's Law, which states that if something can go wrong, it will.

Projects are particularly susceptible to risk because each project is unique in some measure. The degree of uniqueness can vary dramatically. Thus a state-of-the-art semiconductor research project will have more unique features than a project to carry out the one-thousandth installation of a small telephone switch. This uniqueness means that the past is an imperfect guide to the future. We are never completely sure what the future holds. There is always a risk that things will not go as planned.

Official recognition of risk as a special concern of project management came in the late 1980s, when the Project Management Institute declared risk management a part of its core Project Management Body of Knowledge (PMBOK).

PERSPECTIVES ON RISK

It seems as if everyone is involved in risk management these days. In business school, students learn how to measure the risk of a stock portfolio. A low-risk portfolio is one whose performance analysts can predict with a high degree of certainty. A high-risk portfolio is one whose performance can fluctuate dramatically.

Civil engineers look at risk from the perspective of system failure. On many civil engineering projects, system failure can have dramatic consequences. A bridge that collapses, a nuclear power plant that experiences a meltdown, and a building that cannot withstand a 7.5 Richter scale earthquake reflect risks that have both economic and safety implications.

Insurance companies have been in the business of risk analysis for centuries. They insure clients against losses. In effect, they allow their clients to deflect risk by transferring responsibility for losses from the clients onto themselves. They stay in business by estimating the likelihood that their clients will suffer losses and weighing this against income generated through insurance premiums.

Definitions of acceptable risk are different for stockholders, civil engineers, and insurers, reflecting the varied consequences of undesirable outcomes. Although a 10 percent probability of a downside loss is acceptable in a business context, it is totally unacceptable in the building of a nuclear power plant, where a nuclear accident can lead to the loss of thousands of lives.

RISK AND VARIABILITY

Ultimately, what ties the different perspectives on risk together is the concept of variability. Risk is fundamentally a measure of the extent to which a given outcome might deviate from what is expected or desired. Consider the performance of two stocks over a period of a year. Stock A's price averages $20.00 a share. During the year, its lowest price is $19.50 per share, and its highest reaches $20.50 per share. Stock B's price also averages $20.00 per share. However, it hits a low of $10.00 per share and a high of $30.00 per share. The variability of its price is substantially larger than that of stock A. From an investment perspective, stock B presents a greater investment risk than stock A.

In many cases, variability can be measured quite precisely. It is known that many phenomena, such as body weight, height, the volume of soda distributed by a bottling machine, and IQ, are distributed normally (that is, according to a bell-shaped curve). Events that occur rarely can often be described by a Poisson distribution. Statisticians are thoroughly familiar with the properties of a plethora of distributions, including uniform, beta, gamma, hypergeometric, and binomial distributions. If we know the statistical distribution of some phenomenon, we can make probabilistic guesses about the occurrence of a specific event.

The usefulness of distributions in predicting outcomes has been applied in project management for decades and is embedded in its best-known technique: PERT (Program Evaluation and Review Technique, developed by the United States Navy in 1957). The people who created the PERT scheduling technique realized that any estimate of the duration of a proposed task is subject to uncertainty.

This can be illustrated in a numerical example. Suppose we are trying to estimate the amount of time it will take for paint to dry on a newly painted chair. Historical evidence tells us that on warm, dry days, the paint may dry in as little as three hours. On cool, humid days, however, it may dry in seven hours. Most typically, it dries in four hours. These three data points can describe critical points in what is called a PERT beta distribution. The three-hour estimate is our optimistic estimate, the seven-hour estimate our pessimistic estimate, and the four-hour estimate what is most likely to occur. The PERT beta distribution associated with paint drying on our chairs is pictured in Figure 4.1.

Given this array of possible outcomes, how long does it take the paint on an average chair to dry? PERT beta allows us to estimate the expected value (the average duration) for paint drying on many chairs. The formula for computing this expected value is

$$\text{Expected duration} = \frac{\text{optimistic duration} + (4 \times \text{most likely duration}) + \text{pessimistic duration}}{6}$$

In our example, we have

$$\text{Expected duration} = \frac{3 + (4 \times 4) + 7}{6} = \frac{26}{6} = 4.33$$

That is, given that the paint may dry in as little as three hours, as much as seven hours, and most likely in four hours, it will, on the average, take 4.33 hours to dry. This value is a *point estimate*. This one number summarizes what is likely to happen after accounting for the variability of the outcome. However, realistically, we know that there is a

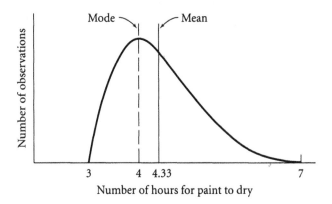

Figure 4.1. Using the PERT Beta Distribution
to Estimate Expected Task Duration.

range of possible outcomes. We acknowledge this in everyday life, when we make a statement such as "It will take you three hours to reach Los Angeles, give or take a half hour." What we want to know is how to compute this "give or take" figure.

In statistics, the "give or take" of an estimate is often computed as *standard deviation*. Over the years, I have taught business statistics to hundreds of M.B.A. students and have seen the beads of sweat form on their upper lips as we discussed the implications of standard deviation. To many of them, standard deviation is an arcane concept akin to the equations describing the second law of thermodynamics. In reality, standard deviation is a simple, user-friendly concept. It is basically a measure of the "slop"—the variability—of our estimate. In the example of paint drying on our chairs, a rough estimate of the standard deviation of our PERT beta distribution can be obtained with the following equation:

$$\text{Standard deviation} = \frac{\text{optimistic duration} - \text{pessimistic duration}}{6}$$

Substituting our paint-drying data into this equation, we have

$$\text{Standard deviation} = \frac{7-3}{6} = \frac{4}{6} = 0.67$$

Thus we can say that typically the paint on our chairs dries in four and one-third hours, plus or minus two-thirds of an hour.

The concept of standard deviation is important in risk analysis. Standard deviation measures the variability of an estimate. Risk is concerned with variability. Thus standard deviation can be taken to be a measure of risk. The larger the standard deviation of an estimate, the greater its variability and concomitant risk. For example, experience may show us that task A costs $10,000 to carry out, with a standard deviation of $1,000. Task B also typically costs $10,000, but its associated standard deviation is $3,000. The precision of our estimate of the cost of task B is weaker than for our estimate of the cost of task A. Thus the risk associated with task B is greater than that associated with task A.

Note that the PERT beta distribution is a generic statistical distribution. Although our example employs the distribution to estimate task duration, it can be used to estimate other things as well. For example, it can be used to estimate costs. If the cheapest cost to do a job is $3,000, the most expensive is $7,000, and the most typical is $4,000, we use the PERT beta formula to estimate that the expected value for cost is $4,333. As another example, it can be used to estimate human resource requirements. If historically the fewest people we have needed to do a particular job is three people, the most is seven, and the most typical number is four, then using the PERT beta formula we estimate the expected value to be 4.33 people.

RANGE OF RISKS

The concept of risk is closely tied to the concept of information. When information is lacking, uncertainty increases, which leads to greater risk. When pertinent information is bountiful, uncertainty decreases, leading to a parallel decrease in risk. Clearly, a key strategy for managing risk is to increase the amount of information we can feed into the decision process. More will be said about this later.

To appreciate the range of risk we face on our projects, we can picture a continuum ranging from total uncertainty to total certainty. With total uncertainty, everything is unknown. We lack data, either because we have never collected any or because the data are inherently difficult to compute. Here risk is high because there may be a great variation in the outcomes that can occur. We are just not sure what these outcomes might be.

With total certainty, everything is known. We can predict the consequences of actions with 100 percent accuracy. Here risk is zero, since there is no variability in outcomes.

Of course, in most decision-making situations, the uncertainty we face lies somewhere between the two extremes. On tasks that we have carried out many times, we know from experience what the range of outcomes will be. In the chair-painting example, data from past experiences tell us that it might take the paint as long as seven hours to dry or as little as three hours and that most typically it dries in four hours. Although we do not know with 100 percent certainty how long it will take for the paint to dry, we nonetheless have a good idea of what to expect.

In contrast, we also encounter surprise situations, which can be labeled "unknown unknowns" (the Defense Department calls these *unk unks*). For example, a competitor can produce a major advance in an integrated circuit design that makes our technology obsolete. Or a war in the Middle East may cause oil shortages that invalidate all our project material cost estimates.

In general, to get a better handle on risk, we should strive to reduce the unknowns.

SOURCES OF RISK ON PROJECTS

In project management, a little paranoia is healthy. We don't just suspect that risk lurks behind every shrub, pillar, and door; it really does! Risk is everywhere. The only time we do not encounter risk is when we make decisions with total certainty, and such circumstances are extremely rare.

Our principal concern is to learn how to categorize the risks we encounter. One useful categorization is the distinction between risks that arise in the environment and those that arise internally. Sources of risk coming from outside our organization include changes in government regulations, the introduction of new competitive products, and major technological breakthroughs made at a university lab. Environmental risk sources coming from within our organization (but outside our work unit) include such things as the appointment of a new vice president in charge of our division, budget cuts associated with declining corporate profitability, and the assignment of resources to our project coming from other work units.

A major feature of environmental risks—whether inside or outside the organization—is that they are largely uncontrollable. At best, we strive to identify them so that we can be prepared to deal with them.

Sources of internal risk include unreliability of worker performance, office politics, and unchecked expenditures. We often have some measure of control over such risks. For example, good human resource management practices will help reduce problems of worker unreliability, awareness of political agendas will mitigate the impacts of office politics, and close monitoring of expenditures will reduce the likelihood of cost overruns.

Of course, risks can be categorized in other ways as well. A common approach is to categorize them functionally. *Technical risk* comprises the risk factors associated with the development or operation of the deliverable. Our concern here is with "bugs" and glitches. Software modules that ran beautifully when tested independently fail when we try to run them as an integrated product. A soldered electrical connection won't hold because of the vibration of a motor. A chemical compound we have spent millions of dollars to develop becomes unstable at temperatures above 35 degrees Celsius (95 degrees Fahrenheit).

Technical risk is highest when our projects tread new terrain or when they entail working with highly complex systems. Basic research and systems integration projects are notorious for their technical surprises. Risk is lowest when we revisit familiar ground.

Market risk is the risk that the product or service we develop will fail in the marketplace. Business history is replete with tales of products that overcame enormous technical obstacles only to fail commercially. The best-known example is Du Pont's Corfam, a synthetic leather that cost a fortune to develop but was ultimately rejected by consumers.

Financial risk comprises risks having to do with cash flow and profitability. Many companies with excellent products have gone out of business simply because they ran out of cash to pay the bills. Cash shortages can result if accounts receivable are not collected promptly, if a key customer disappears, if money is tied up in equipment, or if financial reserves are limited. Similarly, a company will not stay in business long unless it achieves profits. There are countless ways for companies to fail to achieve their profit objectives.

Human risk arises from the fact that the human players in projects—project staff, managers, customers, vendors—are complex and only marginally predictable beings. Projects are constantly plagued with problems of human resource reliability, competence, and availability. They are further buffeted by the consequences of political struggles, the turnover of key players, and the fickleness of customers. If one were to create a detailed list of risk factors affecting a specific project, the list of human risks would surely be the longest.

RISK-REWARD TRADE-OFFS

We are willing to assume risks because we anticipate that the rewards of our venture will more than offset the losses. The higher the potential rewards, the greater the risks we are willing to incur. This is a well-established principle of business, and we see evidence of it everywhere. Investment in over-the-counter start-up companies can return 80 cents on the dollar in a year; it can also lead to massive losses of our investment capital if the companies perform poorly. In contrast, we can be reasonably sure that an investment in stable blue chip stocks will not result in major losses; by the same token, we should not expect to make a killing on them.

The risk-reward trade-off is also seen on our projects. Companies typically set higher hurdle rates (required return) for high-risk projects than low-risk ones. Risk-averse companies eschew such projects and build portfolios of humdrum, predictable projects. The chief danger they face is that they will not likely be leaders in their industry if they do not dare to innovate. Risk-taking companies, in contrast, weigh their project portfolios heavily in favor of high-risk, high-payoff projects. The chief danger they face is bankruptcy if their projects do not hit pay dirt!

Management science has developed a relatively simple tool for weighing the risks of failure against the opportunity for success. It is called *expected monetary value.* I will illustrate this approach with a simple example and will leave it to your imagination to see how more sophisticated variations on the basic principles can provide powerful insights into the risk-reward trade-off.

Suppose that a company's marketing experts estimate that a project to develop product X may ultimately generate $1 million in net revenue. After taking into account such things as technical risks, market risks, and financial risks, they calculate that the overall probability of developing a successful product is 70 percent. Meanwhile, the company's costing experts estimate that all costs associated with bringing the product to market, including project costs, tool-up expenses, production expenses, and marketing costs, will be $300,000.

If we were to envision this project occurring millions of times, we could say that the expected value of the company's gains would be $1 million (potential gain) times 0.7 (probability of achieving these gains). Thus the expected value of gains would be $700,000. The expected value of losses would be $300,000 (investment outlay) times 0.3 (probability of not achieving gains), or $90,000.

The expected value of *net gains* (expected gains minus expected losses) is therefore $700,000 minus $90,000, or $610,000. This tells us that given the probabilities of gains and losses, coupled with estimates of the dollar value of anticipated gains and losses, it appears that we have a winner.

RISK AND TIME HORIZONS

In general, there is a positive correlation between level of risk and projected time horizon. That is, the farther off an event is in the future, the less certain we are of its exact composition, and the higher the probability that some unanticipated action will affect it adversely. We encounter this reality in our daily lives. We have a precise sense of what we will be doing one hour from now. We are less sure of what we will be doing one week from now and even less sure of our activities one year into the future.

On our projects, the highest level of risk is found at the very outset, when we face a long and uncertain future. As the project proceeds and we begin achieving our milestones and gaining experience, the risks associated with completing the project generally decrease. In the last hours of the project, after the deliverable has been built and fully tested, the risks of not completing the work become very low indeed.

Even as risks are decreasing, there is a countervailing force at work: as time goes by and we commit human and material resources to the project, our *stake* in it increases. In the earliest stages, we have invested little in the project, so if we walk away from it, we have lost little. However, if we walk away from a project when we are far into the life cycle, we stand to lose a great deal.

The interplay of risk and stake is depicted in Figure 4.2.

RISK EXPOSURE

Clearly, the size of the investment required for a project has a bearing on whether it will be supported. From the perspective of risk, the chief concern is how much we have at stake in the project. The size of the stake is called *risk exposure*. The larger the risk exposure, the more we will lose if things go wrong. In general, we would like to maximize benefits while minimizing exposure to risk.

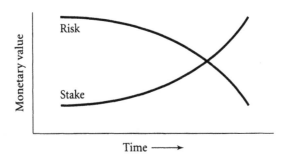

Figure 4.2. Risk Versus Stake.

Table 4.1 shows the kind of risk-reward dilemma we often face in making decisions about how to proceed on our projects. To keep the example simple, we will assume that the dollar values portrayed represent real value (that is, the cost of capital is zero, and there is no time value of money). Project B is clearly more profitable than project A ($1,100 versus $800).

Note that risk exposure is greater in project A than in project B in the early years. In the first year, project A requires outlays of $700 compared to outlays of $300 for project B. In the second, third, and fourth years, project B's total outlays are larger than project A's. If there is a reasonable probability of failure in the early stages of these projects, project B has the lower risk exposure. In year 4, the risk balance begins to shift. Although the total outlays for project A ($1,000) are lower than for project B ($1,200), the cash inflows offset outlays better in project B than in project A. From a five-year perspective, it is clear that over the life of the projects, the overall risk exposure of project A is lower than that of project B.

Project A

	Outlays	Income	Profit	Cumulative Profit
Year 1	$ 700	$ 0	$-700	$-700
Year 2	200	0	-200	-900
Year 3	100	700	600	-300
Year 4	0	600	600	300
Year 5	0	500	500	800
Total	$1,000	$1,800	$ 800	$ 800

Project B

	Outlays	Income	Profit	Cumulative Profit
Year 1	$ 300	$ 0	$ -300	$ -300
Year 2	300	0	-300	-600
Year 3	300	600	300	-300
Year 4	300	800	500	200
Year 5	0	900	900	1,100
Total	$1,200	$2,300	$1,100	$1,100

Table 4.1. Comparing Variability of Risk over Time.

PROJECT RISK MANAGEMENT

When project professionals encounter risk on their projects, what can they do about it? An obvious answer to this question is that they should *manage* it. Project risk management is a broad concept that can be approached in different ways. Two standards have emerged that provide project teams with useful guidance on managing risk. One is Australia/New Zealand Standard 4360:1999, (A/NZS 4360:1999, 1999), and the other is the standard promoted by the Project Management Institute in its *Guide to the Project Management Body of Knowledge* (2000). Both standards share common perspectives inasmuch as they recognize that managing risk requires identifying and understanding risk events, analyzing their impacts, developing strategies to handle them, monitoring them, and treating them when they actually arise. Here we will review the *PMBOK Guide* approach to managing risk.

The *PMBOK Guide* sees managing risk as made up of six processes: risk management planning, risk identification, qualitative risk analysis, quantitative risk analysis, risk response planning, and risk monitoring and control. Each of these processes will be discussed briefly.

Risk Management Planning

If risk is going to be managed effectively on projects, then project team members must approach the effort consciously by *planning* to deal with it. When planning the overall project, time must be set aside to deal specifically with a risk management plan. This plan should address how the team will approach risk. For example, it may specify that potential risk factors might be surfaced by highlighting them on an issues log that is reviewed during weekly status meetings. In organizations that have developed conscious risk-handling processes, the risk management plan would focus on adopting these processes into the specific context of the given project.

Risk Identification

Risk identification is a process of uncovering potential risk events in order to avoid unpleasant surprises. It should be undertaken systematically. It can focus on both internal and external risks, those that are predictable versus those that are unpredictable, those over which we have a measure of control versus those that are largely uncontrollable, and those that are technical versus those that are nontechnical.

As organizations gain experience in identifying risks, they should document their findings. At a minimum, they should develop a checklist of risk factors that must be dealt with on typical projects. If possible, different risk factors should be weighted according to their importance. An example of some risk factors and their associated weights for a data processing project is shown in Exhibit 4.1. The actual document from which these risk factors were taken contains a total of seventy-five risk factors, so what is shown here is just the tip of the iceberg.

What is the status of the project team training plan? (Weight = 2)

a.	No training plan required	N/A = 0
b.	Complete plan in place	Low = 1
c.	Plan under development	Medium = 2
d.	No plan available	High = 3

What is the documentation approach for the proposed/existing system? (Weight = 3)

a.	Excellent standards closely adhered to and carried out as an integral part of system and program development	Low = 1
b.	Adequate practices, but not uniformly adhered to	Medium = 2
c.	Poor or no standards; where standards exist, minimal adherence	High = 3

How much is the development affected by external systems? (Weight = 5)

a.	All critical intersystem communications are controlled through interface control documents; standard protocols are utilized; interfaces are stable	Low = 1
b.	All critical intersystem communications are controlled through interface control documents; some protocols may be nonstandard; interfaces change infrequently	Medium = 2
c.	Not all critical intersystem communications are controlled through interface control documents; some protocols may be nonstandard; some interfaces change infrequently	High = 3

How many output reports are projected? (Weight = 1)

a.	Less than 10	Low = 1
b.	10 to 20	Medium = 2
c.	More than 20	High = 3

Exhibit 4.1. Typical Items Appearing in a
Listing of Risk Factors for a Data Processing Project.

Qualitative Risk Analysis

Risk analysts will have a good sense of what risk events might arise on a project after going through a risk identification exercise. Now they should turn their attention to answering the question, What are the consequences should these risk events arise? They can address this question in two ways: by conducting either a qualitative risk analysis or a quantitative risk analysis.

Qualitative risk analysis strives to determine the impact and probability of the risk events being reviewed. Impact can be described according to a qualitative scale—for example, none, minor, medium, serious, catastrophic. Similarly, the probability of the event's arising can be described according to a scale—for example, highly unlikely, unlikely, somewhat likely, likely, highly likely, where each of these labels of likelihood can be assigned a probability value (e.g., highly unlikely = .1; unlikely = .3; somewhat likely = .5; likely = .7; highly likely = .9). The combination of impact and likelihood can be captured in a probability-impact matrix. Figure 4.3 offers a rendering of this matrix.

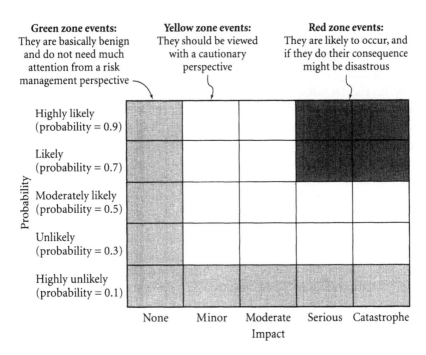

Figure 4.3. The Probability-Impact Matrix.

Quantitative Risk Analysis

Certainly, a well-done qualitative risk analysis will provide risk analysts with a good sense of what they may encounter on their projects. They will have even better insights if they can conduct a quantitative risk analysis. By modeling risk scenarios quantitatively, the analysts can carry out a series of "what if" analyses that will enable them to predict such things as the impact on cost or schedule or resource needs associated with the occurrence of a particular risk event. More will be said about modeling risk shortly.

Risk Response Planning

At this stage in the risk assessment, risk analysts have a good idea of what risk events can arise (through risk identification) and their consequences (through qualitative and quantitative risk analysis). Now the question they face is, What can we do about it? Risk response planning is concerned with developing strategies to cope with risk events. Whereas risk identification and analysis provide us with an understanding of what can happen on the project, risk response planning furnishes us with actions we can take either to avoid a risk event or to dampen its impacts. Common risk-handling strategies include risk transfer (also called risk deflection), risk mitigation, risk avoidance, and risk acceptance.

With risk transfer, we plan to shift the consequences of risk events onto another player. We commonly do this when we purchase insurance. For example, when our insured car suffers a fender bender, the insurance company assumes the burden of paying for repairs. Other standard risk transfer techniques include warranties and contracts. In the case of warranties, a vendor may offer a no-questions-asked replacement policy for a period of ninety days for electrical appliances it sells. With contracts, we have agreements to apportion risk among the signatories: If bad event A occurs, George pays; however, if bad event B occurs, Martha pays.

Risk mitigation focuses on lessening risk by fixing problems that may elevate risk levels. For example, an inspection of a grinding machine may find that one of its belts is a bit loose, which may lead to the production of defective parts. By tightening the belt, we lessen the likelihood of defects.

Risk avoidance recognizes that one way to steer clear of untoward events is to avoid doing things that can get us in trouble. For example, we may find that we have increased the likelihood of a database system crashing by 1,000 percent if we add a new module routine to the program. Solution: Don't add the module! Avoid doing things that create problems.

Finally, with risk acceptance, we recognize that the world is filled with risk and that we need to learn how to live with it. So when we carry out risky initiatives, we establish contingencies to deal with troublesome consequences. For example, research and development projects are notoriously risky because we have little foreknowledge of what will happen on them. In order to deal with unfortunate possibilities such as cost overruns and schedule slippages, we set aside contingencies to cover their possible occurrence.

Risk Monitoring and Control

Until now, we have approached risk management in a largely passive way. We have tried to anticipate the happening of untoward risk events through a series of preemptory exercises. This is the fundamental nature of *risk assessment,* a largely intellectual exercise. But once a project is under way and we actually encounter the occurrence risk events, we need to handle them aggressively. No armchair risk assessment here! With risk monitoring and control, we take a hands-on approach to dealing with risk. We attempt to solve the problems we encounter and continually monitor to see whether our actions are producing the desired effects.

THE NEED FOR DOCUMENTATION

The importance of effective documentation cannot be overstated. Most organizations sit on a mountain of data that can provide valuable insights as to how they are doing their jobs. They have schedule and budget data embedded in their time sheets. They have additional budget data in their monthly budget reports, detailing how money is being spent. Project proposals provide a glimpse of what the organization said it could do in the preproject phase, statements of work detail project obligations, and postmortems describe what actually happened. Technical documentation, including the results of technical testing, generally exists in abundance. Most important, enormous amounts of information reside in the heads of the project participants.

Managers face two problems in dealing with all this information. First, they do not see its inherent value. To them, it is just a bunch of facts and figures cramming the corporate file cabinets. Because they lack sufficient background in data analysis, they find it difficult to picture how the data can be fashioned into something worthwhile.

Second, there are logistical problems in converting all the data into useful information. Who is going to do it? What steps should they take? How will it be reported and incorporated in project management? This second problem is not as intractable as it sounds, even in this era of budget cutbacks. Local colleges and universities are wonderful sources of low-cost, skilled talent. Graduate students in economics, engineering, statistics, and related disciplines are eager to find part-time employment with local organizations. They generally have the skills, discipline, and energy to carry out assignments like this.

Ultimately, the purpose of the documentation is to provide baseline data on what it takes to do a job. If a software writer promises us that she can write her software module in three weeks, we can show her data demonstrating that no one has written such modules in less than eight weeks. If upper management pressures us to shave 20 percent off our cost estimate on a bid, we can employ our historical model to illustrate the budget and schedule consequences of such an action. The important thing is that by collecting and employing historical data, we are creating an environment in which our perceptions of the future are based on informed judgment, rather than on seat-of-the-pants guesses or estimates pulled out of the air.

MODELING

The advent of the personal computer has given project managers the capability to carry out risk analyses that would have been unthinkable until recently. As I mentioned earlier, computerized PERT/CPM software packages allow us to create mathematical models of our projects, integrating schedule, budget, and resource management factors. Once the model has been created, project staff can put it through its paces, playing all manner of "what if" games. What if our budget is cut by 10 percent? What if the testing personnel arrive a week late? What if three additional people are made available to design our software product? Questions such as these can be readily addressed with project scheduling software.

Of particular relevance to risk management is software that allows project analysts to conduct statistical simulations of pertinent budget, schedule, and resource allocation scenarios. Most of these simulations employ the Monte Carlo approach. The use of this approach is best explained through illustrations.

Table 4.2 compares how much time it takes George and Martha to prepare for a picnic. On the average, their performance is identical: both typically take ten minutes to prepare sandwiches, six minutes to gather equipment, and four minutes to pack the car. Thus on the average, each takes twenty minutes to prepare for the picnic. However, experience shows that George's performance on these tasks is less predictable than Martha's. This is reflected in the larger standard deviation values associated with George for each of the tasks.

Let us assume that the variability of both George's and Martha's performance can be described by the bell-shaped curve. The only difference between their curves is the standard deviation. With Monte Carlo simulation, the values for each of the activities can be allowed

	George		Martha	
	Estimated Duration	Standard Deviation	Estimated Duration	Standard Deviation
Make sandwiches	10 min.	3 min.	10 min.	1 min.
Gather equipment	6 min.	2 min.	6 min.	0.5 min.
Pack car	4 min.	2 min.	4 min.	0.5 min.
Total duration	20 min.		20 min.	
Maximum duration (simulated)	31.6 min.		23.1 min.	
Minimum duration (simulated)	9.4 min.		16.8 min.	
Standard deviation of total duration	4.3 min.		1.3 min.	
25% chance that value lies beyond:	22.6 min.		20.7 min.	

Table 4.2. A Schedule Simulation.

to fluctuate randomly according to their respective bell-shaped curves. Because of the larger standard deviations associated with his efforts, George's durations will fluctuate more wildly than Martha's.

We generated one thousand possible scenarios, assuming random fluctuations in duration generated by the bell-shaped curve. The results of this "experiment" are reported at the bottom of Table 4.2.

Owing to the high level of variability in George's performance, we see that it may take him as much as 31.6 minutes to prepare for the picnic or as few as 9.4 minutes. On the average, it will take him 20 minutes. Martha, in contrast, performs in a more predictable manner: it may take her as much as 23.1 minutes or as little as 16.8 minutes to make her preparations. On the average, it takes her 20 minutes. Clearly, there is a greater risk in depending on George than on Martha, even though their performance is equal on average.

Table 4.3 illustrates the use of Monte Carlo simulation in projecting costs. Let us say that our organization's professional cost estimators base their estimates on the most likely costs of each task. They

	Estimate (based on "most likely" costs)	Best Case Costs	Most Likely Costs	Worst Case Costs
Design	$3,500	$3,200	$3,500	$4,500
Development	$36,000	$33,000	$36,000	$42,000
Testing	$3,000	$2,800	$3,000	$3,200
Production (number of units × unit cost)	$312,000			
Number of units	1,200	1,200	1,200	1,200
Unit cost	$260	$220	$260	$330
Total cost	$354,500			

Simulation Results, Assuming Numbers Generated Randomly
Using a Triangular Distribution

	Best Case	Mean Value	Worst Case
Total Cost	$308,114	$367,736	$439,298

Probability that total costs will be greater than $375,000 is 21.6%.

Table 4.3. Cost Estimation Simulation.

gather these data by reviewing previous project experiences. Using these data, they determine that the estimated cost for carrying out a project is $354,500.

As the table indicates, there is actually quite a bit of variability associated with each estimate. For example, experience shows us that design might cost as little as $3,200 or as much as $4,500. Most frequently, it costs $3,500. When we have optimistic, pessimistic, and realistic estimates such as this, we can allow Monte Carlo simulations to generate random data according to a triangular distribution. We have done precisely this in Table 4.3. The results of the simulation, involving one thousand iterations, show us that the expected value of costs is higher than originally predicted: $367,736 versus $354,500, Furthermore, the simulation shows us the range of costs we might expect, from a minimum of $308,114 to a maximum of $439,298. The simulation also alerts us to the fact that there is a fair probability that total costs will exceed $375,000 (a 21.6 percent probability). The frequency distribution associated with this simulation is pictured in Figure 4.4.

CONCLUSIONS

Risk is ubiquitous. It is part of the natural order of things. Although projects have been facing risks and their consequences for millennia, only in recent years has risk management become a widespread concern

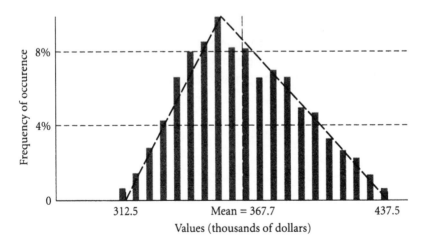

Figure 4.4. Frequency Distribution of
Project Costs Derived from a Monte Carlo Simulation.

of business and government. Some of the newly found interest in risk is a consequence of the chaotic management environment that has developed recently. Global competition is keen, product life cycles are shortening, consumer loyalty is gone, large companies are undergoing massive downsizing—nothing is certain. In such an environment, it is natural for people to strive to make order out of chaos.

I believe that the interest in risk management has also been piqued by developments in information technology. No single event in history did more to stimulate interest in risk management than the "Y2K problem." Beginning the late 1980s, companies and governments throughout the world recognized that when calendar dates changed after 1999, there was a danger of catastrophic computer failures. Big and little organizations set up Y2K offices whose principal function was to identify and correct potential problems triggered by the arrival of the year 2000.

Software developments have also stimulated interest in risk management. Project scheduling software now enables ordinary project managers to create sophisticated models of their projects on their PCs; this previously required the power of mainframes and battalions of programmers. Once the project is modeled, it can be used to explore the full range of consequences arising from different actions.

As we have seen, statistical simulation software brings the power of Monte Carlo risk analysis within reach of ordinary project staff. The software used to run the Monte Carlo simulations described in this chapter can be purchased for $200 to $500 and can be learned, with proper instruction, in an hour or two.

Whatever the origins of the current interest in risk management, it is clear that risk analysis is here to stay. A solid understanding of risk, its implications, and management is now a required item in the project manager's tool box.

CHAPTER FIVE

Satisfying Customers

Knowing Who They Are, What They Want, and When They Are Right or Wrong

A key to surviving and thriving in these competitive times is to win customers and then keep them. Obsession with customer satisfaction is what is driving management change today. It underlies the total quality management (TQM) movement, the speed-to-market effort, and attempts at corporate reengineering.

This obsession with customer satisfaction is leading to great improvements in standards of living and quality of life. Goods and services are better than ever—and cheaper to boot! However, there is a cost associated with achieving customer satisfaction. Organizations must rethink how they do business. As customers move from the periphery to center stage, old ways of doing business no longer work. The organization's shift toward a customer focus may lead to discomfort among the workforce as employees adjust to new ways of operating. It may lead to high levels of anxiety, since customer-focused organizations tend to be lean and jobs may have to be pared.

Obsession with customer satisfaction is part of the new project management. Evidence of this is seen in the explosive growth of customer-developer teaming arrangements. A move in this direction was presaged by Hanon, Cribbin, and Heiser in their classic 1970 work

Consultative Selling. This book pioneered the ideas that high-value organizations are in the business of selling solutions, not hardware, and that customer satisfaction is best achieved through partnering arrangements between buyers and sellers. It was not until the late 1980s that organizations began adopting these ideas on a grand scale.

Customer satisfaction will not happen by accident. Exhortations to do our best and to keep the customer smiling won't do the trick. Customer satisfaction will occur only through conscious efforts to alter the way we approach our work. We must not only change our attitudes but also change the way we organize our efforts. This chapter explores some steps that can be taken to increase the likelihood of customer satisfaction on projects.

WHO ARE OUR CUSTOMERS?

An important first step toward achieving customer satisfaction is to determine exactly who our customers are. Note that this is quite different from the usual approach, which is to ask, "Who *is* our customer?" The point is that we must recognize that we are always dealing with multiple customers.

Consider a project to install point-of-entry terminals at a chain of thirty retail stores. These terminals allow sales staff to enter sales data directly into the company's central computer as sales are being made. The project team—employees of the seller of the hardware, software, and services—faces a plethora of customers in the buying organizations. The managers and salespeople at each of the thirty retail stores are one set of customers, as are the information systems department, the finance department, the accounting department, the purchasing department, the human resource management department, the facilities management group, and upper management at headquarters.

Note that each of the customers enumerated here has a different set of interests. Salespeople want ease of use, the accountants are most interested in how sales data can be consolidated, human resources is interested in how personnel will be trained to use the new system, and so on. There are few shared interests among the different sets of customers. There may in fact be substantial differences. For example, the information systems group is likely to be most interested in functionality ("Let's make sure it's state-of-the-art"), whereas salespeople are concerned with usability. Anyone who has worked with computer systems recognizes that the conflict between functionality and usability is often great.

The project team often faces the difficult task of sorting through the contending needs of different customers in order to define customer needs and requirements—a challenging undertaking. Satisfaction of one set of needs may generate hostility from customers with opposing interests. A successful needs definition process depends on compromise and balance. For needs to be defined effectively, the project team members must possess well-developed people management capabilities and must thoroughly understand the business of the customer organization. These skills have not been prized in project management until quite recently.

Identifying customers is complicated by the fact that we must often deal with internal customers as well as external ones. If I am developing a new financial reporting system for my company, the principal customer organization with which I will deal is the finance department, an internal customer. In most of my project actions—on projects with external or internal customers—I am also concerned with satisfying a broad array of internal players whom I identify as my customers, including my boss, the functional managers with whom I must work, and higher levels of management.

Thus the project staff need to recognize that there is nothing obvious or trivial about identifying who the customers are. It entails careful study. If project staff do not realize this truth, they are likely to be in for some nasty surprises.

MEETING CUSTOMER EXPECTATIONS

Before we organize our efforts to satisfy both our internal and external customers, we must have an understanding of what leads to customer satisfaction. In particular, we must recognize that customer satisfaction is tied to customer expectations. If we fall short of these expectations, we will have unhappy customers. So what are these expectations?

First, customers expect that the product or service that they receive is usable. For example, an end user receiving a new computer expects that the computer will function as a useful device when set up according to the instructions. This end user's expectations will not be met if after stoking up the computer for its first run, an error message appears on the monitor stating that the system is nonoperational because of a chip failure on the motherboard. In this state, the computer is unusable, and the customer will be dissatisfied.

Similarly, in a project to write user documentation for a new hardware product, copyeditors (an internal customer) may expect that the chapters they receive for editing are complete—that there is no missing text. They certainly do not wish to begin work only to find out when they are nearly done that they have to redo the job because crucial information was missing in the original package submitted to them.

Second, customers expect us to keep our promises. If we say we will deliver a product or service by March 15, they will have that date etched into their memories. A March 16 delivery will fall short of their expectations. If we say that the product or service will cost them a certain amount, that is what they plan to pay for it. They will not sympathize with us when we tell them that we have to assess a 20 percent surcharge because of unanticipated delays in the delivery of a crucial part. If we say that the product or service will meet certain minimum performance standards, they will hold us to these standards. Anything that falls short of these standards will disappoint them.

Third, customers expect us to serve them competently and graciously. They expect that the people assigned to do a job know what they are doing. It does not always work this way. We have all experienced the repairman who spends countless hours diagnosing a problem in our equipment by endlessly swapping parts when all that was wrong with the equipment was that it was not plugged into the electrical outlet. Customers also expect that the people providing products or services behave in a friendly, well-mannered fashion. Surly behavior does nothing to improve project performance. Its predictable outcome is to generate customer unhappiness.

Finally, customers expect us to understand their needs and wants and to address these effectively. This means that we must understand the environment in which they function, the constraints they face, and the solutions they seek. We must sympathize with their struggles. Much of our energy must be directed at satisfying their needs and wants.

In the final analysis, what customers expect is that we will alleviate their problems, not add to them. They want things to go smoothly and according to plan. To a large extent, customer satisfaction is as much rooted in the avoidance of hassles and surprises as in the achievement of specific goals. Customers want to see positive results. They don't want to listen to a litany of our problems and hear excuses for poor performance.

UNDERSTANDING CUSTOMERS' NEEDS AND REQUIREMENTS

The importance of doing a good job of identifying needs and specifying requirements cannot be overstated. To appreciate this, we must recognize that the definition of needs sets off a series of events that ultimately results in the production of a deliverable designed to satisfy the defined needs. Thus needs are what get the project ball rolling. Requirements are then developed from our understanding of needs. They serve as the basis of the project plan, which is built around the needs. A major function of the plan is to provide us with step-by-step insights into what it takes to satisfy the requirements.

If we do a bad job at the earliest stages of the project life cycle, this will have ripple effects throughout the project's life. No matter how detailed and carefully contrived the plan may be, it will be a bad plan if it addresses misunderstood needs or poorly specified requirements. Similarly, project control efforts will come to naught if the needs and requirements analyses are poorly done. If the plan is no good, who cares if the variance between plan and actuals is nearly zero? It should be apparent that the success of a project hinges on the quality of the needs and requirements analyses.

Perhaps the single most important step we can take to ensure the proper identification of customers' needs is to hire competent needs analysts. There are many pitfalls in defining needs. Inexperienced project personnel are likely to fall into a majority of them, causing customer unhappiness and jeopardizing the project. In hiring competent needs analysts, what should we look for? Let us examine the traits of the most effective needs analysts.

TRAITS OF EFFECTIVE NEEDS ANALYSTS

In reviewing candidates for the job of needs analyst, one should choose individuals who possess the following six characteristics.

First, because the project is directed at meeting customer needs, the analysts must have a strong ability to deal with customers and extract from them a sense of what they truly need. The analysts must be part psychologists who can understand what makes the customers tick and part sociologists who can discern the social milieu in which the customers function.

Second, they must have good political skills. This means they must recognize that all customers are not equal in a political sense. Some are more significant to the success of the project than others. They must also recognize that some needs and requirements, no matter how compelling, may not be addressable for political reasons. For example, a needs and requirements analysis of a production process at Alpha Computer Corporation may determine that certain manufacturing efficiencies could be realized by using a Beta Computer Corporation computer to drive a machine tool, but such a solution—which suggests dependence on a competitor's product—may be politically unacceptable in Alpha's environment.

Third, they must be technically competent. They should be able to match customers' ill-defined needs to possible solutions. This requires a solid grounding in the technical aspects of the problems being addressed. Good human relations skills by themselves are insufficient for properly defining needs and specifying requirements.

Fourth, they must be open-minded and possess a good imagination. Open-mindedness is necessary so that they do not close off possible solutions to problems because of a narrow outlook. A good imagination is important for a number of reasons. For example, with a good imagination, they can anticipate different problems that might arise given alternative ways of positing project needs and requirements. In addition, a good imagination will encourage creative solutions to problems.

Fifth, they must have a high tolerance for ambiguity. Because customers do not generally know precisely what they need or want, they will send the needs analysts mixed signals. This can be frustrating for the needs analysts, who may begin to develop the impression that customers are not terribly bright people who are hell-bent on making life difficult. Without a high tolerance for ambiguity and an appreciation of the difficulties customers have in articulating their needs, project staff may develop a paranoid streak ("The customers are out to get me!") and may begin to view them with a certain disdain ("How can I be expected to respect people who don't have the foggiest notion of what they want?").

Finally, they must be articulate. They should be able to take fuzzy suggestions and insights offered by customers and forge them into clear statements of needs, which can in turn be translated into clear and useful requirements.

The traits listed here are certainly desirable in project staff members charged with defining needs and specifying requirements. Unfortunately, they are not commonly found in most project staff members, who tend to view needs definition and requirements specification narrowly through a technical prism. They do this because their project-related training has typically been technically oriented. The needs analysis for an avionics project may be carried out by an electrical engineer, for a financial database project by an accountant, or for an office automation project by a computer scientist.

These individuals generally have little in their background or personality to enable them to satisfy most of the desirable traits in our list. Their technical background has done little to provide human relation, political, or communication skills that can make them more articulate. On the contrary, their rigorous "hard" background often encourages them to view "soft" skills with disdain. As a result, they often lack the sensitivity necessary to define needs and specify requirements that will satisfy customers operating in the real world, where technical fixes seldom work as intended. Let's look at some common outcomes emerging from needs and requirements analyses carried out by project staff lacking the basic skills necessary for doing a good job.

• *Gold-plating of needs.* Here the needs analysts serve up a Mercedes-Benz when what the customers really need is a Hyundai. The technical perfectionist may find it difficult to suggest simple and direct solutions to needs when this provides customers with less functionality than they could have with more sophisticated solutions.

In part, gold-plating is rooted in professional pride. Technically competent systems analysts are understandably reluctant to waste their abilities on mundane solutions to problems. In part, it is also a consequence of the training that technically competent needs analysts have received. In this training, they are constantly exposed to state-of-the-art developments and have little or no experience with humbler solutions to problems. They develop an outlook that anything less than state-of-the-art solutions are second-rate.

• *Selective filtering of needs.* The essence of selective filtering of needs is captured in the old adage that states, "To a four-year-old boy with a hammer, all the world is a nail." What we have here are people defining things narrowly in the context of their particular experiences, values, and expertise. We encounter this frequently in our lives. A psychologist might think that the world's problems could be solved if world leaders underwent a bit of psychotherapy. To a Marxist economist, the world's problems could be solved by putting the means of production into the hands of the proletariat. A Protestant minister might argue that the world's problems could be resolved through a reconciliation of sinners and God. And so on.

In the case of projects, it is easy for needs analysts to fall into the trap of defining customers' needs according to their own particular areas of expertise. An analyst who is an authority on relational databases may see such databases as the solution to all problems. The analyst then interprets customer needs and requirements from the perspective of relational databases, even though this might not be appropriate. What such analysts are in fact doing is replacing the customers' true needs with their own need to employ their expertise.

• *Operating in a patronizing fashion.* Working with customers can be enormously frustrating for project staff. Because customers typically have only a vague notion of what they need, they may behave in ways that project staff perceive as fickle, ignorant, illogical, and spiteful. For project staff lacking good human relations skills, a coping strategy to deal with customer foibles might be summed up as, "These people obviously don't have the slightest idea of what they need, and the technology we're dealing with here is way over their heads. Since I am the expert, I'll call the shots and give them what I know they need, even if they disagree with my judgments." The problem with this approach is that it may result in customer rejection of the final deliverable, since customers perceive their needs differently from the expert.

STEPS FOR IMPROVING NEEDS DEFINITION

Given the problems inherent in defining needs effectively, it is evident that defining needs properly is not easy. Let's examine some steps that project personnel can take to improve the likelihood that they will define the real needs of customers rather than some distortion of those needs.

Step 1: Understand the Present System in Its Total Context

Most guides to designing and implementing hardware and software systems suggest that the first step systems analysts should take is to study the existing system. This includes doing such things as gaining a detailed understanding of the functions performed by the current system, identifying information flows within the system, listing inputs into the system, and listing outputs emerging from the system. The rationale is that we must understand how things are being done now if we wish to understand how they can be done better.

This is good advice as far as it goes, but it doesn't go far enough. The approach tends to put blinders on project staff, forcing them to focus only on the technical dimensions of the problem they face.

Step 1 goes beyond conventional systems analysis advice. Understanding the technical dimensions of the current system is of course vital to understanding why customers feel that the system should be replaced with something better suited to meeting their needs. However, needs analysts must go beyond purely technical investigations of problems. They should strive to understand the present system in its total context. What is the organizational milieu in which the system functions? Who are the relevant actors? What is the political environment like? What is the hidden agenda? Without a thorough grounding in these broader issues, needs analysts will end up with a myopic view of what is really needed to satisfy customers.

Step 2: Identify the Various Customers and Prioritize Their Needs

Step 1 should provide the needs analysts with a good idea of who is affected by the project and who has an interest in its outcome—these are customers in the broadest sense of the term. They include different players in the customer organization as well as individuals in the project organization. Since there are always multiple customers, needs analysts performing step 1 should be able to generate a list of several individuals.

In step 2, the analysts refine the list of interested parties and strive to determine the nature of their interests. Actors who are only peripherally involved with the project can be dropped from the list. Of those remaining, analysts should focus especially on individuals whose actions (or inactions) will have a measurable impact on the project and its deliverable. Their stake in the project should be identified. Furthermore, recognizing that the relevant actors have different interests—interests that may in fact be at cross-purposes—needs analysts should try to sort out these interests and develop a rough sense of how they should be prioritized.

If the project deliverable is something that will be sold commercially in the open market (for example, a toaster or a piece of software), step 2 includes conducting a market research study that examines the preferences of consumers in detail.

Step 3: Put Together a Needs-Defining Task Force

Having completed steps 1 and 2, the needs analyst should have a rough idea of the customers, their interests, and the technical dimensions of the problem. This information is gathered through interviews, observation, and a review of organizational procedures. In most needs analyses, the analysts are now deemed ready to define the needs carefully so that they can serve as the basis of functional requirements.

Unfortunately, careful needs definition at this point is probably premature. Since a major objective of project management is to produce deliverables that satisfy customers, it is now time to involve customers actively in the needs analysis. This can be done effectively by creating a needs-defining task force representing the different sets of customers. For example, an office automation task force may be composed of representatives from key constituencies, such as secretaries, management, professional workers, and the information technology group.

The task force can strengthen the needs analysis in at least three ways. First, since it is made up of representatives of different constituencies, it allows for the cross-fertilization of ideas. The resulting suggestions regarding customer needs will therefore be more robust than if needs were identified by only one or two people.

Second, the task force allows the different customer groups to develop a consensus about their needs through give-and-take interaction. This shifts some of the burden of decision making from the needs analysts to the customers themselves. Furthermore, whatever priorities emerge through this process are likely to be less arbitrary than if determined by a single individual.

Third, because relevant customer constituencies play an active role in defining their needs, they have, in effect, "bought into" the project. Later on, they will be more likely to cooperate with project staff as the project develops and more likely to be satisfied with the final deliverable than they would have been if a statement of needs had been foisted on them by an outsider.

The customary partnering technique of rapid prototyping (see Chapter Three) in effect employs task forces in this way to develop customer-focused requirements.

Step 4: Educate the Customers

Customers generally do not know what they need with any degree of precision. A major function of needs analysts is to work closely with customers to help them develop a more precise sense of their needs. An important step can be taken in this direction by educating customers. Most obviously, they should be given some understanding of the technical issues involved. What are these issues? What kinds of deliverables can be developed to address them? What are the capabilities of the deliverables? What are their limitations?

It would also be useful to educate customers in some of the rudiments of project management so that they can gain a better appreciation of the practical aspects of what it takes to address their needs. In particular, the needs analysts should explain to them that their needs will inevitably be shifting and that such shifts put a tremendous burden on keeping the project on track. By recognizing that it is natural to have shifting needs and by further understanding that this causes problems in the execution of projects, customers are likely to be more careful in how they formulate their needs in order to minimize the most serious kinds of disruptions.

CUSTOMERS' RESPONSIBILITIES IN DEFINING THEIR NEEDS

The responsibility for putting together a good statement of needs does not rest solely on the needs analysts. A good statement of needs is the product of a partnership between the needs analysts and the customers. For their part, customers must do their share to maximize the likelihood that the needs statement does indeed meet their needs.

Customers can do many specific things to help out in the needs definition effort. For example, they can document the problems they are facing as they see them, what they perceive their needs to be, and how they currently carry out their work.

Although their specific contributions may vary from situation to situation, customers should be aware of at least two universal realities. First, they should recognize their limitations and realize that such limitations are natural and do not reflect deficiencies. The extent of their ignorance can be substantial. In general, they do not really know what they need and do not have the skills necessary to uncover those needs precisely. They do not possess expert knowledge of the technologies embodied in possible solutions to their problems. They are unaware of alternative solutions and the respective consequences. They do not know what it takes to design, build, install, and maintain an effective deliverable. If they insist that they know exactly what their needs are at the outset of the needs definition effort, and if the needs analysts take them at their word, there is a good chance that needs- and requirements-related problems will arise later in the project.

Second, customers should recognize that the project management process is a grand exercise in compromise, from defining needs all the way up to writing the final documentation at the conclusion of the project. Their needs are not going to be satisfied perfectly. Because there are multiple customers involved in projects, their needs must be reconciled with the often conflicting needs of fellow customers. Because all projects operate under resource and time constraints, the articulation of customers' needs will be tempered by budget and schedule realities. Customers should also reconcile themselves to the inevitability of compromise if they want a workable needs statement to emerge from the needs definition process.

ORGANIZING TO ACHIEVE CUSTOMER SATISFACTION

The achievement of customer satisfaction requires constant and conscious effort. It will not happen by accident. It entails commitment on the part of the whole organization to make it work. For example, a customer-support environment must be created enabling project staff to respond quickly and incisively to customer concerns. Top management must be willing to share decision-making authority with project workers. Accounting systems must be created to support the efforts of grassroots decision makers. And so on.

A five-pronged approach is helpful in organizing for customer satisfaction. First, the corporate culture must be changed to support a customer-focused approach. In some organizations, this may be tantamount to calling for a revolution. Old ways must be abandoned and new ones adopted. In this process of changing the corporate culture, we must never forget that change involves more than just adjustments in attitudes. It requires nothing less than a restructuring of the way the organization does its business so that a customer-support system can be effectively developed and maintained. It also requires a shift of the power locus. Project managers and other project staff—the front-line troops who encounter customers on a daily basis—must be empowered to do what it takes to ensure customer satisfaction.

Second, every effort must be made to develop projects as islands of stability in a sea of change. A primary feature of life today is breakneck change. Product life cycles are measured in months, currency exchange rates vary from minute to minute, worker mobility is ever-increasing, and so on. Unbridled change is one of the greatest threats to project success. Sources of change on projects include customers changing their minds about what they want; management turnovers that lead to shifts in priorities; competitors introducing products that make our efforts obsolete; and reinterpretations of requirements as the deliverable makes its way through marketing, design, prototyping, production, handover, and postproduction.

Third, the organization must adopt a "total life cycle" outlook on its project efforts. This means that projects should be viewed from a cradle-to-grave perspective. The process begins with the identification of customer needs and wants. The primary objective of the project should be to satisfy these needs and wants. With the life cycle approach, we recognize that the process does not end with the handover of the deliverable to customers. Customers must be able to operate the deliverable and to maintain it as well. Consequently, project staff must do their work with one eye always on the operation and maintenance of the final product. The life cycle does not end with the handover but extends well beyond it.

Fourth, mechanisms must be established to ensure customer satisfaction. This translates into the development of methods and procedures that make certain that customer sensibilities will not be violated by oversights and sloppy procedures. We must strive to create a situation where it is impossible for any customer to "fall between the cracks."

Fifth, everything possible must be done to improve the capabilities of project staff. This requires a new look at their role. As was stated earlier, project staff have traditionally been viewed as mere implementers; they have played little or no role in actually developing plans. The management skills necessary to fulfill the traditional role are not very demanding. Staff simply need basic scheduling knowledge and the technical skills to follow a plan. Consequently, traditional project management training has focused intensively on working with scheduling tools such as Gantt chats and PERT/CPM networks.

With a customer-focused outlook, however, the role of project staff changes dramatically. They are no longer mere implementers of plans developed by others. They must be able to respond quickly and effectively to customer requirements. To do this, they must be able to operate like independent entrepreneurs concerned with both satisfying their customers and maintaining profitability. Consequently, they need to develop a profound appreciation of basic business concepts, such as opportunity cost, the time value of money, and benefit-cost principles. (To learn more about identifying and developing qualified project staff, see my book *Project Management Competence*.)

Let us take a deeper look at each of these five issues.

Issue 1: Reformulating the Corporate Culture

The concept of corporate culture is important. Corporate culture effectively defines the limits of what an organization can do. If an organization's underlying culture harks back to past glories and is hostile to new ideas, no amount of restructuring will transform it into an innovator. If the culture cherishes the perquisites of power, it is unlikely to be metamorphosed into a flat organization. If the culture is engineering-driven, customer needs and requirements are apt to be overlooked.

In recent years, an enormous amount of attention has been directed toward understanding and transforming corporate cultures. There has been a general outcry to reformulate corporate cultures to allow organizations to operate more effectively in a competitive environment. Advice on what should be done flows from many quarters. Today, the key source of advice comes from proponents of corporate business process reengineering. For the most part, this advice is good.

Although the details for action differ from adviser to adviser, the basic thrust is constant: the corporate culture should encourage flatter, more democratic operations; it should empower employees; it should be obsessed with satisfying customers; it should encourage faster production of products and services; and it should be open to the outside so that the organization can deal effectively with outsourcing and strategic alliances.

Although discussions about the need for reformulating corporate cultures abound in the management literature and the boardrooms of corporations, very little of the dialogue has been directed specifically at project management. What impact does corporate culture have on the way projects are carried out? What cultural postures are most conducive to meeting project needs? The answers to these and related questions call for a corporate culture that has the following features.

A FOCUS ON VALUE. *Value* should be a word that appears frequently in the conversations of project employees. In exploring different decision alternatives to further the project's goals, staff should weigh each alternative according to the value it adds to the organization in general and the project in particular. For example, when choosing vendors' products to be used on a project, the question staff should address is which product offers the most value and not which product is cheapest. Similarly, when choosing a design, material, or function to incorporate into an emerging deliverable, the question to answer is which alternative offers the customers the greatest value.

A focus on value requires that decision makers take a *range* of factors into account when making their decisions. Decisions should not be based on price alone, nor should they be based purely on performance. These two factors should be considered together. Other factors should be given consideration as well, including the physical appearance of the deliverable, its overall appeal, and its life expectancy. Ultimately, a focus on value compels organizations to place greater emphasis on quality. Today in many organizations the concepts of value and quality are viewed as interchangeable.

ENCOURAGEMENT OF UPSIDE-DOWN THINKING. As mentioned in Chapter Three, Charles Handy (1989) talks convincingly about the need for upside-down thinking in today's organizations. In a static world, the past serves as an excellent guide to the future. Experience dictates clear solutions to problems. However, in the turbulent world we face today, a prescription to conform and follow the old ways leads to disaster. In such a world, people have to be able to break out of the mold occasionally. Otherwise, the organization will find itself in a rut. Upside-down thinking allows different ideas to compete with each other. It creates an environment that the best professionals find stimulating and challenging and allows the organization to rejuvenate itself continually.

THE SHARING OF POWER THROUGHOUT THE ORGANIZATION. All employees should be viewed as decision makers. They are *not* cogs in a machine. The traditional hierarchical organization does not operate effectively in a world characterized by constant dynamic change. Investing all power in the hands of top management implies that top management has the solutions to all problems. In a static world, top management may indeed know most of the solutions. In a turbulent world, though, no one grasps more than a small fraction of the answers. Interestingly, rank-and-file employees are often better informed than their "superiors" in such circumstances since they have firsthand knowledge of a rapidly evolving situation. By the time managers in the rarefied heights of the hierarchy receive information on what is happening, circumstances have changed.

The need to empower project managers is particularly acute. Currently, they possess large amounts of responsibility without corresponding authority. One reason for this situation is that they do not own the resources they need to employ in their work. Their resources are borrowed from different functional groups. Information systems consultants come from the data processing organization, design engineers from the engineering division, editors from the media department, and so on. Other problems include the frequent requirement that they run projects that they had no role in selecting or planning, lack of profit-and-loss responsibilities, lack of skills and information needed to do a good job, and frequent rotation of assignments.

A LONG-TERM VIEW. When change is rapid, it is tempting to adopt a short-term view of life. Change leads to uncertainty, and there is less uncertainty in the short run than in the long run. We can be pretty sure that whatever long-term guesses we make will be wrong. So, the argument goes, let us focus on the short term.

Unfortunately, most worthwhile achievements are carried out in the long run and consequently require a long-term outlook. A simple landscaping project requires a five- to ten-year time horizon (trees and shrubs do not develop fully overnight). An urban renewal project may require a ten- to twenty-year outlook. When in 1961 President Kennedy announced a project to send humans to the moon, he set the target date as the end of the decade.

On projects, many forces reinforce a short-term perspective. For example, account executives are concerned with making a sale. Once a project contract is signed, they turn their attention to other opportunities. If they made promises to the customer that project staff cannot fulfill, they are not held accountable. The constant turnover of personnel in U.S. organizations encourages a short-term outlook as well. On most projects, you can be certain that at least one key player (the project manager, the project sponsor, the CEO, the procurement head, or key members of the client organization) will be gone within six to nine months. The departure often leads to painful changes in the project requirements, which are in turn important contributors to time and cost overruns. In this situation, long-term considerations are sacrificed to short-term exigencies.

The corporate culture must extol the virtues of a long-term outlook. It must cast a cold eye on all undertakings that focus narrowly on short-term results. It must also convey the attitude that short-term setbacks are tolerable when they lead ultimately to long-term gains. The best way to let people know the importance of this outlook to the organization is to create incentive systems that reward long-term behavior and to develop organizational structures that make it difficult to be a short-termer.

TOTAL CUSTOMER FOCUS. Clearly, a significant organizational requirement leading to customer-focused project management is the nurturing of a culture that is obsessed with customer satisfaction. Customers must be seen like royalty. Customer satisfaction must be touted as the highest goal. All decisions must be assessed according to their impacts on customers.

Given such a focus, project management takes on a new meaning. The traditional view of project success—doing the job on time, within budget, and according to specs—gives way to a new perspective—producing a deliverable that satisfies customers. The traditional orphan stages of the life cycle—concept and closeout—become crucial. Concept is important because it is here that customers' needs are identified. Everything that follows on the project should be geared to addressing these needs. Closeout is important because it is here that the project team prepares to hand over the deliverable to customers. This is the moment of truth, when the team learns whether it has indeed satisfied customers or not.

A customer-focused culture requires a new attitude toward customers. They should not be seen as irritants that get in the way of doing the job. Their confusion about the technical requirements of the project should not be viewed as a sign of obtuseness. Their inability to define what they want and need should not be interpreted as fickleness. Instead of being seen as antagonists, they should be viewed as *partners* in the project. In the final analysis, they are the experts on their needs and requirements. The project team and the customers work *together* to reveal these needs and requirements and to develop a deliverable to satisfy them.

Issue 2: Focusing on Stability and Continuity

A prime cause of cost and schedule overruns on major federal government projects is budgetary instability. Although major projects occur over several years, congressional funding is provided on a year-by-year basis. The problem is that each year, things change dramatically, and as a consequence, congressional priorities shift.

One major source of change, of course, is political elections. Congressional representatives are elected every two years, senators every six, and presidents every four. At each election, there is a possibility that the congressional actors overseeing a project's funding will change. And even if the actors don't change, there is a strong probability that their outlooks will shift with the political winds. If national defense is a political hot button one year, members of Congress will trip over each other to sponsor costly defense projects. If the next year defense issues fade into the background and the budget deficit is the key political concern, defense project budgets may suddenly be slashed, forcing contractors to lay off critical workers and shut down facilities. If in the following year there is an international crisis and defense issues become paramount once again, massive amounts of money may flow to defense contractors again. The costs of rehiring workers and reactivating facilities will of course be substantial, and the original project schedules will be unachievable. Cost and schedule overruns are effectively hardwired into the system.

To gain a full appreciation of the potential of budgetary instability to create havoc, consider what can happen in the federal environment over a five-year period of time. During this period, there may be three congressional and two presidential elections. The opportunities for opening and closing and then reopening the funding spigots for projects are limitless.

Unfortunately, parallel sources of instability exist in the private sector. At the highest levels, CEOs, COOs, divisional vice presidents, CFOs, and other senior executives come and go. With the arrival and departure of each of these actors, major shifts in priorities are likely to occur. We encounter a similar shuffling of key players at the project level. Project managers are rotated out of jobs, technical personnel leave the company in search of greener pastures, reorganizations move projects from one unit to another, divisions are spun off through leveraged buyouts, and new divisions are brought in through mergers and acquisitions. And all this churning is occurring in *both* the developer organization and the customer organization. As in the federal case, this kind of instability leads to time and cost overruns and to the development of patchwork deliverables.

Shifting actors are not the only source of project instability; other causes abound. For example, purchasing policies that award contracts to low bidders typically lead to a continual rotation of suppliers as this year's low bidder is replaced by next year's low bidder. Sales commissions awarded once an item is shipped may encourage the shipping of goods at the convenience of the account executives, contrary to the requirements of the plan. Transfer of project responsibility from one group to another as the project works its way through the life cycle opens the door for regular reinterpretation of project requirements. Changes in the environment (for example, inflation, the entry of new competitors into the market, or new technology) may stimulate reinterpretations of the project charter. And so on.

Clearly, effective project management requires that the project team be able to cope with all these forces of instability.

Issue 3: Assuming a Life Cycle Perspective

Many projects get into trouble because of the piecemeal approach taken in executing them. The people who select the project are not the people who design the deliverable. Those who create the project plans are not the individuals who are responsible for executing them. Those charged with operations and maintenance of the deliverable in the postproject stage generally did not participate in any aspect of its development.

This reality was revealed in a study of 113 project professionals whom I asked to describe their degree of involvement in five distinct phases of the project life cycle: concept, planning, execution, closeout, and operations and maintenance. Thirty-two percent of the project managers who responded reported that they most typically worked on only two of the five phases. Only 20 percent worked on all five phases. Furthermore, only 29 percent reported involvement in the concept phase—meaning that they were responsible for carrying out efforts in which they had no inputs during the formative early stage.

These data suggest situations that are natural breeding grounds of discontinuity. There is no integrating force to ensure that the project sticks to its goals. In fact, there are many forces of *disintegration*, with different actors pursuing their own agenda as the deliverable makes its way through the life cycle. The consequences of this are dramatic. For one thing, we can be assured that what comes out of the pipeline is not what was initially put into it. The danger here is that what comes out is no longer geared to the customers' wants and needs. In addition, it is likely that the basic design underlying the deliverable will become a patchwork as different actors have the opportunity to tweak it to their own requirements. So even though we set out to design a horse, we wind up with a camel. Ultimately, problems of discontinuity translate into shifting baselines, which in turn yield cost and schedule overruns.

Effective project management requires a life cycle approach to running the project. Efforts must be taken to ensure that the project is seen in its entirety at all times. The implications of such an outlook are substantial: deliverables are now designed to be operable and maintainable, requirements remain steady regardless of life cycle stage, and key actors who work on the project throughout its life develop a commitment to the project in its entirety, not just to pieces of it.

Assumption of a life cycle approach is not easy. As we saw earlier in this chapter, there are many disintegrative forces at work, including personnel replacement, low-bid-focused procurement systems, and the dynamism of the environment.

Issue 4: Establishing Methods and Procedures to Ensure Customer Satisfaction

Projects are inherently complex undertakings. They are made up of interrelated parts, meaning that the failure of one part may have significant downstream consequences. They are unique, so past experience is an imperfect guide to the future. They entail the use of borrowed resources that may not be available when they are needed. They operate in a management quagmire where accountability is unclear and key actors who follow their own agendas may operate at cross-purposes.

Such an environment is ideal for errors and omissions. There is a constant lurking threat that the best intentions will go awry, that promises made will not be kept. Customers are likely to be chronically disappointed.

Chaos need not reign supreme on projects. It can be contained to a degree by the implementation of thoughtful methods and procedures. These are commonly embodied in something called an M&P (methods and procedures) document. This document lays out the rules governing the procedures that should be followed in executing a project. Since all actors should abide by these rules, regardless of their skills area or their position in the organization, the rules add an important element of continuity and consistency to the project.

The central importance of methods and procedures is reflected in the directives of two major quality initiatives active today: ISO 9000 and CMM. IS0 9000—sponsored by the International Organization for Standards—have become the de facto world standards of quality in the manufacturing and service sectors. In the ISO world, quality is assessed by reviewing the adequacy of an organization's processes. CMM (the Capability Maturity Model)—a quality initiative sponsored by Carnegie-Mellon University's Software Engineering Institute (SEI)—assesses the quality of information technology operations. As with ISO 9000, CMM quality assessments are based on reviewing the adequacy of an organization's processes.

Methods and procedures should focus intensively on making sure that nothing falls through the cracks. For example, they may require that customer walk-throughs be conducted at periodic intervals. Furthermore, they may describe the steps that should be taken when conducting the walk-through. These walk-throughs serve at least two important functions: they assure customers that they are not being ignored, and they protect the project team from accusations that customer views were not solicited.

Methods and procedures should also detail how project staff should deal with pressures to change requirements. The M&P document should spell out how change requests should be submitted, evaluated, and implemented. Only through such procedures can the inevitable problem of shifting baselines be managed.

The establishment of effective methods and procedures requires that special attention be given to documentation. Projects are filled with documentation. Common documents include the project charter, the statement of work (SOW), the project contract, preliminary design review (PDR) and critical design review (CDR) documents, monthly progress reports, specifications, performance appraisal documents, punch lists, user manuals, and engineering change proposals.

Anyone with substantial project experience recognizes that documentation has the characteristics of both Dr. Jekyll and Mr. Hyde. On the positive side, when documents are tied to critical milestones, they provide project staff with a mechanism for pacing themselves through the life cycle. Furthermore, they supply the project with an audit trail, providing both the project staff and the customer with information on what has been done. Finally, they impose a discipline on the project, requiring project staff to pay attention to crucial management issues and to do their job in a consistent fashion.

On the negative side, an emphasis on documentation—and the whole methods and procedures exercise, for that matter—can lead to excessive bureaucratization. A time may arrive when project staff are spending more hours filling out forms in triplicate than doing their project work. Bureaucratization can discourage staff initiative and encourage managing "by the book." It slows down project staff response time to various project exigencies and customer requests. Excessive bureaucratization can ultimately reduce productivity and erode the organization's competitive position.

Clearly, effective project management necessitates a balance between the need for the discipline of established methods and procedures (and their attendant documentation) and the need for flexibility and responsiveness to customer requirements.

Issue 5: Strengthening Project Staff Capabilities

Recently, I was looking at power tools in a large hardware shopping center. Nearby, a customer was asking some questions of a salesclerk.

"Is this the power drill advertised as being on sale in today's newspaper?" the customer asked, holding up a box.

"Yes, it is," the clerk answered.

The customer peered at the box carefully. "It says on the box that this is model 5062. Isn't the drill that's on sale model 5060?"

The clerk took the box and read the label. "It does say model 5062," the clerk said. "I think somebody must have mislabeled the box."

"So this is definitely the drill that's on sale?"

"Uh . . . yes."

"Now does this drill run at two speeds?"

"That's correct."

"Wait a second. It says on the box that it is only a one-speed drill."

And so the conversation went. It was clear that the salesclerk was a fount of misinformation. The fact that he didn't know what he was talking about never stopped him from proffering incorrect information. People listening to his advice were going to have serious difficulties on their home projects. And their anger would be directed not only at him but at the store that employed him as well.

Customer satisfaction demands that the sellers of goods and services—whether salesclerks, project managers, or technical specialists—be highly competent in their work. The perception of incompetence will alienate customers and result in lost business.

Until recently, competence in project management meant that project staff possessed the technical skills to do the job and sufficient management skills to work with budgets and schedules. However, today's customers are demanding more of project staff. In particular, they see project staff as *business partners*. They expect them to know the customers' business and to possess basic business skills.

Thus project staff are increasingly receiving training in business fundamentals. In particular, they are studying the rudiments of such topics as capital budgeting techniques, contracting basics, decision-making methodologies, forecasting, and reading financial statements.

WHAT TO DO WHEN CUSTOMERS DON'T COOPERATE

I do a lot of traveling around the world. When I began traveling extensively, I was at first surprised and then delighted to find that project workers everywhere—from Buenos Aires to Birmingham to Sydney to Toronto to Singapore—were sensitive to the need to adopt the perspective of a new project management. They were customer-focused. They realized that customers expected them to offer business solutions as well as technical solutions. They were sensitive to the radical transformations occurring in their own organizations: downsizing, outsourcing, and flattening.

An important revelation I had in dealing with these people was that one of their most common complaints was that customers were not behaving responsibly on their projects. Specifically, project managers everywhere revealed to me that a prime cause of schedule slippages and cost overruns on their projects was customers who did not meet their obligations. They complained that customers held them tightly to meeting milestone commitments. Yet when it came time for customers to meet their own obligations, they were lax in doing so.

For example, a frequent complaint was that customers were slow in responding to inputs coming from the project team. The team might send the results of a systems test for customers to review and approve and then find themselves waiting for months for a customer response. Of course, delays in customer turnaround caused major schedule slippages on their projects, which were often blamed on the project team.

Most of the project managers I spoke with attributed these problems to disorganization in the customer organization. I looked into some of the complaints in detail and found this diagnosis to be a bit superficial. My suspicion is that the majority of the delays in customer turnaround were tied to political problems existing in the customer organization. It should be recalled that the idea of the customer—a monolithic entity with a consistent worldview—is a myth. There are always multiple customers who have conflicting interests. The power balance among these customers often shifts. For example, a player from the financial department whose views prevailed during the project definition phase is promoted to a different division, leaving a power vacuum. The vacuum is filled by another player from the information technology group whose views differ dramatically from those of the previous dominant player. Suddenly, project priorities in the customer organization shift to reflect the new power balance.

Thus the customer organization may be reluctant to respond to system test results because a positive response indicates customer approval of the direction the project is taking. However, shifts in the political winds may give the customer organization second thoughts about the project's goals. The result: decision paralysis.

So what is the project team to do in such a situation? Three possible responses stand out.

First, remind the customer organization of its contractual obligations. Point out to key authorities the schedule and budget consequences of the customers' inaction. Make it clear that if they do not abide by the contract, the contractor's obligations become null and void.

Many project managers are reluctant to take this step. They fear that by focusing on the contract, they will alienate their customers and lose future business. I respond with a standard pair of questions: Why were they so silly as to enter into a one-sided contract that put all the onus of performance on them? And if customer irresponsibility causes them to lose money on their project, why are they worried about losing business with an organization that has caused them to suffer financial losses—and may well maintain this pattern in future business transactions?

Second, emphasize clearly at the outset of the project the importance to project success of meeting certain key milestones, including those requiring customer inputs. Periodically remind the customers of upcoming obligations. The key point here is to indicate continually to the customer organization that the project team takes its responsibilities seriously and that it expects the customer organization to do the same.

Third, establish a steering committee to oversee project progress. Members should include individuals from the customer organization as well as representatives of the project organization. The members of the steering committee should be powerful individuals so that decisions coming from the committee must be taken seriously. If the customer organization fails to meet its commitments, this fact should be raised before the steering committee for action. Ideally, a powerful steering committee will become an ally of the project team and will pressure pertinent players to meet their obligations.

CONCLUSIONS

With the new project management, project success is defined largely by customer satisfaction. Achieving such satisfaction does not come easily. It requires project organizations to abandon their old technically focused paradigms and to adopt ones that concentrate on customers. It also requires people to recognize that there is no such thing as *the* customer, who possesses a single, consistent view of project requirements. In fact, all projects must address the often conflicting needs of multiple customers.

CHAPTER SIX

Defining Requirements That Bridge the Customer-Developer Gap

An important premise of the new project management is that project success requires a heavy dose of customer-developer partnering. Historically, the development team—charged with producing a technical solution—carries out a customer needs assessment (often rather perfunctorily) and then designs and implements a solution to address the identified needs. The problem with this approach is that the development team often never really identifies customers' true needs and wants. So the solution is not satisfactory from the customers' point of view.

There are a number of reasons why, historically, the development team has been unable to identify customer needs and wants. For one thing, it usually approaches the needs analysis process from a narrow technical perspective, reflecting the team members' personal technical orientation. They typically have only a vague sense of the customers' business concerns. When customers raise business issues, development team members do not understand what is being discussed. Beyond this, many technical people lack the facilitation and empathy skills needed to deal effectively with their customers. They have little patience with their customers' technical ignorance. Their general approach is, "Give me a sense of what you want, and then trust me to develop a good technical solution." Regrettably, the resulting solution misses the mark quite often.

For their part, customers often are ill-equipped to identify their needs and wants. They never really think about what it takes to articulate needs and wants clearly. Also, they do not understand the technical implications of their requirements. Consequently, when meeting with the technical team, they state their requirements vaguely. For example, they might say, "What we need is a data entry form that is *dynamic.*" On the surface, it may seem that this requirement is straightforward. But a little reflection reveals that it is rife with ambiguity. For one thing, the term *dynamic* has specific connotations to a software programmer (as in dynamic programming and dynamic HTML). Use of the term *dynamic* may cause the team to interpret the customers' requirements in unintended ways. Furthermore, this term does not really convey what exactly the customers need and want. Are they seeking data entry forms that are interactive so that when customers enter data into a field, the form provides an appropriate response? If so, which fields should have these interactive features, and which should be static? Are they seeking something else?

The point is, a cultural, knowledge, and communication gap often exists between customers and developers, and this gap makes it difficult for the project team to capture customer needs effectively and then convert them into requirements that lead to customer satisfaction. The gap creates frustration and unhappiness on both sides. Customers complain that the project team is too technically focused and doesn't really understand the business issues that should be addressed. Technical team members complain that customers are continually confused and fickle and don't really know what they need or want.

Usually, the complaints of each side are justified. The development team often *is* too technically focused, and frequently customers *don't* know what they need or want. The question is, how can we best deal with this situation? How can we bypass the usual struggles inherent in converting business needs into technical requirements? If we can resolve this issue, we will have better project solutions. We will also have happier business customers and technical team members.

THE PLACE OF NEEDS AND REQUIREMENTS IN THE PROJECT MANAGEMENT PROCESS

All projects arise in response to somebody's needs. The needs may be selfish ("to increase our profit margins") or altruistic ("to reduce human suffering"). The moral basis of the needs is immaterial. The key point is that projects arise to address people's needs. Consequently, if a project is going to be successful, the project team members must always keep an eye on the needs as they go about their work.

The place of needs and requirements in the project management process is captured in the following arrow diagram:

NEEDS → REQUIREMENTS → DESIGN → PROJECT IMPLEMENTATION

What this schema shows is that needs arise, requirements are created to capture them, requirements serve as the basis of the design of a solution, and the design is implemented by means of project management. Let us look briefly at each element of this chain.

Needs

Needs reflect conditions that must be satisfied in order to enable people and their artifacts to function satisfactorily. For example, if I haven't eaten in several days, I need food to sustain me. Or if workers lack the proper knowledge to do their jobs, they may need to be educated. Or if a database system responds too slowly to customer queries, it may need to be revamped so that it operates more quickly. Needs may be inextricably interwoven with wants. For example, I may so desire to possess a Mercedes-Benz 600SL that I feel I cannot function properly without one. Objectively, no one really *needs* a luxury car. However, desires may be so strong that on a subjective level they are converted into needs.

The needs themselves go through a three-step evolutionary process. First, *needs emerge.* They arise, but at the earliest stage, they are amorphous and barely perceived. To the extent they are unrecognized, no one will act to address them. Then *needs are recognized.* At this stage, the existence of the needs becomes clear, and it is evident that they should be addressed. Note that a key function of market research departments is to scan the business environment for new opportunities with a view to exploiting them—market research groups are in the business of recognizing needs. Finally, *needs are articulated.* The fact that someone recognizes a need is not good enough. The need must be articulated in a way that suggests action. Writing a project proposal is an example of an approach to articulating needs and offering possible solutions to addressing them.

Requirements

Requirements are the physical manifestation of needs. If needs have not been captured properly, the resulting requirements will be off-target, no matter how well they are formulated. They are generally divided into two categories: business and technical.

Business requirements are requirements seen from the perspective of business users. They generally address two broad questions. First, what problems need to be solved? For example, it may be determined that we need to improve our responsiveness to customer inquiries. Or we may need to add a new column to our financial reports to address changes in SEC financial data reporting requirements. Second, what business objectives are we striving to achieve? For example, we may determine that the project should achieve 10 percent profitability or payback within two years or should contribute to a 5 percent growth in market share.

Technical requirements offer guidance on what the deliverable should look like and what it should do. They are broken into two types: First, *functional requirements* are requirements stated in ordinary language. They are formulated once needs are clearly articulated. They are a step in the direction of creating detailed specifications. You crawl before you walk, and you walk before you run. So it is that you develop functional requirements before delving into the formulation of detailed specifications.

Functional requirements are important because they establish customer expectations. When customers authorize the launching of a project, their impression of what will be delivered to them is typically a reflection of the functional requirements. If a deliverable is produced that falls short of the expectations established by the functional requirements, customers are sure to be disappointed.

Second, *specifications* provide clear and detailed guidance on the appearance and functioning of the deliverable. They are written for technical personnel who have ultimate responsibility for developing the deliverable. With good specifications, the technical people should know exactly what they should be producing.

A major challenge for effective project management is to capture business needs and then to convert them into viable technical requirements.

Design

Ultimately, specifications provide the foundation for designing the deliverable. For example, if the technical requirements specify that we should build a box to house a camera that will be used in outdoor nature photography, that the box should be waterproof and should be camouflaged to fit into a wooded setting, and so forth, we will use this information to design a box that best meets the specs. Even intangibles and semitangibles must be designed before they are developed. For example, in writing a script for a television drama, the requirements provided to us might be that the program must be delivered in forty-three minutes; it must be built primarily on dialogue between two protagonists, a man and a woman; it should be targeted to an audience of adults over the age of forty; it should reflect life in colonial India in the 1890s; and so forth. The "design" associated with these requirements will take the form of an outline of the story that identifies key players, a description of the story's locale, and the story line.

Project Implementation

Once a deliverable has been designed, a project can be implemented to achieve the design. To implement the project, we go through the traditional project life cycle: we gear up to launch a project in an *initiation* phase; then *plan* the schedule, budget, resource allocations and technical details; and then *execute* the plan. Even as the project is being executed, we need to engage in *control* efforts to make sure that the project is achieving its baseline goals. Finally, at the end of the project, we need to *close out* operations to make sure the project is brought to a conclusion in an intelligent way.

The concatenation of *needs → requirements → design → project implementation* demonstrates that project success requires us to get each of the pieces right. Too often, project teams focus entirely on implementation. They pay lip service to capturing needs and defining requirements and are also oblivious to the role of design. After all, project management is an action-oriented discipline, so we are eager to roll up our sleeves and get to work. However, if any link in the chain is flawed, the final solution will be defective. This means that project teams must give needs definition, requirements development, and design creation the same degree of attention they give project implementation.

CAPTURING REQUIREMENTS

The development of requirements is a four-step process. First, requirements specialists work with customers to *elicit* the requirements. The big challenge here is to get the technical team and customers working together. As we saw earlier in this chapter, this is not always easy to do, for a variety of reasons. For example, customers do not know how to specify their requirements, and technical team members are often only moderately familiar with business issues. Thus customers and project team members must bridge a serious cultural, knowledge, and communication gap. At this stage, the requirements are largely impressionistic. They are called *candidate requirements.*

Second, the project team needs to *analyze* the requirements. Analysis entails examining their cost, schedule, and systemwide impacts. It also requires the team to prioritize the requirements to see which are "must-haves" and which "nice-to-haves." At this point, the requirements are *informal requirements.*

Third, the project team needs to *formalize* the requirements. The initial elicited requirements are typically abstract and vague. The formalization process focuses on tightening them. The elicited requirements are first stated as informal, general requirements. Then as a consequence of the analysis process, they are narrowed to detailed, *formal requirements.* (When the requirements are very detailed, they become *specifications.*)

Finally, the formal requirements should go through a *verification* process, where a last check is made on whether they are on target. This is done by testing them for *traceability* (Can we trace the formal requirements back to customer needs?) and having all stakeholders review them to make sure that they meet their needs and wants. Once the requirements have been verified as appropriate, they are *accepted* and employed to design solutions that are ultimately implemented by means of project management.

KEY PLAYERS IN THE REQUIREMENTS DEFINITION AND MANAGEMENT PROCESS

On all projects, the definition and management of requirements entail the interaction of a number of players. On small, relatively simple projects—such as a project to organize a conference—the number of key players with crucial inputs is usually small. On large, complex projects—such as a project to build a next-generation fighter aircraft—the list of key players is long and includes scores of people whose perspectives must be taken into account when generating requirements.

In developing requirements, one of the first steps that must be taken is to identify who the key players are. Once this has been done, the next step is to determine how to capture their multiple—and often conflicting—perspectives on what the project requirements should be. Clearly, this process will be messy, particularly when one considers that the players have their individual views on what is important and what is not. Issues that need to be resolved include whose views count the most and, when there are conflicting views on what should be done, how deadlocks should be resolved.

The matter of identifying key players and harnessing their views will be illustrated with two hypothetical examples. The first addresses a project to build an office building in a suburban center. Here we are dealing with a palpable deliverable that is amenable to physical representation in the form of drawings and models. The second addresses a project to create a software system that will support the implementation of a new supply chain management process in a company. Here we are dealing with a deliverable that is fairly dynamic and abstract because it employs technology that is advancing day by day and is based on largely intangible knowledge.

Globus World Headquarters Construction Project: Key Players

The first example illustrates key players and their requirements-related concerns on a typical construction project. While specific players and their viewpoints will vary from project to project in the construction arena, the example offered here covers the principal issues encountered on most construction projects.

Globus Enterprises plans to build a world headquarters along the Beltway surrounding Baltimore. The headquarters building will be part of a larger multiuse complex that will contain a hotel, a six-theater movie house, and a shopping mall. Globus will own 35 percent of the overall complex, and the remaining 65 percent will be owned by a consortium of outside investors.

Key players on the project who will play a significant role in defining requirements include the owners, architects, engineers, the building contractor, and regulators. Each of these players has a perspective on what the requirements should be. Figure 6.1 pictures the relationship of the players to one another. The role and perspectives of each will be discussed briefly.

OWNERS. The owners at Globus are a composite of players who are investing in the project. They are divided into two groups: the management committee of Globus Enterprises and the executive committee of outside investors. Neither group is monolithic. Each group contains subsets of players who are jockeying to have their opinions prevail.

At the highest level of generality, the owners' requirements include such views as the following:

• We want a complex that is attractive, well designed, well engineered, and well built.

• The complex should be built on time, within budget, and according to the specifications that have been established.

• The complex should be designed in such a way that the costs of building maintenance (heating, ongoing maintenance) are minimized.

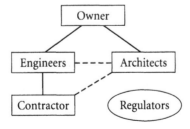

Figure 6.1. Structure of a Typical Construction Project Team.

Because the owners are footing the bill to build the complex, their views on what the project requirements should be are highly significant. Problems can arise, however, when the owners hold conflicting opinions on specific requirements that should be established. For example, the Globus management team may argue that a disproportionate share of project funds should be devoted to building the main headquarters building because management and employees will be occupying it and want to work in a first-class structure. The outside investors, however, may argue that the shopping mall, movie house, and hotel should receive a disproportionate share of the budget since these structures will be revenue-generating and will maximize returns on their investment.

Clearly, in creating processes to capture the owners' requirements for the project, decision rules must be established to resolve disputes that might arise among them. Steps that can be taken to prioritize requirements will be covered later in this chapter.

ARCHITECTS. Architects have the responsibility of designing a complex that will address the owners' needs and wants in an attractive way. Although they are supposed to be concerned with both *form* and *function*, they often emphasize the former at the expense of the latter. In general, they are the champions of the artistic aspects of the effort, and the final complex will reflect their artistic capabilities. Once built, it will be visible to the whole world, so the architects want to design structures that showcase their tastes and design skills.

Interestingly, in their attempt to push the boundaries of design, architects occasionally design structures that cannot be built because the technology does not yet exist to help them realize their vision. This phenomenon is often cited as a major cause for the cost and schedule overruns encountered on the project to build the opera house in Sydney—to fabricate the grandiose "clamshells" that the architect envisioned, a new type of concrete had to be invented. This can lead to tensions between a project's architects and engineers.

ENGINEERS. The engineers' job is to make the architects' vision real. They have to figure out how to build the arches, install the off-spec windows, and hide the plumbing according to the architects' desires. While the architects' concern is with the grace of a walkway, the engineers' is with its load-carrying capacity. Clearly, engineers approach requirements development principally from a technical perspective. They may have little sympathy with the architects' artistic temperament, particularly when the architects' vision creates practical problems.

BUILDING CONTRACTOR. The building contractor's primary concern on the Globus headquarters project is to build the complex within the schedule, budget, and quality constraints defined by the contract. Their job is to implement the requirements defined by the architects and engineers.

REGULATORS. In building a structure, builders may be exposed to a wide range of regulations that they must contend with, including abiding by building codes imposed by the state and local community, obtaining building permits, meeting national safety standards (such as OSHA rules), obeying environmental regulations, and operating within the labor laws (paying no less than minimum wage, for example). Each of the rules and regulations imposed on builders will help shape the requirements they face when building a new structure.

Globus Supply Chain Management Information Systems Project: Key Players

The second example examines key players on a typical information technology project that is launched to address an organization's internal information needs. The players discussed here reflect what has become a standard set of players in information technology organizations. Owing to the dramatic difference between the environments encountered on construction and information technology projects, the major players and their requirements-related concerns are quite different in the two scenarios.

Globus Enterprises is about to launch a project to integrate its supply chain management processes. With the new system, all aspects of order processing, vendor management, and inventory management will be handled by a single, user-friendly, integrated information system. Although the entire Globus organization will be affected by the new system, a smaller group of key players whose perspectives must be captured in order to create effective requirements can be readily identified. They include the project sponsor, solution owner, project manager, subject matter experts (SMEs), business analysts, technology analysts, technology director, testers, and vendors.

As in the construction example, each of these players has a per-spective on what the requirements should be. Figure 6.2 depicts the relationships among the players. The role and views of each will be discussed briefly.

PROJECT SPONSOR. On information technology projects, project sponsors are senior managers who are the ultimate "owners" of projects carried out within the organization. Their principal functions are to define high-level project goals, to use their powerful position to help sponsored projects achieve these goals, and to protect projects from disruptive political actions. Sponsors can help projects by making certain they are properly resourced. The importance of their role emerged in the 1990s, and today it is widely acknowledged that knowledge-based projects without active sponsors will face struggles.

The requirements the project sponsor supports are important, and all subsequently developed detailed requirements and specifications should trace back to them. The sponsor's requirements are invariably *business* requirements and should be explicitly tied to corporate strategic goals.

SOLUTION OWNER. Solution owners are typically upper-level middle managers (such as vice presidents) who are actively engaged in project affairs. In a sense, they are agents of the sponsor, and their job is to see that projects are carried out effectively and that the sponsor's high-level goals are achieved. They will monitor project progress through weekly meetings with the project manager and key project personnel.

	Business players	**Technical players**
Senior managers	Project sponsor Solution owner	Technology director
Project team players	Project manager Business analyst Subject matter expert	Technical analyst Tester

Figure 6.2. Structure of a Typical Information Technology Project Team.

PROJECT MANAGER. Project managers are assigned responsibility for delivering successful projects. They run projects on a day-by-day basis. Their primary requirements-related concern is to ensure that the business requirements being addressed by the project are accurately expressed and converted into viable technical specifications. They serve an important bridging function, making sure that the gap between business and technical issues is properly spanned. Occasionally, they play the role of referee, adjudicating disputes between business and technical members of the project team.

SUBJECT MATTER EXPERT. Subject matter experts (SMEs) are people who have detailed knowledge of how business processes work. For example, SMEs employed in the Globus supply chain management project would include experts on inventory management and control, order processing experts, purchasing specialists, and logisticians. These people possess the business knowledge that needs to be incorporated into the definition of business requirements. The chief problem associated with SMEs is that they often lack the ability to state business needs in terms that can be readily converted into technical requirements.

BUSINESS ANALYST. Business analysts play a significant role in requirements definition. Their primary responsibility is to capture the business requirements of SMEs and other business users and to formulate them in a fashion that is understandable by the technical team. They are in effect interpreters who translate business talk into technical requirements. The best business analysts have a thorough knowledge of both business issues and the technology that will be employed to provide business solutions. In practice, many of them worked in the technical arena earlier in their lives, so they are well acquainted with conditions and concerns the technical team may face.

TECHNICAL ANALYST. Technical analysts have a thorough grounding in technologies currently being employed by the organization. Though they may not be familiar with business issues, they can take the requirements specified by business analysts and convert them into specifications that are addressed by software programmers and other members of the technical team.

TECHNOLOGY DIRECTOR. The technology director is a senior manager on the technology side of the organization's business. Because this player controls resource allocations, it is important that he or she be involved in project planning and execution. In the early stages of a project, the technology director can provide guidance on when resources will be available to work on the project effort. Once the project is under way, this individual can help ensure that resources show up when they are supposed to.

TESTER. Testers can play a significant role in the requirements definition effort on information technology projects. Although their broad charter is to make sure the emerging technical solution functions properly, they must specifically determine whether the system meets the requirements set out for it. It is not enough to have a system that works—the system must address the business needs that led to the launching of the project. If testers are doing their job right, their tests will identify solutions that are drifting from defined requirements. In this case, technical team members will be instructed to adjust their work to bring it back into conformance with the established requirements. For testers to carry out their requirements-policing role properly, they must be explicitly instructed to test the solution against stated requirements.

VENDOR. Vendors can play a major role in requirements definition, particularly if their product is the cornerstone of the information technology solution that will be employed. For example, if the supply chain management solution adopted by Globus is based on a product called SCM Solutions, the business and technical requirements must be defined according to the limitations imposed on them by the SCM Solutions product.

THE COMMUNICATION CHALLENGE: I CAN'T READ YOUR MIND

At its heart, developing effective requirements is about communication. For a project to create solutions that address a business need, business players must be able to communicate their needs and wants clearly enough to enable the technical team members to know what they should focus on. Without good communication, there is no understanding. Since the technical team members cannot read the business players' minds, they will build whatever solution appears to be appropriate to them. Of course, this approach leads to the creation of deliverables that do not satisfy customers.

To clarify the role of communication in developing requirements, it is helpful to examine what is called the standard communication model. This model identifies the principal players in a communication transaction and shows how communication works. By reviewing this model, it is possible to identify barriers to communication. When these barriers are removed, communication improves greatly.

THE STANDARD COMMUNICATION MODEL

The standard communication model is depicted in part (a) of Figure 6.3. It shows that any act of communication involves senders who "encode" their messages so that they can be transmitted. For example,

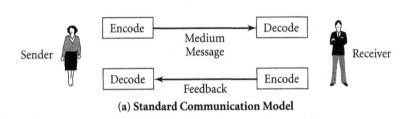

(a) Standard Communication Model

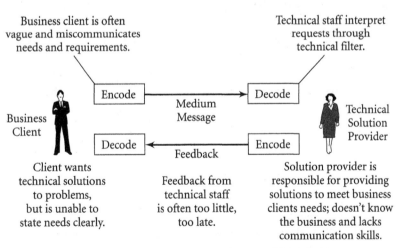

(b) Communication Roots of the Business-Technology Gap

Figure 6.3. The Communication Model.

among French people who will be engaging in verbal communication with their colleagues, the message will be encoded in the French language. The encoded message is then transmitted to receivers through a medium (for example, in face-to-face conversations, the medium is air; in a telephone conversation, it may be a fiber-optic cable). Before the receivers understand the content of the message, it needs to be decoded. For the message to make sense, the encoding and decoding keys must match. In the present case, encoding and decoding revolve around the vocabulary, grammar, and syntax of standard French. When receivers provide pertinent feedback to senders (for example, "I agree with your point"), they close the communication loop.

This simple model is helpful in explaining why communication problems often arise between business players and technical project team members. Part (b) of Figure 6.3 converts the standard communication model into a model that addresses transactions between business players and technical project team members. The barriers to communication leap from the drawing. Consider the following four barriers.

Culturally Rooted Barriers

Owing to cultural factors, the business players' worldview is different from that of the technical team members'. The two sets of players are operating according to different perceptual frameworks. Business players, for example, are concerned with issues such as profitability, time to market, market share, and customer satisfaction. They want technical solutions that will help them increase sales and can be produced quickly. To them, technical concerns are side issues that reside in a black box: their prevailing view is that these issues will somehow be resolved.

Their technical counterparts, meanwhile, are focused on technical concerns such as design, testability, utilization of current technology, and technical integrity. They see nothing automatic about solving technically challenging problems. To these people, the technical issues are the core issues.

It is easy to see how the difference in worldviews between the business and technical players can generate communication barriers. When confronted with feedback that suggests that a requirement they have is not technically feasible, business players may brush off this warning with the statement: "That's just a technical detail that someone can fix." Meanwhile, technical team members who cherish technical perfection may not feel a sense of urgency to develop timely, "good enough" solutions in a cost-effective fashion—and this attitude drives their business counterparts mad.

Vocabulary-Rooted Barriers

Business players generally encode their messages using a business vocabulary while the technical team members operate according to a rather precise technical vocabulary. Both sets of players can have difficulty interpreting the words of their counterparts.

To business players, the technical realm is arcane, filled with strange terms and formulations that require years of education to comprehend—*bits, bytes, baud rates, bandwidth, token rings,* and *SQL* are terms that lie outside their ken. The concepts underlying them are even more obscure. So when business players sit down with the technical team, they describe their needs and wants in decidedly imprecise—and occasionally misleading—terms. For effective communication to occur in this case, it is important that the technical team members be sensitive to this reality. They should not grow impatient with their business clients' inability to articulate their needs and wants in technically meaningful ways. Furthermore, they should be careful not to treat client statements of needs too literally—if a client says, "We need to access this database through a Lotus Notes interface," the technical team should recognize that the client does not really know what the need actually is or how to articulate it meaningfully, and hence the team should not assume that the appropriate solution is based on Lotus Notes, even though this is what the client stated.

Interestingly, the business client's vocabulary may be considered a foreign language by technical team members. Although we don't normally think of businesspeople as "technical," their knowledge is often highly specialized, with its own unique lexicon. Consider how strange terms like *options, puts,* and *calls* seem to a software programmer. Clearly, developing an understanding of vocabulary is a two-way street, involving both clients and technical team members.

Organizations take various approaches to deal with vocabulary issues. One is to employ *business analysts* in the requirements-development effort. As we saw earlier in this chapter, these are typically men and women with technical backgrounds who have developed expertise in the business area. They are analogous to interpreters employed in an international meeting whose job is to translate statements from one language to another.

Another approach is to have a group of stakeholders from different backgrounds get together to articulate needs and requirements. With a group approach, all stakeholders have an opportunity to explain problems they may have with vocabulary—no one will be left out. The most popular group approach employed today is called *joint application development* (JAD). We will cover use of JAD sessions later in this chapter.

Medium-Rooted Barriers

The medium employed for eliciting requirements is often not amenable to effective communication. Clearly, the best approach to overcoming communication barriers is to have face-to-face encounters when eliciting requirements. But even then, communication problems can arise, particularly when these encounters are performed one-on-one. Traditionally, needs and requirements are identified by systems analysts. They carry out their effort by interviewing customers one by one. The interviews are often conducted in an ad hoc fashion and gain only a fragmented view of customer needs. After a number of interviews have been conducted, the systems analysts return to their offices, where they attempt to integrate the perspectives of multiple customers. The results of this effort become the basis of the requirements' definition.

Because traditional one-on-one interviews may lead to a narrow, distorted view of customer needs and wants, today it is generally agreed that the face-to-face requirements-generating sessions should be carried out by assembling a full range of stakeholders in a meeting, where they can articulate their needs and wants in the presence of other stakeholders. This gives all stakeholders the opportunity to comment on requests and insights provided by their colleagues. The requirements that emerge from this process account for the dynamics of the whole group of customers and go beyond the views of individual people stating their opinions in isolation. Once again, JAD sessions appear to provide a solution to dealing with this form of communication barrier.

Barriers Rooted in Inadequate Feedback

Feedback from the technical team is often too little, too late. Frequently, technical team members are not comfortable with the human side of customer relations and so avoid interacting with business clients. Once they have gathered requirements, they may not carry out "sanity checks" to make sure they have addressed the true needs and wants of the business clients. Consequently, customers do not know what requirements the technical team is addressing. Only much later, when a commitment to a particular design has been made, do they see the solution they will be getting, and if they do not like what they see, this will spell trouble for the project.

To avoid regrettable surprises resulting from miscommunication, the requirements-definition process should call for continual customer review of the developing requirements. These review sessions may make the technical team uncomfortable, but they help manage customer expectations and decrease the likelihood of unhappy surprises later in the project life cycle.

TIPS FOR HANDLING REQUIREMENTS

There is no limit to the sage advice that experienced developers of requirements can offer novices. Anyone who has been in the business for more than a few years has long lists of the dos and don'ts of requirements definition. Some of the more useful tips are offered here.

• *Be up front—state the requirement explicitly and have customers sign off on it.* Lawyers are continually telling their business clients to "put it in writing." Verbal agreements sealed with a handshake may seem to be an admirable way to do business because they are predicated on trust and run counter to the litigiousness that permeates our lives. But they are fundamentally flawed. If an agreement is not documented, how do we know what the parties agreed to? This is not a problem so long as things are running smoothly, but what if we hit a rough patch of road and it becomes important to know how rights and responsibilities have been divided between the parties? Beyond this, it is likely that with handshake agreements, the parties have not thoroughly thought through the issues encompassed in the agreement. The very act of articulating something and documenting it is prima facie evidence that someone has engaged in more than trivial reflection on a issue.

Requirements should certainly be stated in writing. The dominant theme of this chapter is that effective requirements management demands that everything be clear. Undocumented requirements do not promote this notion. They encourage multiple perspectives on what should be done, which in turn leads to off-target deliverables and generating conflict.

Beyond this, stakeholders who are affected by a requirement should also sign off on it. Sign-offs serve three important functions. First, when people are asked to sign off on something, this forces them to take it seriously. They are likely to have read the statement and given it serious consideration, because their signature reflects a significant level of commitment and accountability.

Second, their signatures indicate their support of the stated requirement. If people question the validity of a stated requirement, the signatures of key stakeholders demonstrate its legitimacy.

Third, the sign-off is part of an audit trail. If problems arise on the project, the signatures of senior managers indicate that the project team obtained proper authorization to do their jobs. Without the signatures, the team may be accused of operating outside their bounds of authority.

• *Be cautious—assume that if a requirement can be misinterpreted, it will be.* Experienced project workers know that instructions, requirements, and customer or manager intentions are continually being misinterpreted. When specifying a requirement, it is smart to operate under the assumption that the people to whom it is directed do not fully understand it. One technique to check on this is to ask the recipients of the requirement to repeat back to you their understanding of its intent. If project workers do this regularly, their colleagues, team members, and contractors listen more carefully to stated requirements because they know that they will be quizzed on them.

• *Be realistic—recognize that there will be changes on your project and that things will not go precisely as anticipated.* Many people that do not have project management experience operate under the delusion that when well planned, projects can be carried out flawlessly. Regrettably, even the best-planned projects experience surprises triggered by unanticipated developments. There are many sources of change over which the project team has little or no control: economic downturns, the actions of competitors, changes in government regulations, mergers and acquisitions, evolving technology, shortages of key supplies, tight labor markets, and reengineering efforts.

Project managers and their team members can be certain that they will encounter changes to requirements on their project. The issue is not whether there will be change but rather whether they are prepared to deal with the changes that will inevitably occur. To handle change, it is important that the project team be familiar with their organization's change control processes. If the organization lacks effective change control procedures, the team should develop its own and communicate them to customers.

At a minimum, change requests should include all of the following:

Name of individual requesting the change

Date of the change request

Brief description of the request for change

Brief description of project tasks and features of the deliverable that will be affected by the requested change

Cost impacts of the requested change

Schedule impacts of the requested change

• *Be clear—to the greatest extent possible, use pictures, graphics, physical models, and other nonverbal exhibits in formulating requirements.* Rapid prototyping is a successful requirements-defining methodology because customers develop a realistic sense of what is being developed for them by working with a physical prototype of the emerging product. By actually entering data on a data entry form designed for the prototyped system, they have a much better understanding of its strengths and limitations than by reading a one-paragraph description of how the form functions.

In general, verbal descriptions of requirements should be supplemented with appropriate visual displays. By itself, the following instruction can lead to confusion and can easily be misinterpreted: "Compute sales tax based on the Total Sales figure (column 4, line 8 of the Invoice form) and put the resulting figure into the next cell down (column 4, line 9 of the Invoice form)." However, if a clearly marked copy of the Invoice form accompanies the instruction, the intent of the instruction is dramatically clarified.

• *Be patient—don't jump to solutions prematurely when formulating requirements.* When attempting to elicit and articulate requirements, it is easy to identify solutions prematurely. This may be due to impatience. For example, as the technical team grows frustrated with its customers' inability to nail down their requirements, it may interject: "Say no more. We know what you require." If the customers' true requirements have not yet emerged, the offered solution will be off-target.

Most often, premature solutions arise subtly, and neither customers nor developers are aware of it. A common sign of this is when requirements are defined in terms of vendor products—for example, "What we must build is a SAP ERP solution" or "They need to hook their workstations into an Ethernet network configuration." The problem is not that the proposed solution is bad but rather that by seizing on a specific solution too early in the discovery process, the search for good solutions is sidetracked or stopped.

An effective way to avoid the tendency to jump to solutions prematurely is to develop requirements through the efforts of groups of different stakeholders. When different stakeholders are brought together, each wants to be given a chance to present its views to the overall group. In such an environment—where multiple perspectives are presented and discussed—it is difficult to jump to solutions prematurely.

• *Communicate effectively—educate customers and project team members on requirements-related issues that are likely to arise.* Many requirements-related issues are predictable: requirements change, there are difficulties translating business needs into technical requirements, there is a tendency to confuse solutions with requirements, and so forth. The project manager should devote time at the outset of the project to educate customers and team members about these issues to avoid confusion and surprises later in the project.

BRINGING IT TOGETHER WITH
JOINT APPLICATION DEVELOPMENT

As this chapter has shown, there are many impediments to converting business needs into technical requirements, including gaps separating the business and technology cultures, communication problems, conflicting perspectives on what should be done, and forces of change that can make requirements unstable. One approach that has been successfully adopted helps bridge the business-technology gap. The approach is called *joint application development* (JAD). It was developed in the information technology arena to address two issues: (1) owing to rapidly changing technology and brutal competitive pressure, project teams need to develop software solutions at breakneck speed, and (2) to produce software solutions that address true customer needs, requirements must be developed as part of a group effort, where the key business and technology stakeholders meet to work things out in intense working sessions.

The term *JAD* is often used colloquially to describe a freewheeling session where the technical project team gets together with customers at an off-site facility and the group brainstorms day and night until a set of acceptable requirements emerges. In this session, the group is under pressure to come up with something quickly. To emphasize the frenetic dimension of the effort, the JAD team is not even given time off for lunch or dinner or breaks. Food is brought to the group at mealtimes as they struggle to develop effective requirements.

Actually, the formal JAD approach—while it promotes flexibility— has a degree of structure associated with it. Typically, it entails a two-step process, illustrated in Figure 6.4. The first session is called the *planning session*. Its principal objective is to carry out the preliminary work needed to produce requirements. It results in the creation of preliminary requirements. During the planning session, the following actions are taken:

- Provide an orientation to the session (Why are we here? What are we doing?).

- Define high-level requirements, using visuals, stick-on labels, and prototypes.

- Identify steps needed to implement the JAD design session.

- Set out a schedule for developing requirements.

- Document issues and decisions (have a scribe do this).

- Conclude the session.

Joint Application Development (JAD) Sessions

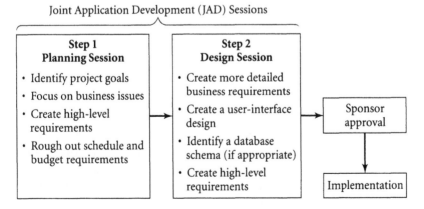

Figure 6.4. The Two-Step JAD Process.

An important feature of JAD is that after the creative brainstorming has ended, a core group is charged with conducting a wrap-up exercise, which should include the following tasks:

- Write a statement of system objectives.
- Conduct and document an examination of systems functions—the needs they address, benefits, and priorities.
- Highlight limitations—functions the system will not address.
- Craft a statement of interfaces with other systems.
- Highlight and document unresolved issues.
- List the next steps to be taken.

As a result of the JAD planning session, the requirements team has a good sense of high-level requirements and has taken steps to identify what should be done to develop detailed requirements. At this point, a JAD *design session* should be carried out to identify the detailed requirements. The design session typically includes the following activities:

- Provide an orientation to the session (Why are we here? What are we doing?).
- Define detailed requirements using workflow diagrams and workflow descriptions.
- Design screens and reports in a prototype format.
- Specify process requirements.
- Define interface requirements.
- Document issues and decisions (have a scribe do this).
- Conclude the session.

As with the JAD planning session, a wrap-up exercise is conducted by a subgroup of the JAD team. The objective of this exercise is to reflect on decisions made during the design session and to document the results. The documents generated by this group serve as the "official" pronouncement on requirements. Following are the tasks required in the wrap-up effort:

• Complete the JAD design document.

• Refine whatever prototypes have been developed.

• Have participants review the document.

• Present the document to the project sponsor.

JAD sessions clearly provide a better basis for defining requirements than the traditional approach of having a systems analyst conduct one-on-one interviews with stakeholders. Today's complex processes demand cross-functional inputs from the full array of significant stakeholders, and the best way to gain their input is to bring them together in a common meeting. By having key stakeholders working together to identify and articulate requirements, JAD sessions lead to the development of requirements that are likely to define deliverables that satisfy customer needs and wants.

CONCLUSIONS

One of the chief challenges for project management today is dealing with the customer-developer gap. To the extent that customers and developers operate in different cultures, speak different languages, and are ignorant of the details of each other's profession, the gap contributes to project failure because the deliverables being developed do not address true customer needs.

The gap is bridgeable, however. Customers must learn to articulate their needs and wants clearly and in terms that make sense to developers. This means that they must do their homework and determine the technical consequences of their requests. It also means that they should understand the peculiar points of view held by their technical counterparts.

Developers, for their part, need to be patient when dealing with customers. They should recognize that because customers are often unaware of the technical intricacies of systems solutions, they may make comments that are off-target and may demonstrate signs of defensiveness when technical questions arise. Developers should also do their homework and learn as much as they can about their customers' business.

It is clear that the customer-developer gap can be bridged only by bringing the two sides together to address project requirements. We are moving away from the view that the development of project requirements is the job of a technically smart systems analyst who works alone. The rise of joint responsibility teams, rapid prototyping, and joint application development suggest that people are learning that the effective development of requirements demands inputs from multiple stakeholders.

PART TWO

Tools for the New Project Management

P art Two of this book looks at the skill sets that project management professionals should possess in order to deal with the issues raised in Part One. The skills required of today's project professionals go far beyond the set of skills demanded of them until quite recently. The traditional view of project professionals as implementers required skills development in the areas of budgeting, scheduling, and allocating human and material resources.

In today's business environment, however, project professionals have responsibilities that go beyond mere implementation. To be effective, today's project professionals must be capable in the political arena, able to forge teams in the matrix environment, competent to make independent decisions, qualified to predict future scenarios, able to deal with outsiders through contracts, and skilled at many other tasks.

Each of the ten chapters in Part Two deals with an area in which skills mastery should be achieved for effective project management. Chapter Seven focuses on political skills. Project managers often assume high levels of responsibility without possessing commensurate levels of authority. This chapter shows how the conscientious cultivation of political awareness and development of whatever authority sources are available can enable project managers to influence outcomes even under these adverse conditions.

Chapter Eight examines one of the most fundamental dilemmas the project professional may face: how to create a sense of team spirit when the team players assigned to the project are borrowed resources.

Chapter Nine reviews decision-making principles and techniques to help project professionals select projects, staff, material resources, and vendors. Techniques are suggested for better decision making, including benefit-cost analysis, peer review, the murder board, and the poor man's hierarchy.

Chapter Ten focuses on one of the leading causes of project failure: poor estimation of costs, schedules, and specifications. Techniques are offered for improving the quality of project estimates, thereby lowering the likelihood of schedule slippages, cost overruns, and the development of poor-quality deliverables.

Chapter Eleven examines two new scheduling tools that have emerged in recent years: time-boxed scheduling and critical chain scheduling. These techniques reflect the realities of scheduling that are ignored by the traditional project management scheduling techniques. Applying them enables project teams to produce their deliverables faster than ever.

Chapter Twelve reviews one of the dominant phenomena of business today: the employment of outsiders to carry out the organization's work. The chapter examines key principles of contracting as they relate to projects and offers suggestions for operating effectively in an outsource environment.

Chapter Thirteen examines one of the most sophisticated techniques of project management: the cost and schedule control system, also known as the earned value method. This cost accounting technique allows project teams to assess cost and schedule performance on projects simultaneously.

Chapter Fourteen reviews attempts to increase accountability on projects. Pitfalls of traditional approaches to evaluation are discussed. The structured walk-through—evaluation with a human face—is highlighted.

Chapter Fifteen examines the measurement of work performance. It shows how the employment of work performance measures enhances project control and increases the likelihood of project success.

Chapter Sixteen looks at one of the hottest developments in project management today: the establishment and maintenance of project support offices. These offices free project staff to do project work rather than get bogged down in paperwork. In addition, they supply organizations with the expertise they need to carry out large numbers of projects, from simple to complex.

As with Part One, the chapters in Part Two have been written as self-contained entities. Consequently, they can be read in whatever order you find useful.

CHAPTER SEVEN

Acquiring Political Skills
and Building Influence

P ractitioners of the new project management recognize that life is often messy. Management practice has a way of deviating sharply from management theory. People do not fit into neat categories and do not behave according to set formulas.

One important messy reality is that on projects, politics is inevitable. All project managers will encounter it in some measure. It is futile to fight it. Wise project managers learn to accommodate it. Although the term *politics* has negative connotations, project managers who master its intricacies come to see its positive qualities. They know that if they are to get the job done, they will have to develop political skills.

WHAT IS POLITICS?

The concept of politics is difficult to nail down. Even dictionaries—normally precise in defining terms—are not very helpful here. Their definitions of politics often have an element of circularity to them, as in "the art or science of political government" (*American Heritage Dictionary*, 1978, p. 1015). To the extent that they talk of politics outside the context of government, they portray it in negative terms, as in "factional scheming within a group" (*Webster's New World Dictionary,* 1964, p. 1132).

Any practical discussion of politics must come to grips with its negative image, because for many people this negative image stands in the way of their developing effective political skills. President John Kennedy caught the spirit of our ambivalence toward politics when he said, "Mothers may still want their favorite sons to grow up to be President, but . . . they do not want them to become politicians in the process" (*American Heritage Dictionary,* 1978, p. 1015). The negative feeling toward politics is captured in adjectives commonly used to describe the politician: conniving, shifty, unprincipled, selfish, corrupt, Machiavellian, amoral. The common theme of these adjectives is the nonadherence of politicians to a clear set of moral principles that guide them in their undertakings.

Although many examples in our daily newspapers appear to confirm this view of politics and politicians, we must recognize that the image of politics as sleazy distorts the true nature of politics. At heart, *politics is the art of influence.* For the most part, politicians do not achieve their goals and the goals of their constituents by virtue of powerful muscles, large bank accounts, or the use of military force. Politicians are successful in their work only to the extent that they can effectively influence others to do their bidding. For example, elected politicians must first influence the electorate to vote for them. Once elected, they maintain their influence by serving their constituents' needs. To do this, they influence other politicians to back their positions. When politicians lose this ability to influence the outcome of events, they become powerless.

Another feature of politics is that it is the lubricant that allows the wheels of organized human activity to turn without jamming. People are in conflict with each other because they pursue conflicting goals. We see this all around us at all levels of human activity. At the level of the individual, we may find a husband and wife struggling over the household thermostat because one prefers the house warmer than the other does. At the level of the community, we frequently encounter battles between advocates of economic growth and antigrowth forces who want to maintain the aesthetic integrity of the community. At the national level, there are struggles between those who desire strong government social programs and those who champion a laissez-faire role for government. Internationally, of course, the struggle over conflicting goals can have catastrophic consequences resulting in war.

The way conflict is resolved is through accommodation—which is to say, through political efforts. If this does not work, the consequences will be chaos, stalemate, or outright hostile actions. This is what Karl von Clausewitz meant when he said, in his classic book *On War* (1833), "War is the continuation of politics by other means."

Taking these considerations into account, we can improve on dictionary definitions of politics by defining it in the following way: *Politics is the process whereby attempts are made to achieve goals through accommodation and the exercise of influence.*

POLITICS IN PROJECTS

Project environments are excellent breeding grounds for rampant politics. An important reason for this is that authority on projects is diffuse. On most projects, managers do not "own" their resources. Staff are borrowed from functional areas, so they "belong" to someone else. A large part of efforts of project managers is devoted to wangling these resources from functional managers. Their lives are complicated by the fact that they are competing against other project managers and functional heads for these scarce resources like five hungry dogs fighting for a single bone. Obtaining needed resources often entails a good deal of horse trading and the occasional issuance of implied or explicit threats.

PLAYERS TO CONTEND WITH IN THE PROJECT ENVIRONMENT

Authority is diffuse in another sense as well. On most projects, managers find themselves surrounded by many key players who have the power to make or break the project. It behooves project managers to spend some time reflecting on these actors and how they can affect the course of events. Such reflection will identify the many ways that politics creeps into projects. The following are some key players.

Bosses

Project managers work with varying degrees of independence. Some call the shots on budgeting, scheduling, and resource utilization; others are basically baby-sitters. In all cases, they are ultimately accountable to someone above them in the hierarchy. That is, they have bosses.

Bosses can make a big difference in whether project managers have good or bad experiences with their projects. Bosses can affect project performance both materially and psychologically. For example, in an emergency, they can supply their project managers with extra human and material resources. On a psychological plane, fear of a bad performance review by the boss can make a project manager so risk-averse that no hard decisions are made on the project.

There is one important political fact that all project managers should bear in mind: their bosses are not neutral with regard to their project. In fact, their bosses are stakeholders in the project. Bosses themselves have bosses. Their relations with their bosses may be sensitive to the performance of their project managers. Success of a highly visible project may reflect positively on their management ability and lead to promotions and bonuses, whereas failure may assure them of a spot in the organization's gulag.

Bosses are frequently stakeholders in another sense as well: with the acquisition of projects, they can enlarge their turf. A given project may be yet another tool they can employ to strengthen their position in the organization. Even bosses who are totally devoid of ambition are stakeholders in a very mundane sense: if their project managers should run into trouble, this will create administrative and political hassles for them and make their lives generally unpleasant.

The political implications of bosses being stakeholders are significant. It means that politically savvy project managers must view their decisions from their boss's perspective. They must know what their boss's goals are in relation to the project. If they do not do this, they may find their decisions being reversed and support for their efforts declining. Ultimately, insensitivity to the boss's goals may lead to poor performance ratings and denial of future managerial responsibilities.

Peers

I use the term *peers* to refer to coworkers who operate at the same level of responsibility as we do. They are very likely project managers themselves. Because they are our equals in the hierarchy, we have no direct control over them. If we want their cooperation, we must obtain this through influence.

Our relations with our project peers are often filled with ambiguity. On the one hand, they can be our helpmates. They can provide us with crucial information, share their resources, offer us a shoulder to cry on, serve as a sounding board for ideas, and act as our political allies.

On the other hand, they are our competitors, in two senses. First, they compete with us for scarce resources. As a consequence, they may be involved in all sorts of behind-the-scenes machinations to ensure that they can acquire these resources—possibly at our expense. Second, they compete with us for career advancement. As we progress higher in the organizational pyramid, there are more candidates for fewer job slots. The fact that pyramids are crumbling and organizations are flattening only intensifies competition. If our peers have any ambition at all, we can be sure that they hear a little voice somewhere inside them telling them that our successes may jeopardize their advancement.

Functional Managers Who Control Resources

Because project managers do not own their resources, they must borrow them from functional areas within the organization. Project managers expend a good deal of effort trying to acquire needed resources from the functional managers who control them.

Their chief concerns in acquiring resources revolve around the following questions: Can I acquire resources that satisfy the technical requirements of the project? Will they be of good quality and do what it takes to get the job done? Will I have enough of them? Will I be able to obtain them when I need them? Will I be able to keep them for the time I need them, or will they be pulled off the project to fight fires somewhere else?

Sometimes the acquisition of these resources is straightforward. For example, the project manager may tell the head of data processing that she needs a database specialist for a two-month period beginning on September 9. After checking a resource calendar, the DP head may make arrangements guaranteeing that her request will be satisfied.

However, obtaining resources is generally more complex than this. Project environments are dynamic. Plans change—schedules slip, budgets are cut or augmented, new tasks emerge, people become ill, new staff sign on, and so on. In such an environment, the acquisition of resources becomes a major challenge. Success in getting the people we need when we need them may depend more on our powers of persuasion over managers who control resources than on our ability to fill out resource request forms properly. That is, in acquiring resources, political skills can be important.

Customers

Not long ago, customers played only a peripheral role on projects even though the purpose of these projects was purportedly to produce a deliverable that would satisfy them. The reason for this was confidence in the superior expertise of the project staff. The assumption was that by dint of their education, experience, and great intelligence, project staff knew what was best for customers. Why muddy the waters with heavy customer involvement in the development of the deliverable?

An important feature of the new project management is the belief that customers are kings. In fact, project success and failure are defined in terms of satisfying customers. A project is said to fail if its deliverables are not used, underused, or misused by customers. In the new project management, the view that the experts know what is best for customers is regarded as paternalistic and self-serving.

As pointed out in Chapter Five, close contact with customers carries a major consequence that is relatively new to project management: project staff must develop good people skills so that they can interact productively with their clients. Staff have to become politically astute because they are dealing with players who are beyond their control and who possess different goals from their own. This means that staff must be able to put themselves into their customers' shoes to appreciate their needs more fully. Staff must also be willing and able to live with compromise, since their vision of what is best for the customers will often differ from the customers' perception of what is best.

Unfortunately, the development of good customer relations skills can be stressful for many project staff members, who went into computer programming, electrical engineering, or accounting because they were attracted by the work itself rather than by a desire to interact with people. For the most part, these individuals have little political savvy. Yet to work effectively to produce deliverables that satisfy customers, they must develop some.

Vendors

On the surface, it would appear that there should be few political problems with vendors, seeing that project managers have a degree of control over them. After all, if vendors fail to deliver, project managers need not pay them.

This view hides a reality that experienced project managers are acutely aware of: getting something out of vendors is a complex process. Following are some common problems in dealing with vendors:

- The deliverable arrives late, causing a schedule slippage.
- The deliverable does not meet the agreed specifications and is unusable.
- The invoice price of the deliverable is higher than the estimated price originally quoted, contributing to cost overruns.

When these kinds of problems arise, how should they be dealt with? Or better yet, what can be done to avoid them in the first place? The answers to these questions are not obvious and must be worked out in the specific circumstances. Frequently, the answers involve more than threatening nonpayment for goods, canceling the contract, or instituting a lawsuit for breach of contract. A project staff's primary objective in dealing with vendors is to get the needed goods and services from them in as effective a manner as possible. If vendor problems translate into budget, schedule, or requirements problems for the project, it is small consolation that we can withhold payment.

As with so much in project management, dealing with vendors requires political skills. With these skills, project staff can anticipate problems before they arise and identify ways to pressure the vendors to meet their obligations. Without these skills, project staff are at the mercy of events that lie beyond their control.

Others

A great many other project players can be involved in political activity, including the following:

- Purchasing department—for example, their foot-dragging in placing orders can lead to slow deliveries of needed supplies and services.
- Information resource management—for example, their insistence that we buy a computer that meets organizational standards may lead to the procurement of a device that does not fully meet the project's needs.

- Contracts office—for example, their narrow interpretation of contract clauses may not allow for needed changes in the requirements for a deliverable to be supplied by a contractor.

- Secretaries—for example, their lack of commitment to project work may lead to delays in progress and poor-quality reports.

BEING A BETTER POLITICIAN

Some people seem to be born politicians. They appear to have an instinctive capacity to size up the political dimensions of different situations and know what to do to have their will prevail. Being politically astute is as natural to them as taking a stroll.

Most of us are not born politicians. Furthermore, our upbringing and education do not prepare us for the political realities of life because our parents and teachers are as politically naïve as we are. In fact, given the prevailing view that politics is dirty, we are encouraged to avoid anything that smacks of political maneuvering. As a consequence, when we enter into political situations, we are like lambs being led to the slaughter.

Common Political Pitfalls

There are many ways that we can get into trouble politically. Following are some of the more common political pitfalls.

ACCEPTING THINGS AT FACE VALUE. One thing that politics shares with such diverse undertakings as psychoanalysis, the new physics, Eastern religions, and magic is the view that *things aren't as they seem*. Reality occurs at many different levels. Plato captured this in *The Republic* in his allegory of people trapped in a cave who perceive moving shadows on the wall to be reality since that is all they have ever experienced. Behind this reality, of course, there is a deeper reality of three-dimensional objects passing in front of a light, casting the shadows that fall on the wall. *The Republic*, incidentally, is not only a great philosophical work but also a political statement. The Greeks—inventors of democracy—did not perceive of politics as a shameful thing.

Good politicians are adept at penetrating through the superficial to identify the real issues. For example, the office head says he wants to automate the office to increase productivity. The astute project manager who knows the boss well may recognize that what the boss really wants is a modern-looking facility—an office filled with machines that hum rather than machines that clunk. This knowledge provides the project manager with important insights that increase the probability of project success.

INSENSITIVITY TO POLITICAL REALITIES. Some people have the political finesse of a bull in a china shop. Their primary trait is to make waves through their actions. To them, concern for the political consequences of their actions is overridden by a philosophy of "Damn the torpedoes, full speed ahead!"

Frequently, these individuals fall into the trap of not making much effort to do needed political spadework before they carry out their undertakings. Consider the case of the project manager who appointed a twenty-three-year-old hotshot as a task leader in charge of a group of people in their forties and fifties. When warned that the age differential between the task leader and the staff might cause morale problems for the project team, he responded, "I don't care. These old-timers will be gone in a few years. We've got to give our young blood the chance to learn how to manage effectively." His goal to speed up the professional development of young staff may have been admirable. However, his insensitivity to the views of the older project team members ultimately led to a revolt that made the life of the twenty-three-year-old so miserable that he soon left the company. Had the project manager done a bit of political spadework, he might have softened the team opposition to the young manager, or else he might have seen the futility of putting a youngster in charge of old hands.

THE HYPERPOLITICIAN. Sometimes project workers can get into trouble by being too political. These individuals thrive on gossip and behind-the-scenes manipulation. They hold no firm views on anything, preferring to bend with the prevailing political currents of the organization. They are, in fact, a caricature of the weasely politician.

The problem is that in playing the role of the stereotypical politician, they are not being politically effective. Their political machinations are transparent to all. The ultimate goal of effective politicians is to *influence others* to do their bidding, not to engage in backslapping and backstabbing on a large scale. More often than not, the ability to influence others requires subtlety and a quiet appreciation of what others need, want, and feel. Hyperpoliticians lack this subtlety.

Hyperpoliticians can get into trouble in a number of ways. For example, through their blatant political maneuverings, they may lose the respect of their fellow workers, who may perceive them as lacking substance. This will ultimately limit their career development and their ability to get others to cooperate with them. Another common pitfall facing hyperpoliticians is that their political maneuverings may backfire on them. The alliance they make may come apart so that yesterday's ally becomes today's enemy. Furthermore, yesterday's enemy is likely to remain today's enemy as well, leaving them with few friends.

THE HYPOPOLITICIAN. Diametrically opposed to the hyperpolitician is the hypopolitician. Whereas the former pursues too much of a good thing, the latter underperforms politically. Hypopoliticians eschew politics for a number of reasons. Some see it as an unprincipled undertaking, and they do not want to be sullied by it. Others view it as silly and demeaning and avoid politics for fear of being branded as superficial. Still others who have a natural tendency toward introversion are uncomfortable with the demands for extroverted behavior required of a politician.

The big problem hypopoliticians face is that they are either avoiding or ignoring something that will ultimately affect them. Politics on projects is inevitable owing to the very nature of projects and the environment in which they are carried out. By understanding politics and developing basic political skills, hypopoliticians can improve their project performance. By avoiding politics, they diminish the degree of control they can exercise over their projects.

A GUIDE TO ACTION

Until now, the discussion has concentrated on exploring the general nature of politics on projects. At this point, we turn our attention to a program of action, where we address the question, What do we need to do to become more effective politically? I offer a four-step approach:

Step 1: Develop a positive attitude toward politics.

Step 2: Lay a solid foundation for political action by developing a base of authority.

Step 3: Identify key elements of the environment.

Step 4: Identify and implement a course of action.

Step 1: Develop a Positive Attitude Toward Politics

A principal theme of this chapter is that politics is inevitable on projects, so we might as well learn to live with it and to use our knowledge to become more effective managers. We must dispel the notion that politics is an inherently sleazy or frivolous activity and should recall that it is fundamentally concerned with *achieving goals through accommodation and influence.* Inasmuch as we rarely have direct control over much of anything on our projects, it behooves us to become masters of accommodation and influence in order to gain some control over our efforts so that we can achieve our objectives.

Step 2: Lay a Solid Foundation for Political Action by Developing a Base of Authority

A fundamental problem for project managers is that they have responsibility without authority. As we have seen, the reason for the absence of authority is that project managers typically do not own the resources they work with. Instead, their resources are borrowed.

Why is authority important? Because it provides us with the capacity to get others to do our bidding. Without authority, we have no clout, no leverage over our staff and colleagues. Without authority, we must depend on the goodwill of others to get the job done. We are not really in control of our project.

Clearly, a major objective of effective project managers should be to develop a base of authority. This authority base, coupled with an awareness of the environment in which they operate (discussed in step 3), will give them the fundamental skills and resources needed to navigate the political waters of the project. There are many different kinds of authority. This chapter focuses on a handful that are relevant to most project situations. These will be discussed in detail later.

So effective political action requires the development of authority. It is authority that gives project managers a measure of influence over their staff, their bosses, and their peers. However, proper use of this authority demands that they have a good appreciation of the environment in which this authority will be applied. This brings us to the third step that must be undertaken to develop good political skills: the development of a good sense of the environment in which we operate.

Step 3: Identify Key Elements of the Environment

In *The Politics of Projects* (1983), Robert Block points out that to operate effectively as project managers, we must have a solid grasp of the environment in which we work. An important talent possessed by all successful politicians is the ability to divine what is happening around them. Accordingly, his book devotes a great deal of attention to describing how to carry out a politically savvy environmental assessment. This can be achieved by addressing three basic questions:

• Who are the players?

• What are their goals?

• Who am I?

WHO ARE THE PLAYERS? Politics is a process of people interacting with people, so it makes sense to undertake a systematic survey to identify the players that will be affected by our project or will have an effect on it. The important thing about this survey is to create as long a list of potentially relevant players as possible at the outset. In creating a long list, we reduce the likelihood that w have overlooked key players. Later on, we can shrink the list to manageable dimensions by eliminating marginal players.

In deciding who the key players are, we should not simply focus on individuals who are in the upper echelons of the organizational chart. The important issue is not where people stand in the hierarchy but whether they have the capacity to affect the project outcome either positively or negatively. If this serves as the guideline for identifying key players, then we see that on a database development project, humble data entry clerks might be key players; on a market survey project, telephone interviewers might be key players.

Consider what a list of key players in a hypothetical office relocation project might look like:

• *Players within the organization:* upper management, project staff, office director, purchasing department, budget office, people being relocated, managers of the operations being relocated, data processing department, maintenance department, facilities management group.

• *Players outside the organization:* customers, architectural consultant, interior design consultant, real estate agents, moving company, insurance company, electric power company; if the move entails building a new facility, the list of outside players might grow explosively, including key players such as the general contractor, subcontractors, the zoning board, and the county permits office.

Each of these players has the power to affect the project. That is, each of them, through their actions or inactions, can influence the project schedule, budget, and specifications.

WHAT ARE THE PLAYERS' GOALS? The creation of a list of key players alerts us to the people to whom we must devote some attention because they can affect the outcome of our project. Once we have identified them, we need to find out what motivates them. Knowledge of their goals provides us with insights into how we should deal with them.

Discovering the goals of key players requires us to develop the skills of a psychologist. Not only are we concerned with the players' stated goals, but we are interested in their hidden goals as well. Identifying hidden goals is not easy since not only are they hidden from us, but—to the extent that they operate at a subliminal level—they may also be hidden from the players themselves.

In the office relocation example, the office director may have presented the following goals to upper management in order to gain their support for the move:

- To move to larger facilities in order to accommodate a growing workforce
- To move to facilities with modern amenities
- To be located nearer to customers

However, she may have harbored an additional goal that she did not articulate: to move away from headquarters so as to gain a degree of independence of action. Furthermore, she may have unconscious goals of which she is only dimly aware. For example, she may be an inherently restless person who periodically needs a major change to recharge her batteries. Conscious awareness of all these goals gives the project manager special insights into the character and desires of a key player. With this knowledge, the project manager will have some guidance on what to do and what to avoid.

Many project professionals have difficulty identifying the goals of key players. Some are simply insensitive to the needs and wants of other people and lack empathy. Others are uncomfortable playing the role of psychologist. This is especially true of introverted technically oriented individuals, who are more comfortable with things than with people. Given the difficulty that many people have in identifying key players' goals, it may be wise to conduct this exercise in a small group where two or more heads may be better than one.

WHO AM I? This is the "know thyself" step. To be politically effective, project managers must know their own strengths and limitations, particularly as they bear on the project at hand. For example, how well does the project mesh with their values? Do they see it as a Mickey Mouse effort that misuses their talents? Do they resent the fact that the enormous workload interferes with their weekend plans? If the match between the project requirements and their goals is a poor one, this will negatively affect their attitude and commitment to the project, which will in turn hamper their political effectiveness.

Other important knowledge project managers should gain about themselves can be obtained by addressing the following questions:

- In the eyes of my colleagues, am I physically and socially attractive?
- Do I have good written and oral communication skills?
- Do I have a good grasp of the technical and administrative issues involved in this project?

For detailed guidance on understanding oneself better, read Richard Bolles's *What Color Is Your Parachute?* (2000), one of the most successful business books of all time. The central premise of this book is that individuals cannot be successful in planning a career if they do not understand their wants, needs, and capabilities thoroughly.

Step 4: Identify and Implement a Course of Action

Steps 1 through 3 have prepared the political groundwork that enables project managers to factor important political considerations into their decisions. Only now are they ready to offer solutions to problems. Unfortunately, most project managers skip steps 1 through 3 and begin the decision-making process at step 4. That is, they define the problem and begin offering solutions before they have an appreciation of the political issues that underlie the matters they are addressing.

Having done their political spadework, project managers will have a different perspective on the situation than they otherwise would have had. The real nature of the problems they face will look different when viewed through political spectacles than when political issues are ignored. What may originally have seemed a straightforward technical matter is now seen as something more complex, something fraught with traps and hidden obstacles. Armed with their knowledge of the political landscape, managers are in a good position to blaze a trail through the thicket.

Of course, mere awareness of key issues is not enough. Effective political action requires that project managers use their awareness effectively. They must *behave* in a politically appropriate manner. For example, they must know when to employ finesse in their dealings with others and when to use a club. They must avoid gaffes such as saying the wrong things to the wrong people at the wrong time. They must develop a good sense of timing, knowing when to introduce new initiatives and when to pull back. They must identify how much pressure they can apply to pursue an objective, being sure not to be too aggressive or too timid.

BUILDING AUTHORITY

Over the years, I have been maintaining a list of the different kinds of authority that project staff employ. Each time I come across a new form, I add it to the list. The full list has some thirty distinct kinds of authority that I have identified. Many of these border on the trivial or are counterproductive, so I offer here an abridged list.

Formal Authority (Positional Authority)

People who are new to project management and technical people who see the world as governed by clearly defined rules tend to depend heavily on formal authority. They believe that the very status of project manager confers on them a substantial degree of authority. They see themselves as bosses. They expect others to recognize their authority and to respond to it appropriately.

Unfortunately, this is not how organizations work in the real world. Formal authority is often not very helpful to project managers unless it is accompanied by what is called *borrowed authority.* That is, for formal authority to be effective, it must be closely associated with the will of someone who is an obviously powerful player—typically someone in a high position in the organizational hierarchy. When this condition exists, the requests of the project manager can be interpreted as requests of the powerful player. Going against the project manager is in effect going against the will of someone with clout.

In the *PMBOK Guide* (Project Management Institute, 2000), formal authority is called "positional authority."

Technical Authority (Expert Authority)

Technical people tend to view the world through a prism of technical competence. The value of their bosses, colleagues, and subordinates is often measured in terms of their perceived intelligence and technical abilities. A great source of frustration for technical staff is to work for someone who they feel is a technical lightweight. They may be distressed that this individual's lack of know-how is hampering their efforts. They may also resent that they are subordinate to someone whom they perceive as inferior to them intellectually.

The implications of the technical ethos are clear: project managers working directly with technical staff must possess some degree of technical authority if they are to earn the respect of the staff. It should be noted that this reality extends beyond the purely technical environment of scientists and engineers. Accountants, marketers, attorneys—any staff members with finely developed skills—require a fairly high level of technical competence in their supervisors. When such technical authority is absent, it is easy for staff to dismiss the efforts and desires of their bosses and colleagues with "Don't take him seriously because he isn't all that sharp technically."

Technical authority is not achieved easily. The expertise that underlies it is gained through education and experience over an extended period of time. If we do not have it when we assume our project responsibilities, we face a disadvantage that cannot be overcome easily.

In the *PMBOK Guide* (Project Management Institute, 2000), technical authority is called "expert authority."

Charismatic Authority

People who possess charismatic authority are able to get others to do their bidding through the force of their personality. The benefits of possessing some measure of charismatic authority are obvious. A major benefit is that charisma can serve as an important component of leadership. Through the sheer force of personality, the charismatic leader may be able to get project staff to commit themselves more fully to the project—to work long hours, to take risks they normally would avoid, and to be creative in problem solving.

There are two common problems with charismatic authority. First, when things go wrong—as they often do on projects—project staff may come to question the basis of this authority and may perceive the charismatic leader as a master of form who lacks substance. The same charisma that serves as the basis of managerial strength may become an object of derision.

Second, it is not clear how project managers can develop charisma. Some argue that it is an inherent component of personality—either you have it or you don't. Others maintain that the fundamental elements of charisma can be learned. Most likely, it is not an either-or situation. That is, some people can acquire certain charismatic traits through study and practice, whereas others are going to be hopelessly uncharismatic no matter how many hours they spend trying to learn how to win friends and influence people.

Purse-String Authority (Reward Authority)

People who control resources can parlay this into a significant source of authority. With purse-string authority, we face a classic carrot-and-stick reward situation: those who cooperate with us are rewarded by gaining access to needed resources; those who do not are denied these resources. Clearly, there is strong incentive here for staff and colleagues to see things our way.

The big problem with purse-string authority is that most project managers have little control over resources. The people assigned to their projects are borrowed resources who report to other managers. In addition, they often have only marginal control of their budgets.

Having said this, I would like to add that the picture is not as bleak as it may seem. With a little imagination, project managers and staff can see that they control more resources than they might think. For example, they have a measure of control over one of the most precious of all resources: *time*. They can reward the hardest workers with time off. (As one of my colleagues at a Fortune 500 company quipped, "To reward their good behavior, I occasionally give my finest workers a Saturday off from work.") They may also be able to adjust staff schedules for the convenience of individual workers.

Project managers also control work assignments. As a reward for effective work, the best workers can be given the most challenging assignments. To the extent that project managers regulate the allocation of equipment (for example, computers, photocopy machines, and fax machines), this can be seen as a resource to be employed. The rewards and punishments that can be employed by project managers to build authority are discussed in more detail in Chapter Eight, which looks at team building in a matrix environment.

Purse-string authority is basically the same as "reward authority" as described in the *PMBOK Guide* (Project Management Institute, 2000).

Bureaucratic Authority

The essence of bureaucratic authority is captured in the words of Lyndon Johnson, who was one of the most effective politicians in the U.S. Congress. He advised, "Learn how the system works so that you can work the system." The great appeal of this form of authority is that with a little effort, anyone can develop it. The basis of bureaucratic authority is knowing the rules by which the organization runs and using this knowledge to achieve desired objectives. It is common knowledge that in a parliamentary debate, the individuals who have mastered Robert's Rules of Order have an edge over those who have not. Similarly, those who have mastered the rules of the organization have an edge over those who are only marginally aware of these rules.

What are the rules that should be mastered? They come in a great many varieties. There are rules for the hiring and firing of personnel, rules governing the types of equipment that can be acquired, procurement rules, contract rules, budget cycle rules, ethics rules, leave-time rules, rules impinging on our personal conduct outside the office . . . rules of every stripe and color. Most of us view these rules as impediments to doing a good job. We have minimal tolerance for them and follow them with little or no enthusiasm—we may even ignore them outright. We do not appreciate how with a little study, we can turn these rules to our advantage. To see this, consider the following example.

Emily Ando was overwhelmed with the administrative chores associated with the project she was managing. She was spending more time filling out time sheets, budget reports, requests for tuition remission, performance appraisals, and so on than she was doing active project work. She went to her boss, Maureen Reilly, and told her of her problem. She asked Ms. Reilly for administrative help. Ms. Reilly said she would see what she could do.

One month later, Emily still had no help. She went to Ms. Reilly and reminded her of her plight. It was clear that Ms. Reilly had forgotten about Emily's request. Emily pleaded once again for administrative help, and once again she received assurances that Ms. Reilly would look into the matter. Two weeks later, Emily stopped Ms. Reilly in the hallway to inquire about progress in obtaining administrative assistance. Ms. Reilly was vague in her response. Emily was getting nowhere.

By chance, the same day that Emily had her last encounter with Ms. Reilly, she ate lunch with a budget officer who complained to her about the increase in his workload now that the end of the fiscal year was approaching. "Suddenly, everyone is worried about the money they haven't spent this year. They know that if they don't spend it, they lose it." Emily knew practically nothing about the budgeting process in her organization, so she had her companion explain it to her briefly. She learned that a department's unspent money was returned to the general fund at the end of the fiscal year.

When she returned to her office, she immediately telephoned Jack Marx, who maintained Ms. Reilly's department budget and was on good terms with Emily. She asked him about the department's budget status, explained her need to him, and learned that there was a $25,000 line item in the budget for college interns that had not been spent in three years.

The next day, she met with Ms. Reilly and told her about the intern position and how the department would once again lose the money obligated for the position. Ms. Reilly was shocked to learn that this money was not being used by her department and immediately authorized the creation of a job slot titled "project administrative intern." Three weeks later, Emily had a young graduate student taking over the administrative duties that had plagued her for so long.

By gaining knowledge of how the budget system worked in her organization, Emily Ando was able to have her will prevail. Whether she recognized it or not, she was behaving in a politically effective manner.

Other Sources of Authority

The five sources of authority discussed so far are the most common types of authority that project staff are likely to encounter, but many other sources of authority exist. Let us briefly look at a few.

AUTHORITY BASED ON COMPETENCE. I put this at the top of the list because it promotes my view that one of the most powerful weapons individuals have is their competence (Frame, 1999). My experience suggests that people who are very good at what they do achieve a level of respect that translates into power. Highly competent individuals add value to their organizations. They make their managers and colleagues look good. People ignore them or mistreat them at their peril. They epitomize the maxim "Nothing succeeds like success."

FOLLOW-THROUGH AUTHORITY. One element of competence is the capacity to actually do what you promise. Follow-through is a scarce commodity. I have asked several hundred managers, "Of the promises made to you over the past year, what percentage were actually kept?" Answers typically range from 5 to 20 percent. One company I worked with in the 1970s was populated with highly talented scientists, most of whom held doctorates from world-class universities. The president of this company told me that the single greatest frustration he faced was the fact that "despite their considerable talent, our people can't seem to bring things to closure."

Imagine the power of being perceived as a person who keeps his or her promises!

AUTHORITY BASED ON TRUST. Managers who can keep a confidence, who avoid the sordid aspects of politics, and who function consistently according to well-defined standards can develop a strong measure of authority based on the trust others put in them. Too often, people operate according to what is expedient. Those who resist expedient solutions, even when this may lead to short-term discomfort, are a minority of the general population. If their general trustworthiness is recognized, they are powerful.

MANAGEMENT BY INTIMIDATION. Sad to say, there is a place for occasional cage rattling in project management. Workers who consistently come to the office late and leave early might respond positively to managers who are not afraid to raise the decibel level of their voices. Vendors who have been promising for three months that a crucial part is in the mail might actually deliver the part in response to explicit threats of negative action. However, as a dominant approach, management by intimidation is seldom effective. In the long run, it is a demotivator. Furthermore, it breeds resentment, so those who live by the sword should be prepared to die by the sword.

AUTHORITY BASED ON PHYSICAL APPEARANCE. Many studies have demonstrated that how you look helps define the perception other people have of you. Each year, thousands of bright young executives spend a substantial portion of their incomes in an attempt to "dress for success." Actually, the issue is not whether the Rolex watch you recently bought will lead to a promotion. Rather, it is that you should be sensitive to what is considered an appropriate appearance in a given circumstance. The owner of a health spa is not going to inspire confidence in the efficacy of her weight reduction program if she herself is grossly overweight. A biker wearing a three-piece suit will be viewed with suspicion by his Harley-riding colleagues. In many software shops, a plaid flannel shirt, blue jeans, biker boots, a beard, and a ponytail are standard attire for programmers. This same ensemble would raise eyebrows in the boardroom. The point is, project staff should recognize that their physical demeanor has an impact on their authority. They have the power to increase or diminish their authority through their personal grooming habits and their sartorial choices.

AUTHORITY OF INITIATIVE. Back when I was chairman of the Management Science Department at George Washington University, I found myself in a position closely akin to what project managers face. I had ultimate responsibility for the actions of a large number of tenured professors, adjunct faculty, doctoral teaching fellows, and office administrative staff (sixty people in all), yet I had no direct control over any of them. In my department, the department chair was not a boss but rather a servant of the department, an enabler who kept things running smoothly. I quickly learned that the best way for me to establish authority over my flock was to initiate things. I alerted faculty to the availability of grants and contracts and helped them write proposals; I offered clerical assistance to faculty and graduate students who were serious about publishing their research results; I raised money to purchase desktop computers for all the faculty and some of the doctoral students. Through these initiatives, I operated in a proactive fashion. The targets of my actions were put into a reactive mode. I initiated, and they responded. This served me well as the basis of my authority. It also served my department well in that faculty, staff, and graduate students got the support they needed to operate more effectively.

Similarly, project managers can undertake initiatives to strengthen their authority. For example, they may request staff to suggest better ways to carry out tasks, present new project ideas to their bosses, or provide functional managers with suggestions on how to do their jobs better. In taking the initiative, they operate proactively, placing others in a reactive posture. With initiative comes a certain measure of control.

For this approach to work, the initiatives that are undertaken must be sound and achievable. They must capture the imaginations of the individuals to whom they are directed. If they are introduced properly and are well received, they will confer an aura of leadership on the individual introducing them.

CRISIS AUTHORITY. In Chapter Three, I mentioned that some of my Japanese students had pointed out that a common way to establish authority in Japanese organizations is to announce crises. For example, it may be a Friday afternoon, and the project team members are ready to return home for a weekend with the family. Just before they are scheduled to leave, the project manager rushes breathlessly into the room and describes a major crisis that has just arisen. To meet this crisis, the team members will have to stay late for work this evening and are expected to work on Saturday and Sunday as well.

It is interesting to note that in the Japanese language, the word crisis *(kiki)* does not have negative connotations. In fact, the two Chinese characters used for writing *kiki* (*wei ji* in Mandarin) signify "danger" and "opportunity." With crises there are opportunities!

Crisis authority is commonly employed in the East. Even in the West, the occasional raising of a crisis can be an effective way to build authority. A well-motivated team will rise to the challenge and will be willing to sacrifice some personal time for the good of the project. However, as a long-term strategy, the continual raising of crises is bound to fail. Westerners are willing to go only so far to meet the needs of the team. Their individualism requires that their personal needs take priority over the team's needs. A manager who is constantly dealing with crises is perceived to be out of control.

OLD BOY NETWORK. Many of my students tell me that an important source of authority in their organizations is not *what* they know but *whom* they know. They are, of course, describing what has come to be known as the "old boy network." In this era of sensitivity to gender-specific language, some of my female colleagues talk about "the sisterhood." Actually, what is being described here transcends sexual stereotyping. The key point is that decisions are made to a great degree on the basis of personal connections.

I don't see anything inherently wrong with these personal networks as long as their influence is moderate. They are one of the many communication channels that exist in a typical organization. They may enable the organization to get things done when formal communication channels become clogged. We all belong to some personal networks. We should use our connections when doing so helps us achieve our objectives. These personal networks become a problem when they are the dominant mechanisms by which actions are carried out. When this occurs, they are no longer simply another communication channel. In fact, they lead to the repression of the free flow of information because they tend to become the only meaningful communication channel.

Other forms of authority that have come to my attention include name-dropping, weaseling, mothering, blackmailing, mentoring, and tendering. I'll leave it to your imagination to deduce what these forms of authority entail.

USING AUTHORITY EFFECTIVELY

Recall that the whole purpose of developing authority is to have our will prevail over others in an environment where we have little clout. For this to happen, we must develop several bases of authority. Being strong in only one area is not enough. For example, if all we possess is technical authority, we run the risk of being branded as narrow-focused techno-nerds. Or if all we have is charismatic authority, we may develop a reputation for possessing a lot of fluff and little substance.

In respect to authority, the old adage that "more is better" holds true. Effective project managers should develop as many bases of authority as possible. This should be done consciously. Project managers should periodically—say, once a month—ask themselves, "What can I do to strengthen my base of authority?" They should then go through the list of the various sources of authority to identify areas where they can strengthen themselves. They should ask question such as, How can I build up my formal authority? My technical authority? My bureaucratic authority?

MANAGING OUR MANAGERS

To be effective, project managers must know how to manage their own managers. A complaint frequently made by project managers is that the powers above them in the organizational hierarchy are not supportive. Lack of support can take a number of forms. For example, higher-level managers may not provide the resources they promised, may be unclear in defining their goals, may not use their power to open doors for team members, or simply may not listen to what team members have to say.

I suspect that responsibility for the problems of managing our managers rests equally on the unsupported managers and on their bosses. Often when I investigate the accusation that a manager's boss has not been supportive, I find that the complainants have not operated in a manner deserving support or have not clearly articulated their need for support. Their bosses do not support them because the bosses are unaware that a need for support exists.

However, truly nonsupportive managers do exist, and it is unfortunate when we are assigned to work with them. I have encountered many individuals for whom it would be horrible to work. I feel great sympathy for the people they "supervise."

Let us look first at steps that project managers can take to better articulate their need for support and then at ways to deal with a truly nonsupportive boss.

Articulating the Need for Support

If project managers want the support of their bosses, they must do whatever they can to be continually in the bosses' field of vision. Project managers who disappear for three months in order to work in isolation should not be surprised if their bosses do not support them. They have fallen into the classic trap of "out of sight, out of mind."

Project managers can maintain their visibility in a variety of ways. One is regular status briefings. Once a week, managers can brief their bosses on project progress. In doing this, they keep communication channels open. When problems arise, they can be addressed as part of a regular programmed process so that bosses don't get the impression that the only time the project achieves visibility is when it is in trouble. Furthermore, if bosses are made part of the regular decision-making process, they develop a stronger stake in the project's success. Their support of project efforts is likely to increase.

Regular written reports are another way to maintain project visibility. Monthly status reports keep upper management apprised of project developments. Exception reports can be generated when problems arise that need their attention. Periodic milestone reviews alert them to the accomplishment of major components of the project plan. In addition to offering upper management information on project developments, these written reports also allow project managers to maintain an audit trail of their actions. If they are accused of keeping their bosses in the dark about some matter, they need merely pull out the pertinent documentation to show that this is not true. The point here is that project managers should not view reports as an administrative pain; rather, they should recognize that reports, when used effectively, enable them to operate more effectively.

Dealing with the Truly Nonsupportive Boss

I have been fortunate in my personal work experience. I have never worked for a nonsupportive boss. But I know such people exist. I encounter them occasionally in my consulting assignments and hear about them from students in both my university classes and my training classes.

Working for nonsupportive bosses can be exceedingly unpleasant. If their lack of support stems from incompetence, their employees may find themselves trapped in a situation where bad decisions—or perhaps no decisions—are made, where goals are ill-defined, or where managerial ineptness leads to insufficient resources and overcommitments. If lack of support is rooted in simple meanness, employees must struggle to survive the machinations of a bully boss.

There is no simple solution for dealing with the truly nonsupportive boss. The most obvious step the unfortunate employee can take is to move to a better job environment. Even the world's greatest managers will fail if they must operate in an inordinately hostile environment. Of course, this may not always be possible, since there are limits to job mobility in most organizations.

A more proactive step is to overwhelm the nonsupportive manager with competence. *All* managers cherish employees who can solve problems for them. Effective employees make their managers look good. In general, all managers, including nonsupportive managers, will willingly support employees who make their lives easier and who offer them the opportunity for glory. The obvious problem of logic here is that it may not be possible for competent employees to demonstrate their competence if they do not have the support needed to allow them to shine. Still, they are better off striving for excellence than retreating into a protective shell.

Another approach project managers can use to deal with the truly nonsupportive manager is developing powerful allies who can protect them from the consequences of their manager's bad management practices. Examples of powerful allies might be their boss's boss, managers who control resources, and their boss's peers. A danger inherent in this approach is that it can backfire. The boss may view the project manager as insubordinate. Others may perceive the manager as a political operator and not a team player.

CONCLUSIONS

Politics is inevitable on projects. Wise project professionals will therefore strive to develop good political skills. Possession of such skills will improve the likelihood that they can affect the outcome of events in a way that is favorable to them. Without political skills, they will have little control over events.

Unfortunately, not all project professionals are equally successful in developing political skills. Political action is closely tied to personality, and it is evident that some project managers have personalities that allow them to be politically effective while others do not. But for most project professionals, there is some hope. This chapter has made no attempt to change personalities. What it proposes is essentially a method that project personnel can use to increase their political *sensitivity*—their awareness of the political currents on their projects and recognition of the outcomes of political action and inaction.

At the heart of the method is the project manager's effort to be conscious of political issues—through periodic reviews of the list of sources of authority or through periodic enumeration of the individuals who will be affected by the project and who can have an impact on its outcome. At a minimum, increased political sensitivity will help project professionals reduce the number of political blunders they make. Beyond this, it may suggest courses of action that can strengthen their ability to have their will prevail in an environment where they have substantial amounts of responsibility without corresponding levels of authority.

CHAPTER EIGHT

Building Teams with Borrowed Resources

When we think of teams, the image of a sports team immediately springs to mind. Standard team-related concepts, such as team spirit, are usually pictured in the context of athletes striving together to develop the ability to defeat their opponents. Coaches and athletes are popular dinner speakers, and the topic of their speeches often centers on team building.

Unfortunately, the similarity of sports teams and project teams is remote. Sports are characterized by clarity: the rules of the game are known and can be found in the rule book; the goal of the game is clear—to win; the core group of players is fairly constant; they have clearly defined roles; they learn to function as a unit through constant practice; in the heat of the game, team members can identify each other readily by the color of their uniform; and the team is offered strong guidance on how to perform through the directives of the coach (who, incidentally, yields carrots and sticks and therefore is a boss).

Projects, in contrast, are characterized by fuzziness: often there are few clearly established rules governing the project effort; the project goal is often obscure, partially because most projects have multiple goals that may be contradictory; the team is composed of a constantly changing set of players who are used as needed and then returned to their functional homes; team member roles are unclear; team members do not have an opportunity to practice their skills as a unit—sadly, the project is the practice session; and project managers are not bosses.

The reason that project teams do not look like sports teams is that they employ borrowed resources. If you wanted to design a management approach that would make team building truly difficult, you would invent the matrix management concept! Matrix management provides the underlying principles that govern most project activity. Imagine sports events being carried out like projects: each week, the composition of the team would change, players would get their weekly playing assignments through a lottery system, team size could fluctuate, the rules of the game would differ, and coaches would have no power over their players. When applied to a sports example, the standard practices employed in project management appear laughable.

How can team spirit be built in such an environment? I recall a class I held several years ago in which, after a discussion of difficulties in team building on projects, one student asked plaintively, "Is it hopeless then? Is it basically impossible to build a sense of team identity on projects?"

This question caught me off guard. The tenor of our discussion certainly suggested a feeling of hopelessness, but experience counsels that there are highly motivated project teams out there in the real world. I have been a part of such teams and have seen many other examples in my career. Still, I was not sure how to answer the student's question, so I took the Socratic approach.

"What do you think?" I asked the whole class. "Is it hopeless?" The class members' response was exciting. The gist of their answer was that no, it is not hopeless. A large number of students talked about approaches on their projects that had contributed to team building. The exercise was so successful and elicited so much student participation that I have used it in every project management class I've taught since that time. Thousands of people have participated in the exercise.

I soon noticed that the "tricks" for team building employed by my students fit a pattern. From class to class, they were saying the same thing. Basically, their advice fell into three categories. One set of tricks involved making the team as tangible as possible. Most project teams are so dynamic as to be only marginally tangible. Team membership is constantly changing. To build commitment to the team, the team itself should be made as concrete as possible, since most people are reluctant to charge into the fray on behalf of an abstraction.

Another set of tricks focused on identifying rewards for good behavior. Clearly, because most project managers have little or no control over resources, they are not able to effect elaborate rewards. However, with a little creative thinking, they will see that a good reward system can be built even when control over resources is limited.

My students called the third category of tricks "the personal touch." The point is that through their personal actions and attitudes, project managers can motivate their borrowed staff to walk the extra mile. And if they possess a bad attitude, they will demotivate their staff quite easily.

Let's take a closer look at each of these three areas of team building.

MAKING THE TEAM AS TANGIBLE AS POSSIBLE

Project teams are highly dynamic. Team members are constantly changing. For example, on a project to provide external customers with a product, the team may be weighted heavily with members from the marketing department at the outset. As the project evolves along its life cycle, needs analysts and requirements specialists may join the team and play a central role. Most of the marketing staff may drift away and attempt to generate new business elsewhere. Once needs and requirements have been established, designers may begin playing an important role as the needs analysts and requirements specialists in their turn drift away. When a solid design has been developed, builders take over. As they build whatever it is they are making, they are periodically assisted by testers. Documenters also enter the picture periodically, generating systems documentation, user documentation, training manuals, and the like.

The example offered here is quite typical. It is not evident that the various individuals who play a role on the project really see themselves as part of a larger entity, a cohesive team. Why should they? Like the blind men, all they encounter are pieces of the elephant. The lack of a cohesive team identity can rule out any feeling of belonging. Team building will not occur under such conditions.

Very often, project teams are an abstraction. Only the project manager and possibly some members of senior management may see the team in its entirety. The team members themselves see only snippets. If project managers want a motivated team, they must work to make their teams as concrete as possible. How can this be done? Following are frequently employed approaches to make the team more palpable.

Hold Productive Meetings

The most obvious purpose of meetings is to convey information to the participants. A less obvious purpose is to reinforce the identity of the group. At meetings, the players get to see each other in the flesh. There is nothing abstract about sitting in a room with a dozen of your teammates, some of whom you may not have seen before. Obviously, meetings are an instrument to make the team more tangible.

A particularly important meeting in project management is the *kickoff meeting*. As the name implies, this meeting is held at the outset of the project and is designed to get things rolling. Features of a typical kickoff meeting include presenting the project charter (a tangible) that defines project goals and authority; identifying team players and issuing a team roster (a tangible), which includes addresses and phone numbers of the team players; identifying key milestone dates, which can be presented via a milestone chart (a tangible); and establishing rapport among the team players.

Another important meeting category is the *status review*. This is a periodic meeting (weekly, monthly) that focuses on defining project progress. Attention is directed to such things as budget and schedule variances and problems in the execution of the project. On smaller projects, it may be desirable to have all team members present during the status updates. On larger projects, this may be impossible, owing to limitations of time and space. In this case, it is advisable to establish rotating attendance at these meetings in such a way that every month or so each team member has an opportunity to meet with all other team members. The value of status meetings to team building is that they remind the players that they are not Lone Rangers but are a part of a larger group.

Meetings need not be formal. Beer-and-pretzel parties, milestone parties, and social functions, like the team softball game, are informal meetings that help reinforce a sense among the team players of belonging to something concrete. Meetings need not even have attendees present in one place: some of my AT&T students tell me that the most common meetings they attend are telephone conference calls.

Create a Team Space

The single best way to give project staff a sense of belonging to a real team is to locate them all at one site. In this way, they see each other every day. Through their constant interaction, they learn something about each other. Colocation does not ensure good relationships—remember the adage that familiarity breeds contempt—but it does affirm a sense of team identity.

The key problem with colocation is mundane: few organizations have the resources or space to put a large number of people into a consolidated area. Even when resources are bountiful, it may not make sense to relocate people to the project area if the project will be completed in a matter of months.

If colocation is not practical, a good substitute is the creation of a "war room." War rooms were popular as command centers for organizations that were preparing for Y2K at the end of the 1990s. I have seen war rooms used to good effect on many projects. They can be quite humble—no more than glorified closets, in fact. Or they can be elaborate "situation rooms." In any event, they are a tangible embodiment of the project effort. The full array of project-related documentation should be kept here. The walls are often filled with PERT charts, Gantt charts, budget curves, and resource-loading charts. Information on the project history can be stored in loose-leaf binders on the bookshelf. A conference table enables project staff to gather in one place to mull over project ideas. An added advantage of a well-configured war room is that it impresses outsiders. I recently came across a project that was granted a major budget increase primarily because top management was so impressed with the demeanor of the war room.

Increasingly, war rooms have gone virtual and have metamorphosed into Web sites. There are few projects of substance today that have not developed a Web presence. The beauty of a Web site is that it offers a central repository of project information that lets team members and managers access important project data from any place at any time.

Create Team "Signs"

Semiotics is the science of signs. A readable introduction to this field is Jack Solomon's *Signs of Our Time* (1988). Semioticians tell us that the signs we employ advertise our aspirations and motivations. They are symbols reflecting deeper realities. Important signs that can help create team identity are a team name and a logo. The power of these symbols should not be underestimated. At a meeting, I once encountered a well-dressed man wearing a tattered navy blue tie. The tie caught my attention because it did not go with his elegant suit. Looking more carefully at the tie, I saw it had a pattern on it.

"Isn't that the Hubble space telescope on your tie?" I asked him.

"It certainly is," he said with pride. He explained to me that he was with Ford Aerospace and that these ties were distributed to all the men who worked on the multibillion-dollar Hubble project. "I wear it nearly every day," he added. Its heavy use was evident. "It's a badge that identifies me to other Hubble team members. Occasionally, I'll have people from another contractor organization come up to me and tell me they are also on the Hubble team."

To this man, the tie had taken on great significance as an insignia identifying his connection with a prestigious project.

A common practice on project teams is to affix the team name and logo to an assortment of items. I have seen team T-shirts, coffee mugs, pens, stationery, caps, and pins. Purveyors of these goods jokingly refer to them as "trinkets and trash."

Publicize Team Efforts

A project public relations effort can solidify a project's image, thereby making the team more tangible. To the extent that a project team is recognized externally, a sense of identity will be forged among its members. One way to publicize project efforts is to make sure that the project is mentioned regularly in the organization's newsletter. In this day of easy desktop publishing, the project may establish its own newsletter for circulation throughout the organization. To further heighten the project profile, team members should offer public presentations on project work whenever possible. The key point of this public relations effort is to increase awareness of the team's work, setting it apart from the rest of the organization.

REWARDING GOOD BEHAVIOR

A second broad approach to team building on projects is to institute a reward system to motivate team members to do their best and to reaffirm good behavior. The obvious problem here is that project managers seldom have control over resources that would serve as the basis of the rewards. They cannot provide raises, offer bonuses, or extend vacations. In most cases, they do not even have responsibility for filling out performance appraisal reviews for their team members. So how can they use carrots and sticks to motivate their teams?

They must use their imaginations. A little thought will show them that they control more "resources" than they might think:

- They can write letters of commendation for good performance.
- They have a measure of control over job assignments and can make sure that good workers get choice assignments.
- They have a measure of control over scheduling assignments and may be able to adjust schedules to accommodate the needs of exemplary workers.
- They may be able to provide "comp time" for workers who have been putting in a lot of extra hours.
- They can recommend employees for corporate bonuses.
- When new office equipment arrives, they can offer it to the best workers.
- They can take workers (possibly with their spouses) to dinner.
- They may have some input into deciding who gets what perquisites (for example, parking spaces, corner offices, offices with windows—in one company I know, an important status symbol is the quality of trash basket one has).
- They can offer team members increased visibility by allowing them to give briefings to upper management.

The central point here is that despite the lack of direct control over budgets and personnel, project managers can establish rewards to motivate their team members. To do this effectively, they must take stock of the things they *do* control and consciously employ them as rewards.

DEVELOPING A PERSONAL TOUCH

The third category of project management team-building tricks focuses on the one-on-one relationship between project managers and their team members. The basic question here is, does the project manager's personal behavior inspire team members to work as hard and effectively as is necessary to get the job done? Most of the suggestions in this category employ common sense. Like the Golden Rule, they are good precepts that should guide all of our dealings with people.

Here are some suggestions for developing good personal touch capabilities:

- Provide positive feedback on performance. Say thank-you now and then. (I have worked with project teams where project managers issue gold stars to employees as an indicator of their pleasure with good performance. It works!)

- Publicly acknowledge good performance. For example, at the status review meeting, point out that a given employee has completed work ahead of schedule.

- Show interest in the team members. Learn something about their background and interests. *Know their names!* (To support their memories, many project managers keep records of team member facts on 3-by-5-inch cards.)

- Be a "shirt sleeve" manager. Demonstrate a willingness to do the dirty work alongside the other team players. (One project manager told me of an incident where his team was working well into the morning hours on an important project. Outside a blizzard was raging, and all the team members would rather have been at home in bed. The project manager showed his concern for the team by calling them regularly *from his hotel in the Virgin Islands.* After the third phone call, the team members were so irritated with their boss that they packed up and went home.)

- Be accessible. Practice an open-door policy and management by walking around.

- Be clear in defining your expectations and in describing work requirements. Staff are justifiably angered by managers who give them vague guidance on what they should do ("Do what you think is appropriate") and then later criticize them for doing the wrong thing.

- Be consistent, and stick to the rules.

- Empower team members to make decisions.

- Acknowledge special occasions—birthdays, anniversaries, and the like.

- When critical milestones have been achieved, celebrate this with milestone parties.

- At least two important don'ts should be observed: don't publicly criticize team members, and when problems arise, don't put the blame on the team.

A word of caution: project team workers are not stupid. If they sense that project managers are employing motivation tricks in a cynical way as a tool of manipulation, they will be turned off. The team-building effort must come from the heart. Otherwise, it will backfire on the project manager and lead to team disintegration.

SELF-MANAGED TEAMS: PROSPECTS AND PITFALLS

I wish to digress for a moment to examine one of the management "hot buttons" of the 1990s: self-managed teams. At present, organizations are actively experimenting with different team structures to help them operate more effectively in a viciously competitive global business environment. These experiments are exciting and demonstrate the vitality of management thought in many leading organizations.

By the mid-1990s, the concept of self-managed teams achieved prominence. Business magazines such as *Fortune* and *Business Week* extolled the virtues of this approach. Books and seminars proliferated on how to employ self-managed teams in organizations. Tom Peters praised them in his influential book *Liberation Management* (1992). Most of the material on self-managed teams focuses on their having produced miracle results in organizations. Few words of criticism are directed at this approach.

With self-managed teams, team members define the approach they will take to getting a job done. Collectively, they make key personnel decisions—work assignments, performance appraisals, and hiring and occasionally firing decisions. The team members call the shots, and upper-management intrusions are minimized.

The press praises self-managed teams as a mechanism to empower workers to do the best job they can. The theory is that when people make their own decisions, they have a greater commitment to executing them effectively. Furthermore, people who are close to the work have a better sense of what is needed to do a good job than managers far removed from the day-to-day action.

When they function properly, self-managed teams can be impressive. Back when I was actively involved in research and software projects, the teams I belonged to were largely self-managed. Our projects were carried out under contract, so the specifications we were to achieve were externally defined. Beyond that, we wrote our own rules. For the most part, our projects were well done and our customers were highly satisfied with our efforts. Top management was delighted with this approach because the team assumed total responsibility for the work effort. When problems arose, the team would figure out how to deal with them. If the solution to a problem required that we work seventy hours for a week, we would work the seventy hours without complaint.

The problem is that self-managed teams often do not work as advertised. To see this, one need merely recall that Yugoslav enterprises were pioneers in the area of self-management. While in Dubrovnik in 1980, I observed self-management firsthand. The self-management I saw there confirmed the old adage that when everybody is in charge, no one is in charge. Yugoslavia never developed the reputation as a world-class producer despite its self-management practices. By the 1990s, the focus on self-management quickly disappeared as the country disintegrated into fratricidal chaos.

Gerald M. Weinberg's concept of *egoless teams* was a variant of self-management that emerged on software projects in the early 1970s (see his book *The Psychology of Computer Programming,* 1971). The basic idea underlying egoless teams is that team members have collective responsibility for their products and should behave as if they are interchangeable parts. Hierarchies and selfishness are out; group focus and joint decision making are in.

I have interviewed people who were members of egoless teams on more than thirty projects. They highlighted a number of pitfalls they encountered in their group-focused efforts. These included the following:

- There is a danger that leadership will be lacking if the group focus requires everyone to buy into team solutions.

- Decision making may be slow if team consensus must be carefully nurtured.

- To avoid group conflict and achieve group consensus, solutions occasionally appeal to the lowest common denominator.

- People have egos.

Whether a self-managed team approach is appropriate must be determined on a case-by-case basis. The idea of empowering a team is certainly appealing. Through such empowerment, vital team energies might be tapped that would otherwise be suppressed. Workers would take a greater interest in their efforts. They would work harder and smarter to achieve the team's goals. Beyond this, there is the democratic appeal of self-management. In the West, we like to think that people should be given as much control over their destinies as possible.

However, self-management is not a panacea. Success is certainly not built into it. It will not succeed unless the following criteria are met:

- Upper management truly empowers team members to make independent decisions.

- Team members demonstrate leadership qualities and are not frightened of responsibility.

- Team members are highly motivated and are willing to do what it takes to get the job done.

- Team members form a cohesive body of players—they are not borrowed resources temporarily assigned to work on the project.

The last point represents a major obstacle in applying self-managed team concepts on project teams. Today, the dominant mode of structuring teams is to employ borrowed resources: when we need particular resources, we draw them from the resource pool; when we are done with them, we send them back home. This approach is too dynamic to lend itself to self-management.

STRUCTURING THE TEAM

To a large extent, the potential problems of self-managed teams are hardwired due to the self-managed team structure. The principal components of this structure are group decision making, lack of a clearly defined leader, and diffuse accountability. Slow decision making, the need for compromise, and potential aimlessness are all potential consequences of this structure.

We will now examine structural issues in some detail, with a special focus on the management consequences of structure. This discussion is an extension of ideas I presented in *Managing Projects in Organizations* (Frame, 1995). Interest in the management implications of structure gained a measure of popularity in the early 1990s under the rubric of "organizational architecture" as a consequence of work done by David Nadler and the Delta Consulting Group (see Nadler, Gerstein, Shaw, and Associates, 1992).

The principle examined here is the converse of one of the most famous dicta in architecture. Louis Sullivan, the great nineteenth-century American architect, promoted the concept that "form follows function." Basically, this means that if you tell me what will happen in a given space (function), that will suggest the appropriate architectural design (form).

We will examine the converse proposition: "function follows form." In other words, if you show me the structure of a project team (form), I will accurately predict the managerial consequences (function) of that structure.

The power of this approach can be seen through a simple example. Let's say we are examining the following rudimentary structural proposition: *A team is getting larger.* What are the managerial consequences of this growth? One is that communication channels between team members grow explosively. (This matter was discussed in Chapter Two; see Figure 2.1.) For example, with two people, there is one pairwise channel (for the purposes of this discussion, we will ignore the two-way flow of information). With three, there are three channels; with four, six channels; with five, ten channels. In general, if there are n people, the potential number of pairwise channels is $n(n-1)/2$.

This explosive growth in communication channels has enormous managerial implications. For example, project managers on large projects spend disproportionately more time on administrative chores than project managers on smaller teams. Consider that the project manager of a five-person team has only ten pairwise communication channels to oversee, whereas the project manager of a twenty-person team (hardly a large team) has 190. Overseeing communication channels translates into all sorts of administrative and tracking chores.

As the number of channels grows, the need for formal structured procedures increases. It reaches the point where on very large projects (in the billion-dollar range), 65 cents out of every dollar goes to maintaining the administrative infrastructure that keeps the project functioning. Only 35 cents goes to directly productive activities.

Additional implications of growing team size are a greater chance of communication breakdown; a need for more office space, desks, and equipment; and less attention spent on the needs of individual team members, among others.

The point is that the managerial consequences of structure can be anticipated. The manager who has just been promoted from head of a five-person team to head of a twenty-person team had better be prepared for the fact that she will no longer have time to do hands-on technical work along with the other team members. She will spend much of her time on the phone, in meetings, and pushing paper.

Following are two case studies focusing on the structural aspects of two projects. These case studies are not hypothetical. They represent real situations that arose in two real companies.

Euro-Lan

Euro-Lan is a European-based systems integrator that specializes in installing local area networks (LANs) for businesses. It recently won a competitive bid to install LANs in the local offices of a large insurance company that had major operations in the United Kingdom, France, Germany, and Spain.

Responsibility for managing the project was given to Euro-Lan's Development Group in Paris because this group was charged with advancing Euro-Lan's LAN implementation capabilities. Euro-Lan operations in France, Germany, the U.K., and Spain each had responsibility for installing the LANs in the insurance offices in their own countries.

Unfortunately, the national operations of Euro-Lan functioned as semiautonomous fiefdoms, each with its own profit-and-loss responsibilities. Consequently, communication between the project coordinator in Paris and his counterparts in Germany, the U.K., and Spain were indirect, going up and down national chains of command as pictured in Figure 8.1.

The functional implications of this structure are obvious and led to serious problems on this project:

- Communication between the project coordinator and his counterparts in Germany, the U.K., and Spain was painfully slow. Consequently, Euro-Lan was unable to respond quickly to customer requests, which led to unhappiness on the part of the client.

- Because any given communication had to pass through so many hands, the likelihood that messages would become distorted was great. By the time a request from Paris reached technical staff in Germany, the U.K., and Spain, it had undergone so much filtering that the actual instructions received varied measurably from country to country.

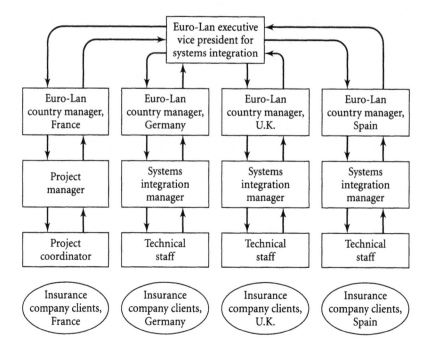

Figure 8.1. Euro-Lan Insurance Company Project.

- The project coordinator lacked even the most rudimentary degree of authority over technical staff in the other countries. A substantial proportion of his requests to these countries were ignored.

- Conflicts between the national groups had to be elevated to Euro-Lan's vice president of systems integration in order to be resolved since the communication structure used in this project made her the key arbiter to deal with cross-divisional problems. The VP became exasperated by the continual bickering on this project as even trivial issues were set before her for resolution.

- Problems induced by the communications architecture on this project were aggravated by financial structural issues. For example, in managing the project budget, Euro-Lan's Paris office allocated the lion's share of profit to Euro-Lan France. Operations in Germany, the U.K., and Spain were basically reimbursed for their costs and were allocated a minuscule profit. This led to a great deal of resentment in the non-Paris operations and chilled any spirit of cooperation that might have existed.

Scan Systems Inc.

Scan Systems Inc. was awarded a contract to replace the bar code scanning equipment for all of Wonder Toy Company's ninety-five retail outlets in the United States. Key players in the project are shown in Figure 8.2. On the Wonder Toy side, a project manager was assigned from the Information Technology Department. Her responsibilities were principally to generate requirements and to monitor the performance of Scan Systems Inc. The IT Department was given a central role in the project. In fact, it was the department that generated the proposal request to which Scan Systems Inc. responded. It was also instrumental in selecting Scan Systems Inc. from among five bidders. The vice president of finance was an important player, since this project was undertaken in response to his request. Similarly, the vice president for operations was involved because bar code scanning enabled Wonder Toy to track inventories.

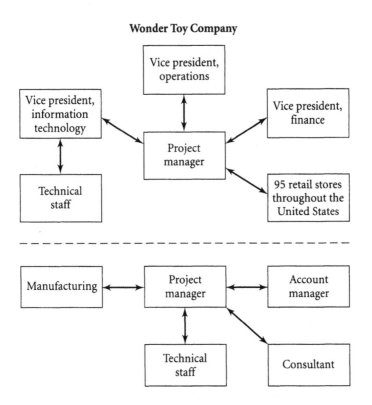

Figure 8.2. Scan Systems Inc.

On the Scan Systems side, a project manager was assigned. He had total responsibility for overseeing the installation of scanning hardware and software in the ninety-five Wonder Toy retail outlets. He had access to about twenty technically capable staff members who would carry out day-to-day activities on the project. Because Wonder Toy required that the software run on the unique B-Zar Operating System, Scan Systems hired a B-Zar specialist as a consultant. The account manager who shepherded the project during the preaward phase and was instrumental in developing the winning proposal continued to work on the project as a customer liaison. Finally, since this project entailed the delivery of some six hundred scanning units, Scan Systems' manufacturing group was actively involved in the project effort.

The Scan Systems project manager was highly experienced with this type of project. He did a "structural analysis" of the situation and saw immediately some structurally based challenges that he had to be prepared to deal with. The following were some of the key challenges:

• Decision-making authority was diffuse on the customer side. Although the Wonder Toy project manager might appear to be a key decision maker, in fact she was a minor player because three powerful players—the Finance, IT, and Operations VPs—could make independent decisions by virtue of their power. In fact, if there is a major divergence of interest between the information technology and finance groups, all decision making can become bogged down.

• Requirements for this project would be difficult to develop because of the contending interests of the different sets of players. For example, the information technology group was likely to focus on technical functionality, whereas the managers of the ninety-five retail outlets were more interested in usability and minimizing disruption to their daily operations.

• The customer side was likely to have a confused image of who was in charge on the Scan Systems side. If the toy company's key players had been working closely with the account manager, they would be likely to perceive of her as the person in charge. If they found the Scan Systems project manager unsympathetic to their requests, they might bypass him by working directly with the account manager. They might also be confused about the role of the consultant. Was he authorized on speak on behalf of Scan Systems?

• Once the project was under way and the technical staff were installing equipment in the retail outlets, there was a danger that local managers would pressure the installation personnel to make unauthorized changes to the configuration of the system.

The Scan Systems project manager's structural "fix" was to make his central role on the project clear to everyone and to insist that consequential communications be routed through him. For example, he told the consultant not to deal independently with anyone in the customer organization. He got the Scan Systems players to agree that they would funnel all change requests coming from the client organization to him. In turn, he told all the key players at Wonder Toy that any requests they had should be directed to him—and that the other players at Scan Systems were cooperating with him to enforce this rule. As a consequence of his proactive stance and structural fix, the project went smoothly. Scanning systems were installed on time and within budget and generated high levels of customer satisfaction.

CONCLUSIONS

The basic unit of project work is the project team. Unfortunately, project environments are so dynamic that teams operating in this environment do not look like regular teams. On projects, team members are borrowed resources. They come to the project, do their work, and then return to their functional homes.

A key concern of project professionals is how to engage in team building in such an environment. Normal conditions that promote team building—for example, colocation of team members, stable membership of players, the availability of carrots and sticks to motivate people—do not exist on most projects.

An additional complication is that project teams today increasingly involve partnering arrangements, in which members from the customer organization are part of the team. Some of the issues involved in partnering were discussed in Chapter Three, which examined a popular partnering arrangement called rapid prototyping.

This chapter has shown that although team building is difficult under standard project conditions, it is not impossible. Caring project managers who employ a little ingenuity can devise ways to build team spirit in an environment that seems rather hostile to it. But they must recognize that team building will not occur by accident. It requires conscious and conscientious effort.

CHAPTER NINE

Selecting Projects That Will Lead to Success

Not so long ago, the common wisdom maintained that the manager's principal jobs were to organize and direct. That outlook was appropriate in the hierarchical organizations that dominated Western business life until recently. Today, however, we live in an age of flattened organizations and inverted pyramids. Much of the organization's work is carried on by outsiders through outsourcing arrangements and strategic alliances. Managers are now charged to empower and support their workforce rather than to direct it. So much of what was standard managerial fare looks positively archaic today.

One thing has still not changed, however. Whatever else they do, managers still have major decision-making responsibilities. This is not to say that they make decisions unilaterally. Now more than ever, in fact, decision making is a cooperative effort between managers, the workforce, and customers. In such an environment, the job of managers is not to call the shots independently but to ensure that effective decisions are made. They can do this in a number of ways. For example, they can create an environment where they, their workforce, and customers can interact productively to arrive at decisions.

Effective decision making does not occur by accident. In this chapter, we examine some of its core elements, particularly as they relate to the selection of projects. The discussion can be generalized to cover other selection decisions as well—choosing staff, vendors, designs, and so on.

THE ESSENCE OF CHOICE

Rational decision making is fundamentally a process of prioritizing options. The best options go to the top of the list, the worst to the bottom. Consider the choice to buy a car. Potential buyers consider a number of selection criteria, including price, performance, styling, safety, and prestige. In the absence of an explicit decision-making methodology such as the analytical hierarchy process, they intuitively assess the performance of the target cars on each of these criteria and then sum up the results. Car A may get top billing on price, performance, and safety but be rated average on styling and prestige. In contrast, car B may receive the highest ratings on styling and prestige but middling ratings on price, performance, and safety.

Which car ranks higher? The answer depends on how the buyer grades practical considerations (price, performance, and safety) versus considerations of status (styling and prestige). If practical considerations are paramount, car A will be chosen. If status considerations dominate, car B will be the choice.

In view of the fact that decision making entails prioritization, whatever decision-making tools we use should have a built-in capacity to rank the options. This is precisely what lies at the heart of the specific project selection techniques that we examine in this chapter. What they all have in common is the goal of ranking the options.

BENEFIT-COST RATIOS

Benefit-cost analysis refers to the attempt to systematically weigh the benefits associated with an option against its costs. This can be done in a highly informal manner, as when we divide a page into two columns, labeling one "pros" and the other "cons." It can be done more formally through the creation of sophisticated mathematical models of benefits and costs.

In this section, we discuss one of the most commonly employed approaches to weighting benefits against costs: the benefit-cost ratio.

The ratio is created by developing a quantitative estimate of benefits (usually measured in monetary terms), developing an estimate of costs, and dividing the latter into the former. Consider the following primitive example of how a benefit-cost ratio might be created to provide guidance on what project to select:

$$\frac{B}{C} = \frac{\text{estimated sales} \times \text{probability of success}}{\text{estimated costs} \times \text{probability of achieving cost target}}$$

Let's assume that the estimated sales volume is $100,000 and the probability of success is 80 percent. These two values multiplied together yield the *expected value* of revenue. That is, $100,000 times 0.80 yields an expected revenue of $80,000.

Let us further assume that the estimated project costs are $50,000 and that the probability of doing the job at this cost is 80 percent. The expected value of cost is then $40,000. Our benefit-cost ratio is determined by dividing the expected value of revenue by the expected value of cost, or $80,000 by $40,000. The resulting ratio is 2.0.

It should be noted that this ratio is not an abstract number. A ratio of 2.0 tells us that for every dollar invested in the project, we can anticipate $2 in benefits. In other words, the ratio is a measure of "bang for the buck." If this ratio accurately portrays the per-dollar impact of an investment, it can be a valuable tool in our project management tool box. The relative merits of two or more projects can be established by comparing their benefit-cost ratios.

In finance, the benefit-cost ratio, when applied to discounted benefit and cost cash flows, is called the *profitability index* because it tells us whether an option is profitable. When the ratio is greater than 1.0, it is profitable, because benefits exceed costs. When it is less than 1.0, it is not profitable, because costs are greater than benefits. A ratio of 1.0 indicates that benefits perfectly offset costs—we neither make nor lose money.

Estimating Benefits and Costs

The benefit-cost ratio is a quantitative tool, and as such it requires that the variables being analyzed be quantified. Most typically, benefits are measured in monetary terms. Our example showed how this can be done. In this particular formulation, benefits are measured by estimating revenue in the simplest way possible.

Computations of benefits can grow more complex than this. An elaborate modeling of benefits can become quite formidable, filled

with exotic integral signs and Greek characters. For example, anticipated benefits might be captured by a mathematical growth function
using integral calculus. The effects of depreciation, salvage value, and
taxes might be factored out, further complicating the formulation.
When all is said and done, the mathematical formula describing benefits might look like something copied from a book on rocket science.

Obtaining data to calculate ratios can be troublesome. Where do
the data come from? Ideally, the organization conducting the analysis
has been collecting data over a period of time and has developed a historical database that can be employed. If it is an important project,
many departments might contribute to the estimating process: the
marketing department might contribute possible sales and price estimates; the manufacturing department, information on projected production runs and costs; and the finance department, data on costs.

It is certain that even the best data will be a bit soft. We are talking,
after all, about gazing into a crystal ball to predict the future, and the
future is always vague. It is therefore a good idea to establish a range
of possible outcomes: a best case, worst case, and a most likely scenario. By uncovering the full range of options, decision makers have
a better sense of the consequences of their actions.

Unfortunately, the reliability of much of the data being generated
through this process may be low because of problems inherent in
making estimates. For example, many of the people involved in generating the data may be amateurs in the realm of cost estimating,
pulling numbers out of thin air. Or perhaps the optimism of key players makes it impossible to see the downside of certain projects. Difficulties of estimation are described in detail in Chapter Ten.

Measuring Benefits as Cost Savings

Clearly, when one is selling a product or service to an external customer, it is easy to construe benefits as income streams. But what of
situations where we do not have income streams? Governments always encounter this situation because they do not operate to generate revenue. This also occurs in the private sector, commonly on
internal projects designed to improve an organization's operations, as
when equipment or information systems are upgraded. For example,
it is difficult, if not impossible, to calculate increases in revenue associated with the purchase of a new financial accounting system.

So how can benefits be calculated when there are no income
streams associated with an activity? One can measure benefits as *cost*

savings. That is, one uses benefit-cost ratios to identify options that will save the organization money.

To see how this works, consider the following example. A government scientific laboratory is looking for a way to analyze blood samples more effectively. Currently, the procedures it employs are labor-intensive. The lab seeks out modern blood analysis machinery that can automate the process extensively. Three products emerge that can help the lab carry out its work more effectively. Each of these products meets the lab's technical requirements for blood analysis. The laboratory decides to conduct a benefit-cost analysis to assist it in selecting the proper piece of equipment.

In calculating benefits, the lab first computes the cost of analyzing blood under current procedures. Then, using data supplied by the vendor combined with estimates made by its own personnel, the laboratory estimates the cost of analyzing blood for each of the three candidate products (net of the costs of purchasing the equipment in the first place, as well as the cost of a maintenance contract). It determines the annual cost savings associated with each of the products to be $120,000 for product A, $80,000 for product B, and $160,000 for product C. Clearly, product C will provide the laboratory with the greatest level of cost savings.

These cost savings must be assessed against the purchase price of the equipment plus additional costs, such as the price of a maintenance agreement. Assuming that the equipment has a useful life of five years, the lab divides the total purchase price by 5 and adds on the annual maintenance fee to derive an estimate of annualized costs for the equipment. The estimated annualized costs are $80,000 for product A, $60,000 for product B, and $160,000 for product C.

In calculating benefit-cost ratios, the laboratory finds that they are 1.5 for product A, 1.33 for product B, and 1.0 for product C. This analysis tells us that from a purely financial point of view, product A gives the most bang for the buck.

Common Problems with Benefit-Cost Ratios

In using benefit-cost ratios, project staff should be aware of a number of common pitfalls.

FOCUS ON THE MEASURABLE. Obviously, this approach has a bias toward what is readily measurable. It tends to ignore things that are hard to quantify. However, sometimes the immeasurable can be very important.

For example, in calculating benefits, have we taken into account the downstream secondary and tertiary consequences of our project? Possibly a seemingly unimpressive project might be laying the groundwork for major breakthroughs in the future. Have the potential downstream benefits been factored into the benefit-cost ratio for this project?

Other hard-to-quantify factors include the amount of goodwill generated by the project, its fit with corporate goals and the corporate culture, and its contribution to building key competencies in the organization (for example, increasing technological capabilities). If factors such as these are not included in the benefit-cost analysis, the resulting ratio will offer a skewed view of the value of benefits in relation to cost.

INADEQUATE SPECIFICATION OF THE BENEFIT-COST MODEL. When computing a benefit-cost ratio, one obvious question always arises: Does the benefit-cost model we have created accurately reflect reality? In statistics, this is called the *specification problem.* There is bound to be some divergence between reality and the model because models are only approximations of reality. The key issue is whether the specified model deviates *dramatically* from reality, providing us with seriously misleading information.

We have just seen that the exclusion of nonmeasurable factors from the model might lead to distortions. But there may be problems even with the measurable factors. For example, our model of benefits may assume that they grow exponentially over the next five years when in fact their growth is linear. Or our model may neglect to take into account the salvage value of a product when this may measurably affect how benefits are calculated.

To minimize the negative effects of model misspecification, the model should be continually tested against reality and subjected to criticism. Alternative forms of the model should also be explored to determine how sensitive it is to variations of its specifications.

SIZE-INDEPENDENT NATURE OF THE RATIOS. Given two project options, one whose benefit-cost ratio is 3.22 and the other whose ratio is 2.80, the "obvious" choice is to support the first option. However, consider the data that might have gone into the construction of these two ratio values:

Option A: $B/C = \$3,220/\$1,000 = 3.22$

Option B: $B/C = \$2,800,000/\$1,000,000 = 2.80$

A review of the data underlying the ratios changes our perspective on the relative merits of the two projects. A large company would find option B more desirable than option A because it involves larger amounts of payback. The payback of option A is "chicken feed." Consider that from an investment point of view, option B is one thousand times larger than option A (that is, it would take one thousand option A projects to equal one Option B project because a $1 million investment is a thousand times larger than a $1,000 investment).

The point here is that benefit-cost ratios are size-independent. They tell us nothing of the dimensions of the underlying investment and payback. There are an infinite number of ways that a ratio of 3.22 can be generated: 0.322/0.100, 3.22/1.00, 32.20/10.00, 322/100, and so on. In comparing two benefit-cost ratios, we want to be sure that we are not comparing an elephant with a mouse.

UNKNOWN PAYBACK PERIODS. If project option C has a benefit-cost ratio of 3.22 and project option D has a ratio of 2.80, option C would seem to be more attractive than option D. However, if the payback period associated with option C's benefits is longer than that of option D, option D might be the more desirable choice. In interpreting benefit-cost ratios, it is generally important to examine the cash inflow and outflow structures associated with benefits and costs, respectively. The overall ratio may blur important information contained in the cash flow data.

THE TELESCOPE EFFECT. In Chapter Ten, which covers procedures for estimating project costs and schedules, the telescope effect is described in some detail. Small errors of estimation can telescope into major errors if these errors occur consistently. For example, if an estimator consistently overstates benefits by 10 percent (and understates costs by 10 percent) in the benefit-cost equation, the resulting benefit-cost ratio will overstate benefits by 22 percent. When such an effect takes place, undeserving projects obtain support based on faulty estimates.

BUSS'S TECHNIQUE
FOR RANKING PROJECTS

In 1983, an interesting article written by Martin Buss appeared in the *Harvard Business Review*. Titled "How to Rank Computer Projects," it described a benefit-cost project selection methodology that does not depend on employing quantitative data but still shares some of the key features of benefit-cost ratios. The following discussion expostulates on Buss's ideas but modifies them slightly in light of my own experience in employing them.

Buss's approach requires that a small project selection team be put together—say, during a quarterly review session—to review a number of project proposals at one time. Ideally, the team members represent different perspectives. For example, a hypothetical team might have one member from the marketing department, one from finance, one from production, and one from engineering.

The team members are charged to go through the pile of proposals and to evaluate each of them according to key project selection criteria. Although each organization can create its own specialized criteria, experience shows that four criteria serve the project selection process effectively: financial, technical, developmental, and organizational. Each of these criteria is viewed from the perspective of benefits and is matched against project costs. The matching of costs against benefit for the four selection criteria is pictured in Figure 9.1. The matching takes the physical form of a three-by-three grid.

Grid A matches costs of the candidate projects against anticipated financial benefits. As the grid illustrates, nine possible scenarios emerge. Project costs can be high while financial benefits are high, moderate, or low; costs can be moderate while benefits are high, moderate, or low; and costs can be low while benefits are high, moderate, or low.

The team begins the process by evaluating the first proposal according to its relative costs and financial benefits. After some discussion, a team consensus should emerge as to which of the nine cells best captures the essence of the project. Let's say that in our example, the team determines that project 1's costs are "medium," and so are its financial benefits. This process is repeated with the other proposals. One by one, the projects are assigned to their appropriate cells in the grid.

Most proposed projects are likely to fall into the cells along the low-low, medium-medium, high-high diagonal of the grid. I call the cells along this diagonal the "you get what you pay for" cells. Along the diagonal, the relative benefits of a low-cost project are low, the relative benefits of a medium-cost project are medium, and the relative benefits of a high-cost project are high. Projects assigned to these cells are analogous to projects with a benefit-cost ratio of 1.0. They neither make nor lose money. Benefits and costs basically offset each other.

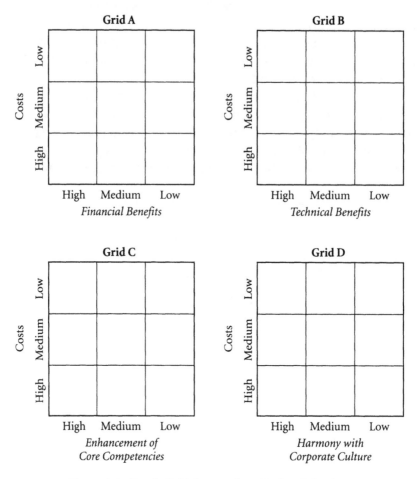

Figure 9.1. Buss's Grid Approach to Project Selection.

The most desirable cell is found in the top left-hand corner: here projects have high benefits but low costs. The least desirable cell is the one in the bottom right-hand corner: here projects have high costs and low benefits. In general, any projects assigned to the diagonal or to the cells above the diagonal are supportable: they do not lose money. Projects assigned to cells below the diagonal are money losers.

Once all projects have been assigned to their cells in grid A, attention turns to grid B. Here project costs are matched against technical benefits arising from the project. A project that leads to a technical breakthrough that can lead to further technical advances would be rated high on the technical benefit scale. One that had no technical benefits would be rated low. As with grid A, each project is assigned to a cell.

Grid C matches project costs against the contributions that the project might make to nurturing the organization's key competencies. By carrying out a project, is the organization's developing the capabilities of its personnel? Is it gaining entry into desirable targeted areas? Is it gaining experience that will serve it well on future projects? If a project is seen to contribute heavily in these areas, it is rated high on the core competencies scale.

Finally, grid D matches project costs against organizational goals and the corporate culture. Key questions addressed here include, Will a project contribute significantly to advancing well-defined organizational goals? Does it reinforce or run against the corporate culture? Projects that go against organizational goals and the corporate culture are doomed to failure and should not be supported.

After all the projects have been assigned to cells in each of the four grids, it is time to make an overall assessment of their value. Buss suggests that the selection team should avoid being too analytical in doing this—for example, by taking a weighted average of each project's "score" for each of the grids. Rather, they should put away the facts and figures and trust in their collective insights. They have spent a substantial amount of time reviewing the proposals and now know each project intimately. As a final step in the selection process, they should assign each project to a cell in a generic overall benefit-cost grid. When all is said and done, which cell does project 1 belong in? Project 2? Project 3? And so on.

Buss's approach to ranking projects is appealing for at least two reasons. First, it offers a method for conducting a benefit-cost analysis that does not require the organization to develop a quantitative model that might be misspecified. Yet it still shares key features of benefit-cost ratio analysis. For example, the cell to which a project is assigned roughly corresponds to benefit-cost ratios greater than, equal to, or less than zero. In addition, the process is rigorous in that the selection team must be explicit about selection criteria.

Second, the approach depends on the informed collective judgment of the members of the selection team. Because the team members reflect a broad range of perspectives, their decisions are less likely to reflect a narrow outlook. They arrive at their conclusions after measured debate on the merits and shortcomings of different projects with respect to different criteria. Through the process of give-and-take discussion, all features of the project—drawbacks as well as strengths—will have been exposed and reviewed. Because any position can be challenged, project optimists will be forced to justify their rosy projections. The Buss approach is very much a Japanese-style management tool.

POOR MAN'S HIERARCHY

An exciting development in management science in the 1980s was the rapid growth in the popularity of a decision-making tool called the Analytical Hierarchy Process (AHP). This technique was developed in the 1970s by Thomas Saaty. Its applications to management decision making are described in Saaty's book *Decision Making for Leaders* (1999). AHP caught people's fancy because it generates quantitative values based on subjective judgments.

A detailed description of this technique is beyond the realm of this book, partly because the math is a bit arcane (involving the computation of such things as eigenvalues and eigenvectors). However, a pared-down treatment can be offered here. Because it is only a shadow of the full AHP, I call it the "poor man's hierarchy." I developed it as an introduction to AHP concepts for managers lacking a solid mathematical background. After teaching it to many managers and employing it on consulting assignments, I found that it is a good decision-making tool in its own right.

The central objective of the poor man's hierarchy is to enable decision makers to rank options in a relatively painless fashion. It does this by having managers compare each of the options pairwise. The point is best illustrated by means of an example. Let's say that a small group of managers and technical staff are brought together to select a new site to establish manufacturing operations. In using the poor man's hierarchy, their first task is to identify what criteria should go into the decision-making process. They choose these criteria after give-and-take discussion. They might ultimately decide that the key selection criteria are availability of cheap labor, proximity of the site to a good highway and a major airport, proximity of the site to key suppliers, cost of land, availability of investment incentives from the local government, and tax policies in the region.

After the criteria have been selected, they are ranked according to priority by making pairwise comparisons between the criteria. The comparisons are made by addressing the following types of questions: Which is the more desirable criterion, availability of cheap labor or regional tax policies? Proximity to key suppliers or regional tax policies? Availability of cheap labor or proximity to key suppliers? These questions are raised for all possible pairs of questions.

The process of asking questions and tracking the answers is facilitated by the creation of a square grid, as depicted in Figure 9.2. The selection criteria are listed along the side of the grid as well as across the top. This enables the decision makers to make sure that they address all possible pairwise combinations of criteria.

Cells in the grid are filled in according to the following rule: if the criterion along the side of the grid is preferable to the criterion listed across the top, a 1 is placed in the cell. If the criterion on top is preferable, a 0 is placed in the cell. Note that the diagonal cells are blanked out since it does not make sense to compare a criterion to itself. Note also that comparisons need only be made for cells above the diagonal. Whatever value is put in a cell above the diagonal, the opposite value will be put into the corresponding cell below the diagonal. For example, the 1 appearing in the cell linking "suppliers" to "land cost" appears as a 0 in the corresponding cell linking "land cost" to "suppliers."

	Cheap labor	Transportation	Suppliers	Land cost	Government incentives	Tax policies	Score
Cheap labor	—	1	1	1	1	1	5
Transportation	0	—	0	1	1	0	2
Suppliers	0	1	—	1	1	0	3
Land cost	0	0	0	—	1	0	1
Government incentives	0	0	0	0	—	0	0
Tax policies	0	1	1	1	1	—	4

Figure 9.2. **Example of the Poor Man's Hierarchy.**

Consider the criterion "suppliers" in Figure 9.2. The 0 in the cell under "cheap labor" tells us that cheap labor is rated higher than access to suppliers. The 1 in the cell under "transportation" indicates that access to suppliers is deemed more important than access to good roads and an airport. Similarly, the 1 under "land cost" indicates that access to suppliers is more important than the cost of land. And so on.

By adding up the numbers across a row, we obtain a total score. This score signifies the number of times a criterion won in its comparisons with other criteria. The higher the score, the higher the number of wins. By implication, the higher the score, the higher the ranking of the criterion. In the example in Figure 9.2, it is evident that the ranking of criteria is, from highest to lowest, cheap labor (5 points), tax policies (4 points), access to suppliers (3 points), access to good transportation facilities (2 points), land cost (1 point), and government investment incentives (0 points).

In making pairwise comparisons, we may produce logical inconsistencies. For example, we may say that A is preferable to B and B is preferable to C, but in comparing A and C we may say that C is preferable to A—a logical inconsistency. In the poor man's hierarchy, inconsistencies will show up as tie scores. For example, "transportation," "suppliers," and "land cost" may all achieve a score of 2. (This will happen if we state that "transportation" is more important than "suppliers" and "transportation" is less important than "land cost.") As Saaty points out in his work, inconsistencies are not inherently bad. They may simply reflect the fact that our model has not taken into account all pertinent decisional dimensions.

The poor man's hierarchy is useful in many contexts. It was noted at the outset of this chapter that the essence of rational decision making is the ranking of options. The whole point of this technique is to assist in the ranking process. It is done very simply, by comparing options two at a time. Thus this technique is a generic decision-making tool. It can be employed to rank projects, vendors, employees, promises, and so on. When my daughter Katy was eight years old, she used it to select whom invite to her birthday party (she wanted to invite twenty friends, but there was enough room for only twelve).

I used it once in a faculty committee meeting established to identify a suitable commencement speaker. The committee members easily generated a list of about fifteen possible prospects. However, we found it impossible to achieve a consensus on how they should be ranked. Finally, I convinced my fellow committee members to rank the candidates through pairwise comparisons. We had no problem at all choosing one candidate over another in a pairwise mode. The whole process took about ten minutes. At the end of that time, we had our overall ranking. Everyone agreed it reflected the consensus of the group. What seemed to be an impossible task when tackled as a whole was easily carried out when broken into small, workable pieces.

THE MURDER BOARD

For project selection to be effective, no proposition should be allowed to go unchallenged. If the project champion states that her project will generate a 20 percent return on investment if supported, she should be prepared to defend that statement rigorously. If the team engineers say that a particular component in their proposed system will outperform existing components by a factor of 5, they should be able to back up their projection.

A highly effective project selection methodology based on the proposition that no idea should go unchallenged has been given the rather macabre name of *murder board*. It is a simple method, in both concept and execution.

With the murder board approach, a panel of reviewers is put together to review project proposals. The panel is made up of people from different parts of the organization. For example, one member might come from marketing, another from finance, another from engineering, and another from production. The panel is charged to scrutinize the project proposal carefully. In fact, members should tear it apart and try to show why it is not workable.

The project champion is charged to go before the panel and make the best arguments possible in support of the proposal. He or she should be prepared to field tough questions and to deal with a skeptical audience. Of course, to be effective, the presenter should have backup documentation and employ it when necessary.

Effective use of a murder board allows organizations to catch problems during the talking stage, before large sums have been committed and designs have been cast in concrete. This process tempers the unchecked optimism of project champions and makes it less likely that their infectious fervor will lead the organization to support unsound ideas. For this approach to work, all parties in the process must recognize that its objective is not to punish and humiliate the project champion but rather to distinguish between solid and shaky propositions.

The murder board approach will likely be used in conjunction with other approaches. For example, the project champion may be required to develop a benefit-cost ratio to support his or her arguments. In the final analysis, the murder board serves as a "reality check," an attempt to make sure that arguments in support of project ideas do not contain the seeds of their own destruction.

PEER REVIEW

The dominant form of project selection in scientific areas is called *peer review*. This approach is employed to select billions of dollars of research projects each year under the auspices of government agencies such as the National Science Foundation, the National Institutes of Health, and the National Institute of Standards and Technology. In addition, it is employed to select projects in industrial labs such as Bell Labs and IBM's assorted laboratories.

With peer review, projects are evaluated by "peers," individuals who are technically competent to assess the technical merits of a proposal. Typically, three or more peers receive a copy of a proposal. They are asked to review the proposal independently. After examining it, they are asked to assess its merits according to a number of criteria. The National Science Foundation criteria, for example, ask for an assessment of such things as the project's technical merits, the competence of key players (in particular, the principal investigator), and the value of the management plan. The assessment is usually noted on a scoring sheet, where each criterion is given a score ranging from 1 (low) to 5 (high).

After the reviewers have all had a chance to score the proposed project, their assessments are collected and examined jointly. If all three reviewers give the project a low score, it will be rejected. If it receives mixed reviews, it is not likely to be funded in this era of tight budgets. Even the enthusiastic support of all the reviewers is no guarantee of funding.

Peer review has long been criticized as a subjective approach that is susceptible to distortion, such as bias in favor of an old boy network. So why is it employed?

The answer is more closely tied to the politics of science than to rational decision making. The scientific community is reluctant to be reviewed by nonscientists and to be accountable to nonscientific selection criteria. It will be interesting to see whether this outlook will be able to survive the tight budgets and social demands for account-ability that we will encounter in the years ahead.

GENERAL RULES FOR SELECTING PROJECTS

This chapter has focused on a handful of rational techniques that can be helpful for decision making. Clearly, there is more to project selection than technique. Before concluding the chapter, I would like to put these techniques into a broader decision-making context. Following are some general rules for project selection that, if followed, will lead to better choices.

• *Rule 1: Be explicit about what is important in choosing projects.* Project selection should occur in accordance with clearly defined se-lection criteria. These criteria should be written in large, boldfaced type. They should be taped onto the walls in the room where selec-tion decisions are being made. They should be ritualistically recited at the outset of each selection meeting. During the selection process, people should not be distracted by the wealth of interesting possibil-ities that the organization *might* pursue—rather, they should focus on what the organization *needs* to pursue, as captured in the selection criteria.

• *Rule 2: Identify explicit procedures for choosing projects and then stick to them.* Project selection should not occur by accident. An ap-proach to choosing projects should be developed and rigorously ad-hered to. Even powerful players in the organization should be required to stick to the procedures. In this way, decisions become less arbitrary. Also, a check can be placed on the powerful players who irresponsi-bly push for a particular project "because it seemed like a good idea at the time."

• *Rule 3: Be prepared to rigorously challenge all assertions.* No state-ment about possible benefits or costs associated with a project should be immune from challenge. Project champions tend to lose sight of possible problems. The picture they paint of project benefits is typi-cally rosy. By the same token, project critics often picture a proposed project in the worst possible light, adducing all manner of facts to back up their position. The most effective way to temper excessive opti-mism or pessimism is to question the veracity of key assertions made by project champions and critics.

• *Rule 4: Constitute a project selection team whose members represent a broad array of stakeholders.* All projects serve multiple purposes and have multiple impacts. Clearly, the project selection team should be made up of individuals who represent a broad array of perspectives. A typical selection team for a private sector project should have members who reflect the varying perspectives of engineering, marketing, finance, and production.

• *Rule 5: Involve key project personnel in the selection process.* In a survey I conducted of a sizable number of project managers, I found that only 20 percent reported being involved in the selection of the projects they work on. For most project managers, the selection decision is made without their input. They are given project management responsibilities after the decision has been made. There are at least two good reasons for including key project personnel in the project selection decision. First, if these people have a role in choosing a project, they will automatically have a stake in it. They will be more energetic in pursuing project goals because they had a role in establishing them. Second, if they are part of the project selection process, they will understand the rationale for conducting a project. In this way, continuity can be maintained between the selection and execution phases in the project life cycle. Too often, when key personnel do not understand the original rationale of a project, they redefine this rationale to suit their outlook, and this leads to problems of continuity.

CONCLUSIONS

The selection of projects is serious business. It should not be carried out in an offhand manner. Too often, insufficient attention is given to whether a particular project idea has real merit. Thus projects may be selected to satisfy the hunches of powerful players. Or they may be selected simply to keep staff busy or to spend end-of-the-year money.

A big problem with offhand project selection is that it leads to the ineffective use of resources. Support of a project to satisfy short-term exigencies may lead to long-term fiascoes. Those making the decisions often forget that by committing resources to a poorly conceived project idea, they are tying up those resources. They have not taken into account the opportunity costs of their decision. If a truly good project prospect arises in the future, they may no longer have the resources to pursue it because their resources are tied up in marginal undertakings.

CHAPTER TEN

Estimating Realistic Costs, Schedules, and Specifications to Ensure Project Success

I spent the late spring of 1989 in Beijing on a World Bank consulting assignment. This was at the time of the Tiananmen Square turmoil. I worked with two groups of project managers, one in the chemical engineering industry and the other in shipbuilding. The environment in which we carried out our sessions was a bit distracting. As we talked about managing projects, we could hear the cheers and chants of student and worker demonstrators outside.

"What do you find to be the single greatest problem of project management in your jobs?" I asked my students.

They answered with amazing consistency. "If we are to get support for our projects," they said, "we must state that we can do the project for nearly nothing. Once the project is authorized, we spend all of our time scrambling for resources."

This problem is certainly not unique to China. In organization after organization, I hear the same refrain: "We are committed to doing the job with insufficient resources." Having worked with many project managers in a large number of organizations, I have reached the conclusion that the great majority of projects being carried out today are underresourced by 20 to 30 percent. What is particularly bothersome about this situation is that cost and schedule overruns are hardwired into these projects. If we are committed to doing 1,000 person-hours of work with only 750 person-hours of labor, something's got to give.

The conscious "lowballing" of cost and schedule estimates is not the only source of poor estimation on projects. Consider the following list of problems. We continually underestimate technical glitches that can arise. The people doing the estimating are generally amateurs. Events arise in the environment that invalidate our informed guesses. Project champions are so blinded by the opportunities their projects present that they don't see the pitfalls. Our clients begin changing project requirements, with measurable budget and schedule impacts. And so on.

To a certain extent, every cost and schedule overrun can be traced back to a failure of estimation. Even when the root cause of an overrun is sloppy project execution, we can complain that the estimation did not take into account the likelihood of such sloppiness.

CAUSES OF POOR ESTIMATION

Problems in estimating costs and schedules have been with us a long, long time. No doubt Imhotep was disappointed more than once by the poor estimates his architects provided him during the building of the pyramids. When we explore the causes of bad estimation, we see why the problem is so intractable: on a typical project, there are *several* causes of difficulties, all functioning at the same time and all conspiring to prove our best guesses to be inadequate. Let's take a look at the key problems.

Inexperienced Guessers

One major cause of poor estimation is that the people making the estimates don't know what they are doing. Most cost and schedule estimates are conducted in the following way: individuals with certain technical expertise and others with responsibility for carrying out tasks are asked to provide estimates of what it will take to carry out their pieces of the project. These individuals generally scratch their heads, think back to past experiences, make a few phone calls, and then come up with their estimates. Usually, there is no consistency of outlook among these individuals. The assortment of scattered predictions they make is then brought together in a haphazard way and offered as the official estimate.

The problem, then, is that most estimates are being made by amateurs. Amateur estimators typically fall into the following traps:

- They tend to be optimistic about what is needed to do the job and consequently understate potential problems.
- They tend to leave things out of their estimates. For example, in estimating the cost to install a computer system, they forget to include the cost of the cable that will link the computer to the printer (this is called the "missing components" problem).
- They follow no consistent methodology in deriving their estimates, so that it is difficult to re-create the rationale for their estimating procedures. It is likely that the estimate they make on a Monday will differ measurably from the same estimate made on a Thursday.

There are two good ways to deal with inexperienced estimators. First, they should be given training on estimating processes. This training will teach them that there is an art and science to estimating. Over the years, methodologies have emerged (for example, parametric cost estimating) that enable individuals to make quite precise time and cost estimates. There are even societies that focus on estimating procedures, such as the Association for the Advancement of Cost Engineering. The students should be required to learn and employ these solid estimating methodologies.

Second, the organization should develop tight methods and procedures for cost and schedule estimates. The procedures can be form-driven so that estimators need merely fill out a form to get the estimates they need. As part of this process, estimators should be supplied with checklists of items that should be included in the estimates. Explicit methods and procedures for estimating will increase the consistency of estimates in the organization and will counter the amateur's propensity to contribute to the "missing components" problem.

Lack of Continuity Between the Preaward and Postaward Phases

Organizations that employ a sales force to sell their products and services encounter a common problem: during preaward negotiations, the salespeople promise clients features and services that the project and production staff cannot provide. The explanation of their behavior is simple. In most organizations, salespeople derive a substantial portion of their incomes from commissions. The more sales they make, the greater their commissions. If they see a sales opportunity slipping, they may be tempted to cut prices excessively or to make product or service commitments that will be difficult or impossible to meet.

Once project staff take over a project in the postaward phase, they may find themselves in a no-win situation. The price of a service provided to the client may be lower than its cost to the company. Technological enhancements may be promised that lie outside of the organization's capabilities. Or commitments may be made to achieving impossible deadlines. What project staff face here is programmed failure. This may manifest itself in outright financial losses or in customer disappointment when expectations are not met. In any event, project staff may find themselves blamed for problems they did not create.

There is no easy solution to this problem. Organizations are often reluctant to take their sales staff off commission for fear that this will dull their killer instincts. What some organizations do is put together an account team that includes sales, project, production, and maintenance people. If the salespeople begin to make unachievable commitments, the other members of the account team can rein them in.

Bad Technical Guesses

As Chapter Four on risk management makes clear, the future is always uncertain. The financial impact of this uncertainty can be devastating when it results in bad technical guesses as to what needs to be done on a project. Newspapers are full of stories about technical problems that hold up progress on projects like Boston's Big Dig project and the Hubble space telescope, leading to massive cost and schedule overruns.

Technical glitches occur on most projects. The simple project to cut a doorway between two offices turns into a nightmare when we discover that the wall separating the offices is not sheetrock but brick. Our attempt to change the oil filter on our car becomes a four-hour ordeal when we discover that the oil filter is just centimeters beyond the reach of our hand. A crucial component on our telecommunications equipment fails on Friday afternoon, right before the beginning of a three-day weekend.

Thorough planning and the employment of good-quality management practices can avert many of these surprises. But others are truly bolts out of the blue that cannot be anticipated. Estimators should therefore assume the worst in making their estimates. They should establish contingency allowances to deal with the "unknown unknowns" that are bound to arise. They should be skeptical of any technical guesses that assume that everything will work fine the first time through.

Changes to the Project

Projects face constant pressure for change. This pressure arises from several sources. Some of it comes from the environment. For example, a competitor's introduction of a new product may lead to changing market conditions that the project team must adjust to. Or government's changes to environmental regulations may force the team to alter the way it does its business. Or macroeconomic fluctuations, such as a sudden surge of inflation, may invalidate key assumptions built into the cost- and schedule-estimating procedures.

Pressure for change also arises from within the organization. For example, technical glitches may require stopping the project until the problems are fixed. Or technical staff may want to redesign something in their search for perfect solutions.

Finally, clients can be a major source of change. As the deliverable becomes more concrete and clients see what they will be getting, they may not like what they see and demand alterations. Or they may be stimulated by what they see and suggest enhancements. Another common source of client-induced change derives from shifts of key personnel in the client organization. For example, the new division director may put the project on hold until he or she has a chance to review it.

A problem with change is that it typically causes some measure of cost and schedule overruns. Consequently, it can lead to failures of estimation. Cost and schedule estimators must factor the effects of change into their estimates. Unfortunately, specific changes are difficult to predict. The best way to anticipate change is to carry out a risk assessment that identifies the overall stability of the project environment (see Chapter Four). If the project is dealing with untried technology, if it is being supported by a cost-reimbursable contract, or if the client organization is in turmoil, it is likely that the project will experience substantial change. In this case, estimators should build large "fudge factors" into their estimates of individual activities, thus providing for substantial contingency allowances.

Beyond this, the project organization should have strong change management procedures in place. Without change management, "scope creep" will ensue. What started out as a modest undertaking will grow into a costly behemoth. Cost and schedule overruns will occur, and the estimating process will be undermined. (More is said about change management in Chapter Three.)

Psychological Factors

As people mull over new project ideas, they often grow excited about the possibilities. The new project may offer interesting technical and marketing challenges. It may also hold the promise of increasing profitability dramatically. Soon there is a psychological commitment to carrying out this project. This can translate into a blinding optimism about the project's prospects.

The impact of unchecked optimism on cost and schedule estimating can be enormous. What is especially disturbing is that optimism can distort the estimates in subtle ways that are not easy to spot. Consider how this occurs in the following story.

THE 10 PERCENT OPTIMIST

Marvin and his development team are very excited about the prospects of building a new Whambangatron. They have roughly scoped out their ideas and now must present a proposal for project support before the project review board. An important component of the presentation will be the business case for the Whambangatron. Marvin must present a benefit-cost analysis describing the business consequences of carrying out the proposed project.

Unfortunately, Marvin is so enamored of the project idea that he becomes a "10 percent optimist." That is, in making his estimates, he unconsciously overstates benefits by a small amount—10 percent. He also tends to underestimate costs by 10 percent. It would seem that the consequences of Marvin's modest optimism would be marginal. Actually, the consequences are dramatic.

To estimate benefits, Marvin predicts that total sales resulting from the Whambangatron will be $1.1 million. In reality, they will be $1 million. He further estimates that profits will be 11 percent of sales, resulting in profits of $121,000 (that is, 11 percent of $1.1 million). In reality, they will be 10 percent, or $100,000 (10 percent of $1 million). After carrying out a risk analysis, he determines that the probability of success for this project is 88 percent, meaning that the expected value of profits is $106,480 (88 percent of $121,000). In reality, it is 80 percent, giving an expected value of profits of $80,000 (80 percent of $100,000).

In estimating costs, Marvin unconsciously shaves 10 percent off of true costs. He states that project costs will be $81,000, whereas in reality they will be $90,000.

In computing a benefit-cost ratio, Marvin divides his estimated benefits of $106,480 by his estimated costs of $81,000. The resulting ratio is 1.31, meaning that for every dollar invested in the project, $1.31 will be generated. In reality, the true benefit-cost ratio is $80,000 divided by $90,000, or 0.89. Because the true ratio is less than 1, the project is actually going to lose money.

Note that Marvin's modest 10 percent optimism has telescoped into a projection that overstates the benefit-cost ratio by 47.2 percent! The project review board will be making a decision on the basis of a flawed estimate, and the project, if supported, will find itself in serious trouble.

The problem here is not that Marvin made imperfect estimates. Most people would be delighted if they could predict the future with 90 percent accuracy. The problem is that his optimistic estimates were *applied consistently* for each variable that went into his benefit-cost equation. This led to a compounding of the estimation error. Imagine what his benefit-cost ratio would be if he decided to boost his estimates by another 10 percent in order to strengthen his case before the project review board!

The best way to deal with the problem of the 10 percent optimist is to place skeptics on the cost-estimating team. No individual estimate should be permitted to go unchallenged.

Lowballing

Lowballing occurs when the project organization says it will do a job for less money than it will actually cost. Obviously, if organizations spend more than they make, they will not stay in business very long. So why do they lowball?

The great hope is that the low bid will get them the job. Once they have it, then they count on making their money through change orders or follow-up business. The lowball bid is the project management equivalent of a "loss leader."

For many years, skilled contractors could play the lowball game and make money on it. This was particularly true in the government arena, where contracts would be awarded primarily on the basis of cost. Project management on these contracts concentrated chiefly on tracking change orders. Each time government wanted a change, it would be billed generously. The nickels and dimes added up, and by the end of the contract, the contractor was in a profitable situation.

The lowballing strategy has lost its appeal in recent years. In part, contractors find that as a consequence of budget shortages, government is not pressing for expensive change orders anymore. So they may offer to do a job at a low cost but may not make up their losses through change orders.

The idea of bidding low in the hope of getting follow-up business has always been problematic. In government work, the logic of such an approach generally does not make sense because follow-up work is competed for openly, and once again, the assignment will go to the low bidder. Even in private sector work, the lowballing strategy frequently backfires. The initial strategy is to get a foot in the door for follow-up business. Unfortunately, because the project is underfunded, it may get into trouble, leading to missed deadlines and quality problems. Given such poor performance, the client is not inclined to conduct repeat business with the project performer.

Customers are increasingly realizing that policies awarding work to the low bidder do not always serve their best interests. At first glance, it appears that competitive bidding in which the low bidder wins leads to cost savings and good bargains. What often happens, however, is that this process creates situations where contractors get in trouble. As a Defense Department colleague once asked me, "Would you want to leap out of an airplane wearing a parachute built by a low bidder?"

The new emphasis is on value. In the early 1990s, the federal government successfully awarded a number of significant contracts based on value rather than cost. Losing low-bid contractors have protested this new policy, but it has been successfully defended by procurement authorities.

Politics

Occasionally, an organization's best cost and schedule estimates are overridden because of political concerns. Professional cost estimators spend countless hours gathering cost information and feeding it into their sophisticated cost models. After some serious number-crunching, a solid cost estimate emerges. This estimate is then forwarded to upper management, who, after glancing at it briefly, crosses it out and puts in a value that is more acceptable politically. Patrick Tyler, in his book *Running Critical* (1986), describes how precisely this kind of scenario at General Dynamics led to one of the greatest cost overruns in history. It also resulted in the tarnishing of the careers of some prominent people, including Admiral Hyman Rickover—father of the U.S. nuclear navy—and General Dynamics' CEO.

Political meddling in cost and schedule estimating is an everyday occurrence in some organizations. To gain support for their projects, project staff doctor their estimates to make them more palatable to powerful players. The best antidote against such political meddling is the establishment of objective, clearly defined procedures for project selection. The procedures should be set up so that no players, no matter how powerful, can unilaterally impose their will on the selection process.

TRADITIONAL APPROACHES TO COST ESTIMATING

Traditional approaches to cost estimating generally fall into one of two categories: bottom-up or top-down. The bottom-up approach is concerned with gathering vast amounts of detailed cost data on each component of the project. Once the data are gathered, they are rolled up for an overall estimate of costs for the whole project. The top-down approach, also called *parametric cost estimating*, eschews the detail and derives estimates on the basis of historical experience. It is a statistical approach.

Bottom-Up Cost Estimating

The bottom-up approach focuses on tracking all cost elements associated with a project. Total project cost is simply the sum of the costs of all the individual elements. The question is how to identify these cost elements in a systematic fashion. The most common approach to doing this is to employ a work breakdown structure (WBS) as a guide to identifying cost elements.

This means that before cost estimates can be made, a detailed WBS must be constructed. Cost data are then gathered at the lowest level of the WBS, which is called the *work package* level. These data are then aggregated to the next WBS level, which provides budget insights into activities reported at this level. They are further aggregated until we reach the highest level of the WBS, at which point we have an overall cost estimate for the project.

The bottom-up roll-up process is illustrated in Table 10.1, where work package data are shown in normal type and rolled-up data in italics. In this example, work package data include both labor and material costs. A more refined WBS can distinguish between different costing categories.

WBS No.	Task	Cost
10.0.0	*Project: Pour concrete foundation*	*$14,900*
10.1.0	*Conduct survey*	*1,200*
10.1.1	Measure foundation dimensions	900
10.1.2	Mark foundation dimensions	300
10.2.0	*Clear debris*	*1,300*
10.2.1	Remove shrubs	700
10.2.1	Remove rocks	600
10.3.0	*Excavate*	*4,700*
10.3.1	Obtain equipment	1,200
10.3.2	Dig hole	3,500
10.4.0	*Pour foundation*	*7,700*
10.4.1	Insert concrete forms	1,100
10.4.2	Pour concrete	6,000

Table 10.1. Bottom-Up Cost Estimating with the WBS.

Note: Work package data are in normal type. Rolled-up data are in italics.

Parametric Cost Estimating

Parametric cost estimating is also called *top-down estimating*. It focuses on formulating cost estimates by examining fundamental parametric relationships. In mathematics, *parameters* is a fancy word for what our high school algebra teachers call *constants*. For example, in the equation of a straight line, $y = mx + b$, m and b are parameters, whereas y and x are variables. There is an additional hidden parameter in the straight-line equation: the exponent of x is understood to be 1.

Parameters define the fundamental structure of the relationships of variables. For example, in the straight-line formula, m represents the slope of the line (how steeply it rises) and b the point at which the line intersects the y-axis. If the parameter associated with x changes from 1 to 2, giving us $y = mx^2 + b$, we no longer have a straight line but rather a parabola.

In everyday life, we encounter many parameters that offer us guidance on how to conduct our affairs. For example, gasoline may sell for $1.25 per gallon. Here the $1.25 is a parameter. If I buy two gallons of gas, I pay $2.50; three gallons, $3.75; and so on. Or consider another example: the speed limit on the highway is 55 miles per hour. If I drive for four hours, I will cover 220 miles.

Similarly, there are many parameters governing the relationship between variables in business. For example: experience tells us that a yard of concrete will cure in so many hours. The learning curve suggests that if we increase the production run of our widgets by 80 percent, their unit costs will decrease by 20 percent. In doubling the height, width, and depth of a structure, we generally increase our material requirements eightfold.

With parametric cost estimating, we identify fundamental parameters that offer us insights into the cost of our project. This is illustrated in a simple example in Table 10.2. The table shows a cost-estimating approach I used for several years to price small-scale research and software projects. In conducting my project business, I often found myself in a position where I would be meeting with a client and the client would raise a point similar to what follows.

"David, since I've got you here, let me ask you something that has nothing to do with our current project. We are thinking about upgrading the management information system that tracks our inventory. . . ." The client would then proceed to describe briefly his requirements for the upgrade.

"So David, what would an upgrade like this cost? Roughly, of course." At this point, the client would typically give me an earnest look. "Don't worry about being precise in your estimate. We won't hold you to it." After he stated this last sentence, I thought I saw the client's nose grow a little bit, like Pinocchio's.

I thus found myself in a situation where I had to respond to a client's inquiry quickly if I was going to exploit a new business opportunity. The client wanted an answer *now*. He didn't want me to tell him I'd get back with an estimate one week from now.

Professionals (500 person-hours @ $40/hour)	$20,000
Technical support (2,000 professional hours @ $30/hour)	$60,000
Total direct wages	$80,000
Fringe benefits + overhead (determined by accountants to be 1.06 × total direct wages)	84,800
Total labor-related costs (fringe benefits + overhead + total direct wages)	$164,800

Table 10.2. Example of a Parametric Cost Estimate.

Generally, I was able to give an estimate that I could live with by using a simple top-down estimating procedure. Let's say that I knew from experience that the work required to do the job would occupy a professional programmer for one-fourth of a person-year. This translates into 500 person-hours of effort (note the useful parameter: 2,000 person-hours a year roughly constitutes one person-year of work). Given my initial estimate of the amount of professional work needed, everything else falls into place due to fundamental parametric relationships.

One person-hour of professional effort costs $40, so 500 person-hours of effort cost $20,000. In my company, experience shows that for every hour of professional effort, four hours of technical support effort are consumed (a parameter), so the proposed project will require 2,000 person-hours of technical effort at $30 per hour ($60,000). Thus labor costs will be an anticipated $80,000. Corporate auditors, who review the financial books carefully each year, have determined that fringe benefits and overhead can be computed by taking direct wages and multiplying them by 1.06 (a parameter). Thus the fringe benefits plus overhead related to this project will amount to $84,800. Total salary-related costs will be $164,800. Note that I had to estimate only one thing: person-hours of professional effort needed to do the job. Once that estimate was made, everything else fell into place.

In addition to the $164,800, we will want to add nonsalary costs to our estimate. Some of these nonsalary costs can be determined parametrically. For example, experience may show us that on a typical project, for each $15,000 of salary-related costs, we spend $1,000 on report reproduction and $800 on travel. Other nonsalary costs may have to be computed according to the specific context of the project. For example, we may have to rent special hardware to create a good platform to develop software that will run on the client's computer system.

The parametric cost-estimating example provided here is very simple. Highly sophisticated parametric cost-estimating models can be developed. One famous model was developed by RCA and is called PRICE. Clients can rent this model to help them perform cost estimates on highly complex projects, such as building a nuclear power plant, installing a telecommunications system, or designing a commercial aircraft. Complex parametric cost-estimating models are made up of hundreds of equations that specify parametric relationships derived from historical data. They have proved to be useful cost-estimating tools.

BOTTOM-UP VERSUS TOP-DOWN ESTIMATES

Which is a better procedure, bottom-up or top-down estimating? The answer, of course, depends on context. Bottom-up estimates require you to develop a detailed WBS. At the earliest stages of a project, this may not be possible since the future is still highly uncertain. It may also be difficult to do this on high-flux development projects. In these cases, estimates may have to be based on a top-down estimating procedure.

Conversely, the building of a detailed WBS is desirable on projects that have been carried out repeatedly. In this case, ample historical data exist, providing project staff with the information they need to construct a good WBS. Large, complex projects also demand WBS-based bottom-up cost estimates. On such projects, there is too much complexity and too much at stake to leave things to chance. Building a detailed WBS on a large project is costly and time-consuming, but the costs of the effort more than offset losses that would be incurred through sloppy planning.

When possible and practical, it might be a good idea to do *both* bottom-up and top-down estimating. One approach can serve as a check on the other. If the resulting estimates are wildly disparate, the estimators had better review their estimates to discover the sources of disparity.

LIFE CYCLE COST ESTIMATING

When I was a boy, my father would occasionally astonish me with some revelation that caught my fancy. Once when we had gone to a drugstore together to purchase a package of razor blades, he took me to the display shelf for razors and showed me the price of different brands. They were all quite inexpensive—somewhere in the range of $2.

"See how cheap these are?" he asked. "The manufacturers sell their razors cheap to get you to buy their product. Where they really make money is in selling you razor blades. So you may pay $2 to buy the razor initially, but over a year you will spend much more than that buying razor blades."

Recently, it has been noted that this same principle is being applied on a grander scale in the selling of automobiles. Automobile dealers today sell new cars at a price that is close to break-even. Where they fatten their profit margins is in after-sales servicing.

We have the same principle at play in the project management arena. Project costs are often small in comparison to postproject operations and maintenance costs. In the software industry, Barry Boehm (1987) has shown that about 70 percent of the money spent on software systems today is directed at maintenance.

Clearly, in pricing something—whether a razor blade or a sophisticated weapons system—cost estimators should take into account the cost over its life. What initially appears to be a low-cost project may turn out to be quite expensive when viewed from a life cycle perspective.

By creating detailed WBSs, project staff can obtain a good sense of what work needs to be done on the project. They can use this information to estimate costs through a bottom-up cost-estimating procedure. Most project staff, however, are unfamiliar with what will happen to the deliverable in the postproject phase. What *are* the key cost elements of operations and maintenance?

Broadly speaking, operations and maintenance costs typically fall into the following seven categories.

Installation

After a deliverable is developed, it frequently must be installed on the customer's premises or in some other appropriate place. For example, a newly developed software system may need to be installed on the customer's mainframe computer, or a telecommunications switching system may need to be installed in the office. Installation can be a project in its own right—it has its tasks, milestones, costs, and specifications. With highly sophisticated systems, the costs of installation can be substantial.

Training

Training costs should not be ignored. To appreciate the costs of training, consider the following example. A client of mine once gleefully recounted to me how he negotiated the price of a scheduling software package (package A) down from $600 per package to $500 per package. The vendor for a competing package (package B) would not come down from its $600 price, so my client decided to purchase ten units of package A.

"I saved $1,000 by going with package A," he chortled.

I smiled at this news. As I smiled, I carried out a quick mental computation of the costs of package A versus package B. From personal experience, I knew that it takes three days of training to get project staff proficient on package A, whereas the training time for package B is two days. At that time, the cost associated with three days of training was about $200 per day per student. The training cost for thirty students being trained on package A would thus be $18,000. The comparable cost for package B would be $12,000, a $6,000 difference. Instead of saving $1,000, my client actually lost $5,000 because of the additional training costs associated with package A. The source of his problem was that he looked only at the shelf price of the product and ignored its life cycle costs.

Repairs

All systems ultimately break down. Sometimes the breakdowns occur because parts wear out. This is a characteristic of mechanical systems. Anyone who has bought or leased a photocopying machine—which has many moving parts—has become well acquainted with photocopy repair service personnel.

Occasionally, the source of breakdowns is embedded in the deliverable—for example, poor design or bug-ridden software. Software that erases a portion of memory each time the F2 key is hit will need to be rewritten.

Preventive Maintenance

When we submit our systems to routine scheduled maintenance, we are undertaking preventive maintenance. We do this, for example, when we take our car for an oil change every 3,000 miles. The purpose of preventive maintenance is to avoid breakdowns by keeping every part of the system functioning effectively.

The impact of preventive maintenance on our life cycle cost estimates will vary dramatically according to the nature of the system we are dealing with. Mechanical systems with many moving parts have a higher need for preventive maintenance than purely electrical systems.

Backup Systems and Disaster Recovery

In many aspects of our lives, we are heavily dependent on the functioning of automated systems to serve us. When the Boeing 767 first came out, pilots quipped that they were now obsolete since the aircraft is almost fully automated. On Wall Street, trading huge volumes of shares per day are made possible through computerized programmed trading. Each day, billions of dollars of transactions are executed between banks through electronic funds transfers. The antilock braking systems of automobiles are computer-controlled.

This dependence on automation has a dark side. What if the computers break down, we lose electric power, or our software is flawed? Will our personal lives or the affairs of our company, community, or country go into a tailspin?

The growing dependence on automated systems has led to a growth industry called *disaster recovery*. Disaster recovery is a risk management approach that is concerned with anticipating problems and developing strategies to cope with them. Consider a bank's concerns about its dependence on computer systems to maintain all of its financial transactions. If an earthquake, fire, flood, software error, or power surge knocks out its main computer system, can the bank continue to operate effectively? What will happen to the billions of dollars of deposits and loans whose records are maintained electronically?

The bank's range of disaster recovery actions varies substantially. At the low-cost end (the "cool site" option), the bank can make an arrangement with other banks to use their facilities in case disaster strikes. This requires that the bank constantly back up crucial data and store the backups in a safe place.

In the mid-cost range (the "warm site" option), the bank can establish the shell of a parallel operation at a separate site. For example, it can rent office space to use in the event of a disaster. Salvaged equipment can be moved to this site, additional equipment rented, and operations resumed.

At the high-cost end (the "hot site"), the bank can continually run a parallel operation at another site. This is the safest option: if disaster hits one site, little is lost because the second site continues to function normally. It is also enormously expensive.

From the perspective of life cycle cost estimating, it is apparent that one cost element that cannot be ignored is the cost of disaster recovery. Even low-cost contingency plans will have a measurable impact on overall costs.

Salaries and Materials Associated with Running the System

Obviously, a major contributor to the life cycle cost of a system is the salaries and material costs associated with running the system. These must be included in the life cycle cost estimate. The material costs include costs of spare parts. With a high-maintenance deliverable (such as a fighter aircraft), these can be considerable—greater, eventually, than the initial cost of the system.

Overhead

Overhead costs include all the indirect costs necessary to keep an operation running, such as electricity, rent, and insurance. Clearly, substantial overhead costs will be incurred in the postproject phase.

STRATEGIES FOR DEALING WITH POOR ESTIMATES

People working on projects often confront situations where they must grapple with the consequences of poor estimates. That is, they find themselves with insufficient resources to do their jobs. The only groups I have encountered that do not routinely struggle with limited resources are those dealing with research and development projects. R&D projects are sufficiently ill-defined that staff can work around resource constraints.

In view of the near inevitability of underbudgeted projects, project staff should develop strategies for dealing with them. The strategies break down into two categories: those designed to avoid bad estimates and those designed to deal with the consequences of bad estimates once the project is under way.

The focus of this chapter until now has been on *avoiding* bad estimates. This can be done by professionalizing the organization's estimating procedures. For example, procedures should be established for developing WBSs and using them to conduct bottom-up estimates. Historical data should be gathered to identify parameters that can be employed in parametric cost estimates. Common estimating pitfalls, such as excessive optimism, political pressures, and poor estimating models, should be recognized and avoided.

Attention now turns to reacting to the consequences of poor estimates. What should be done if it is determined that there are insufficient resources to carry out the job? The course of action to be taken depends on why there are problems, the nature of the project team's relationship with customers, and whether the project is being executed under contract.

First, why are there problems? Is it fundamentally a question of poor execution or of unrealistic estimates at the outset? If the problems reflect poor execution—inexperienced workers, sloppy planning, poor change control—the solution must focus on tightening execution. If they reflect built-in overruns caused by bad estimates, the estimates must be revisited through rebaselining. In either case, if the project is hopelessly bogged down in a cost and schedule quagmire, serious thought must be given to *rescoping*—project management jargon for changing the plan to match reality. It may entail adding additional budget to the project or cutting back on planned tasks (or both).

In trying to understand why problems exist, project staff should determine whether the problems are occurring in a politically charged environment. This is important to know. Political environments are notoriously messy. In such environments, rational solutions are less important than "politically correct" ones. For example, do we find ourselves slipping into a cost overrun situation because our boss has made unrealistic and unachievable promises to customers or upper management? If so, how do we raise the point that the underlying problems have been caused by the actions of a powerful player within our organization? How do we resolve such problems? Questions such as these must be answered in the context of the specific situation. They are always difficult to deal with.

Second, what is the nature of the relationship of the project team to customers? Are the customers kept at arm's length, or are they partners on the project? Is the relationship primarily conflictual or harmonious? Clearly, problems can be worked out best in an environment where the project team and customers pursue common goals and have a good relationship based on mutual trust and understanding. In this case, the developer and the customers will agree to adjustments of schedule, budget, and specifications in order to allow the project to succeed. If the relationship is confrontational, chances are that problems will compound problems. In the worst case, disputes end up in court.

Finally, is the project being carried out under contract? If so, is it a fixed-price or cost-reimbursable contract? With fixed-price contracts, project staff will not receive much sympathy for their problems. A major exception to this rule is when the problems are caused by customers changing project requirements. When this occurs, customers should be charged for their changes and schedules should be updated to reflect the new circumstances.

The whole point of the fixed-price contract is to nail down the requirements for cost, schedule, and specifications at the outset so that they are not subject to continual adjustment. By signing the contract, both buyer and performer agree that a given deliverable will be produced for a specific price and by a specific time according to specific requirements. With such a contract, developers assume the risk of overruns. By the same token, they can capture the benefits of any cost savings that may occur and can translate them into profits.

With a cost-reimbursable contract, project staff find themselves in a more flexible situation. In theory, increased costs in project work can be passed on to the customer. (In practice, spending limitations can be identified, but these do not carry the same weight as the built-in constraints developers feel when they are spending their own money.) There is often a lesser sense of urgency when project staff face cost and schedule problems under a cost-reimbursable contract.

Following are some specific strategies that can be pursued when a project team finds that, owing to estimation problems, it lacks sufficient resources to perform effectively.

Use Data to Illustrate the Problem of Lack of Resources

I call this the intellectual approach. Data and logic can be employed to demonstrate to the powers who control resources that there simply are not enough resources to do the job—that project staff cannot create a silk purse out of a sow's ear. If a convincing argument is made, the resource powers may free up additional resources for the project or may agree to pare back on project requirements.

An excellent tool for illustrating resource limitations graphically is the resource-loading chart, also called the resource histogram. I once worked with a company that was misestimating budgets and schedules by 20–50 percent. I worked with the staff to identify how people's time was committed over the next three-month period. I then plotted the data on a resource-loading chart. The results are shown in Figure 10.1.

This chart clearly shows one explanation for this organization's horrendously poor time and cost estimates: their resource commitments on projects far exceeded their resource capacity. In the case of one resource—a statistician—his time was being allocated to projects as if he could do the work of three people. Of course, he could not. Failure was programmed into his projects.

An interesting aside in this case is that the statistician was largely to blame for the overcommitment of his time. He was unable to say no to requests from various project managers who needed his skills

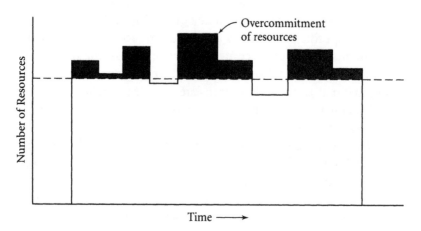

Figure 10.1. Using the Resource-Loading Chart
to Highlight Resource Insufficiency.

because he did not want to disappoint his colleagues. Of course, this short-term desire to please colleagues led to long-term disenchantment with his performance when colleague after colleague found their projects stymied by bottlenecks created by the statistician.

The director of projects in this organization was astonished by the data pictured in the loading charts for all the company's resources. She used the charts in a briefing to upper management. They were equally amazed and immediately increased the budgets for project activities.

Unfortunately, in a politically charged atmosphere, the intellectual approach can fall on deaf ears. In this situation, appeals to rationality may not be effective.

Strengthen Change Control Procedures

Anyone who works in the construction industry knows that a major source of profits comes from change orders. Even fixed-price contracts won through a low-bid process can be quite profitable if change orders are tracked carefully. For example, if the customer wants an electrical outlet moved 18 inches to the left of where it appears in the engineering drawings, the contractor can make the change but will charge handsomely for it. Ultimately, the nickels and dimes add up to fat margins.

The experience of the construction industry suggests that tightened change control procedures may be a significant means to get an underresourced project on track. One problem with this approach is that it may alienate customers, who begin to see the developer as a skinflint who is intent on extracting every penny possible from them.

Prioritize Goals

Project staff members who find themselves overcommitted by 30, 60, 100 percent or more must face a cold reality: they are not going to get all their work done! In the long run, they are put in an untenable situation, and something's got to give. This requires long-term solutions such as increasing staff or reducing workload. In the short run, however, project workers and their immediate managers have got to determine how to handle their efforts over the next month or two. Probably the worst thing they can do is to run helter-skelter from assignment to assignment, plugging leaks. Such an approach will ensure that nothing is brought to a satisfactory conclusion.

What they should do is make some hard decisions revolving around the question of which goals are worth achieving now and which should be abandoned, either temporarily or permanently. In other words, they should establish priorities.

Chapter Nine offers a broad array of approaches to establishing priorities. The approach suggested here is quite simple: employ Pareto's 80-20 rule, which states that most of the problems or opportunities we face (say, 80 percent) are attributable to a small number of causes (say, 20 percent). The rule is employed frequently in quality control. Quality managers are instructed not to expend their energies trying to locate all quality problems but rather to focus their efforts on identifying the core problems that contribute to the majority of problems.

By the same token, project staff who find themselves under-resourced should direct their efforts to high-impact activities. They should systematically identify the 20 percent of actions that can contribute to 80 percent of progress on the project. They should then concentrate on working on these and temporarily ignore low-impact actions. Obviously, what constitutes high-impact and low-impact actions must be determined in the specific context.

CONCLUSIONS

A substantial portion of schedule slippages and cost overruns are rooted in poor estimates of what it will take to do a job. Some of these bad estimates are a result of ineptitude in estimating budgets and schedules. The people making the estimates don't know what they are doing. Others are a consequence of project players—particularly upper management and sales staff—making promises that are unrealistic. Still others are the results of conscious attempts to lowball: offer to do a job for less than cost in order to get the business.

Bad estimates ultimately create problems for the organization. Consistently bad estimates can even lead to bankruptcy as the organization struggles with a string of damaging cost overruns. One unfair consequence of poor estimation is that as project teams incur schedule slippages and cost overruns, the problems are attributed to poor execution, and team members are blamed for their incompetence when in fact these problems are a product of poor estimation.

For organizations to carry out projects effectively, they must estimate as accurately as possible what it takes to get the job done. Through careful estimation, they will spot projects that are likely to be profitable as well as those that will lead to trouble.

CHAPTER ELEVEN

Scheduling Projects with New Tools

The Time-Boxed and Critical Chain Scheduling Techniques

T he explosive growth of Internet usage in the late 1990s and early 2000s led to the coinage of a new term: *Internet time.* This term conveys the sense that in today's era of instant communication, traditional views about time have grown obsolete, if not in ordinary day-to-day life, then in business life. *Faster, faster,* and *faster* are the operative words in business today. It has become common wisdom that the single greatest competitive advantage a company can have is *speed.* In new product development, products that would take six months to transform from concept to market introduction a decade ago are expected to get to market in three months or less. Turnaround time for responses to customer requests is now expected to be nearly instantaneous.

Project management also faces these time pressures. One of the struggles we face on our projects today is that to meet customer expectations, salespeople are promising to deliver in six months jobs that normally take ten months. Of course, this can lead to serious problems when the project team fails to meet its six-month promise date.

In this chapter, we examine two approaches to dealing with schedule pressures on projects. The first, *time-boxed scheduling*, is an approach geared toward cranking out deliverables with astonishingly short lead times. It performs scheduling miracles by forcing customers and developers to recognize that if you want to produce results quickly, you need to reexamine your deliverables and cut out time-consuming features that add little value to the final product.

The second, *critical chain scheduling*, is an approach to scheduling projects that requires us to identify and remove inefficiencies that lead to schedule delays. Its precepts have been taken from manufacturing, where production processes are highly controlled, and applied to the domain of project management, where they are not.

TIME-BOXED SCHEDULING

In the autumn of 1999, a manager at a software company related the following story to me. He was contracted by an on-line stock trading company to produce a software routine that would enable clients to conduct Internet trades using wireless palm computers. His team reckoned that it should take six months to do the job. The problem was that the stock trading company, concerned about competition from other trading companies, insisted that the supplier produce the software in four weeks! At first, this appeared to be an impossible chore. But by using time-boxed scheduling, the software company was able to supply a functioning deliverable in four weeks.

Aficionados of magic shows know that tigers do not really appear out of thin air on stage and that the magician's assistant is not really being sawed in half. These acts are illusions. The same holds for scheduling miracles on projects. There is no way that you can carry out a six-month job in four weeks. With time-boxed scheduling, we are not pulling rabbits out of hats, although it may appear that way. We are, in a certain measure, creating an illusion. Our achievement of meeting impossible schedules is a consequence of cutting back on the original requirements. The underlying premise is, you can't have it all. The trick is to prioritize the functions the deliverable is to perform and to toss out those with low priority.

Thus the key to time-boxed scheduling is prioritization. As we will now see, agreeing on priorities can be difficult.

PRIORITIZING

There are a range of players that play some role on a typical project: the project sponsor, the project manager, team members, a contracting specialist, subject matter experts, contractors, the purchasing department, sales staff, outsourced workers, and an assortment of players on the client side, including the client's representative, users, middle and senior management, client subject matter experts, and so on. Each of these players has his or her own view on what the project should produce. For the purposes of this discussion, we will divide the key players into two categories: users and developers. Although this oversimplifies the typical project environment, it enables us to focus on the principal features of time-boxed scheduling without getting bogged down in extraneous details.

Users and developers are concerned with different things. Consequently, they hold different perspectives on what is important. Users are primarily concerned with the *features* and *usability* of the deliverable. They focus on what it will do and what it takes to operate and maintain it. They want it to do as much as possible, and they want it to be easy to operate and maintain. They also want the deliverable to be delivered as soon as possible.

Developers, in contrast, are primarily concerned with the *functions* that need to be addressed in order to enable the deliverable to operate effectively. Their attention is directed primarily to the technical issues that must be resolved to provide the features and operability that the users want. Their concerns should not be surprising in view of the fact that they are charged with building the deliverable. Temperamentally, they are oriented toward quality and technical perfection. They do not like shortcuts.

When the chief concerns of these two categories of players are compared, it becomes obvious that they have little in common and that getting them to agree on priorities can be tricky. While users insist that a deliverable be produced in an impossibly short time frame, they are reluctant to drop any desired features in order to make the time frame realistic. Meanwhile, the developers resist cutting corners to speed their work, arguing that such action would compromise the technical integrity and quality of the deliverable. So we find ourselves facing a standoff.

Time-boxed scheduling recognizes that it is not easy to get people who hold different points of view to agree on a uniform set of priorities.

Consequently, it directs its attention to enabling disparate groups to come to an agreement on priorities. It requires first-rate small group facilitation skills in order to achieve the needed agreement.

Following are the basic principles of implementing a time-boxed approach to scheduling project work.

BRINGING PERTINENT PLAYERS TOGETHER

At the outset of the time-boxed scheduling process, a facilitator needs to bring key players together in a meeting. This entails bringing together principal customers and technical staff. Others may be included as appropriate.

The primary objective of this kickoff meeting is to establish a realistic sense of what needs to be done if the project is to achieve its aggressive deadlines. The parties must be made to recognize that they are partners in the endeavor. This means that they must work together to achieve the desired results. Customers should be willing to give up some attractive features that they would like to have included in the deliverable, and developers should be willing to create less-than-perfect technical solutions. The central point that both partners must recognize is, you can't have it all.

Clearly, it takes good facilitation skills to get stakeholders to surrender some of what they want for the sake of the project. In general, when seeking compromise, we strive to orient the players toward win-win situations. The philosophy is that if everyone gives a little, we all gain a lot. However, if approached improperly, the quest for compromise may lead to a sense of lose-lose: we all give up something, and none of us gains. Clearly, a good facilitator will always strive to create a win-win perspective and to avoid a lose-lose one.

Customers and developers can be motivated to work together as partners in many ways; four will be suggested here to provide examples of what group facilitation requires at this point.

• *Explain that rational decision-making is based on prioritization.* When the group first assembles and details have not yet been discussed, it is desirable to explain some "theory" of group decision making to the assembled players so that they will understand the prioritization process central to time-boxed scheduling. The point to be made is that all rational decision making is based on prioritization. With prioritization, we rank the alternatives so that the most attractive ones rise to the top of the list and the least attractive ones sink to the bottom. In the end, we choose the alternatives from the top of the list.

This process of prioritization underlies all rational decision making, from deciding what soup to buy at the supermarket to selecting a contractor to build a new house. Consequently, it becomes apparent that effective decision making should have systematic attempts to prioritize built into the decision-making process. Over the years, many tools have emerged to assist in the prioritization process. For decades, engineers have used benefit-cost assessments to help them rank alternatives. Financiers use a variety of tools, such as internal rate of return (IRR) measures. Scientists dealing with basic research projects have focused on subjective prioritization techniques, such as peer review.

• *Explain that time-boxed scheduling requires customer-developer partnering.* To carry out time-boxed scheduling effectively, customers and developers must work together as partners. Traditionally, the customer-developer relationship has been viewed as "us versus them." Customers view developers as too narrowly focused on impractical technical considerations, and developers often regard customers as technically naïve, unfocused, and fickle. Such outlooks create a breeding ground for conflict. It establishes a zero-sum game mentality, which holds that the only way I can win is if you lose.

In contrast to the traditional perspective, a partnering relationship demands that the players work together to achieve their common goals. It is based on a positive-sum (win-win) strategy. For this to occur, each side must respect the views of the other side, and both sides must be willing to give a little in order to gain a lot.

What this boils down to is that customers must recognize that if they want a deliverable delivered early, they must be willing to cut out some of the features they desire. Similarly, the development team must realize that it will have to live with less-than-perfect technical solutions. As partners, both sides must acknowledge that it is not helpful if each sticks to its guns and demands that it get all that it desires.

During these early sessions, each side should be encouraged to raise its concerns before the other side. It is important that each side fully understands the viewpoint of the other side and appreciates why the other side takes the position it does. If carried out properly, this attempt at communication will avert many of the frustrations that would otherwise arise.

- *Excite customers by letting them see that they have a lot to gain and little to lose with time-boxed scheduling.* When customers are asked to prioritize the features they would like to have contained in the deliverable, they may become nervous that too many desirable features will be sacrificed in the interest of quick development. They should be assured that features that are cut out today can be added to future versions of the deliverable. For example, consider the situation where customers want the developer to create a product that has six key features embedded in it. Let's say that normal development time for this product would be six months. With time-boxed scheduling, we may ask the customers to drop four features so that we can produce a deliverable in two months. Two of the dropped features can be added to version 2, which can be delivered by month 4, and the last two features can be added to version 3, which can be delivered by the end of month 6. It is possible, then, for the customers to get everything they desire within a six-month time frame. The advantage with the time-boxed approach is that they will realize viable products earlier than with a traditional development approach.

- *Coach developers to see that good enough is good enough.* The 1978 Nobel Prize winner for economics, Herbert Simon of Carnegie-Mellon University, is perhaps best known for his concept of *satisficing.* Simon showed that in searching for a solution to a problem, the moment a good enough solution is found, it should be adopted and the search should stop. The technical team members of the time-boxed team should be made to see that doing a six-month job in four weeks is an exciting challenge—a challenge that will be met only if the team members are willing to live with good enough solutions. They should recognize that "good enough" is not a synonym for "second rate."

PRIORITIZATION DIMENSIONS

Prioritization must occur along a number of different dimensions. Four are identified here: the marketing, financial, technical, and political dimensions.

Marketing Dimension

As everyone knows who has taken an introduction to marketing course, marketing efforts can be defined by the "four P's": product, price, place, and promotion. Each of these must be taken into account when prioritizing features for inclusion in the deliverable. The most important for time-boxed scheduling is *product:* What features should be included in a scaled-down product that would be most attractive to buying consumers? Beyond the four P's, an important marketing driver is timing—a significant rationale for doing the job at breakneck speed is to get to market quickly to beat out the competition and gain market share. By focusing on the fact that it is crucial that the deliverable be produced quickly, we have a great stick to employ on both customers and developers on the time-box team whose intransigence is slowing down the development effort. If either start dragging their feet, we can remind them that they may cause the initiative to fail if they don't help us meet our deadlines.

Financial Dimension

In designing a product or service, we typically face a range of options that we can pursue, and we should recognize that different options have different financial implications, from the perspectives of potential revenue and costs. When considering what features to include in and exclude from the time-boxed deliverable, pertinent financial issues must be taken into account.

Technical Dimension

The technical dimension is a difficult one to work with because in developing a product or service, certain technical realities must be addressed, and they may defy shortcuts. For example, if a software solution must be developed for the ABC operating system, and the resulting deliverable must be designed around an XYZ protocol, we face severe technical constraints on what we need to contend with in designing and building our time-boxed deliverable. If core technical requirements are not met—as constrained by the operating system and protocol—the deliverable has no value.

Having said this, we should recognize that there are many technical choices that can be made that *are not seriously constrained* by technical requirements. These nonessential technical features need to be identified and prioritized. Those that are considered high-priority can be incorporated into the time-boxed solution, while those that are not can be put aside.

Political Dimension

All organizational decision making has a political component because it entails working with different stakeholders who have different views on how things should be done. In most instances, the time-box team needs to weigh the perspectives of the different players and accommodate them in whatever ways make sense. In cases where the stakeholders are powerful and insistent on having their way prevail, their opinions hold substantial weight. For example, if the director of marketing says, "The new product *will* be colored green," the time-boxed team does not need to spend time debating what color to make the deliverable; it will be green.

The time-box team should recognize that the prioritization effort will be difficult. One reason is that we are prioritizing not only *within* the marketing, finance, technical, and political dimensions but *across* them as well. For example, there will be many occasions when the team will need to consider trade-offs between the marketing and technical dimensions—to achieve a particular marketing goal may require making technical compromises. Do we really want to make these compromises?

TECHNIQUES FOR PRIORITIZATION

As Chapter Nine made clear, rational decision making is basically a process of prioritization. Whether our decisions are based on benefit-cost ratios, the poor man's hierarchy, scoring sheets, peer review, or Buss's technique, we are really engaged in the same process: we are ranking alternatives such that the most attractive go to the top of the list while the least attractive sink to the bottom.

All of the techniques discussed in Chapter Nine can be usefully employed in time-boxed scheduling. I find that the employment of the poor man's hierarchy is especially helpful in getting a group of people to sort through a list of alternatives quickly and intelligently. I also favor the use of scoring sheets, because they not only prioritize the alternatives but also show the degree of consensus the decision makers have in making their judgments.

With time-boxed scheduling, an additional prioritization technique warrants consideration: the 80-20 rule or Pareto rule, named after the Italian economist who developed it, Wilfredo Pareto. What the 80-20 rule does, as noted in Chapter Ten, is focus on a small number of items that have a big impact. For example, this rule is used heavily in sales management, where it recognizes that 20 percent of a company's clients may generate 80 percent of the company's revenue. (Conclusion: keep those 20 percent of the customers happy!) It is also employed in quality management, where 80 percent of quality problems are tied to 20 percent of the potential sources of problems. (Conclusion: you don't need to fix all the problems—just focus on correcting the small number of problem sources that have the greatest impact.)

The 80-20 rule applies to time-boxed scheduling in the following way: you can't deliver all the desired features in a compressed time frame, so address only the handful of features that have the highest impact. Features that are excluded from this version can be included in a future version. By adopting this approach, the deliverable is broken down into manageable portions that can be achieved in short time frames.

Note that the 80-20 rule should not be employed in a literal fashion. No one is saying that exactly 20 percent of the features contribute to exactly 80 percent of a deliverable's functionality. The focus should simply be on identifying a reasonably small number of high-impact features that can be developed in a compressed period of time.

THE USE OF PARALLEL DEVELOPMENT

Prioritization—based on the premise that you can't have it all—is certainly a cornerstone of time-boxed scheduling. But schedules can also be accelerated by using brute force—doing more work in a fixed period of time than you normally would schedule. This can be achieved by carrying out work in parallel to as great an extent as possible. For example, a work crew that is charged with rehabilitating a meeting room in a hotel may be able to get the job done more quickly than normal by having carpet layers lay down carpet even as ceiling tile workers install the ceiling. The safest way to do the job would be to have the ceiling tile workers do their tasks first. Any detritus that falls to the ground can be swept up, and then the carpet layers can be brought in. However, if the project is operating with tight deadlines, having both crews work concurrently can save time.

The example of rehabilitating a hotel room illustrates a feature of parallel development that project managers must keep in mind: parallel development can elevate levels of technical risk. In the hotel room example, the primary technical risk is that trash falling from the ceiling might soil the newly laid carpet. So why are we willing to incur risk? Because there may be another risk associated with slow delivery of a deliverable—a business risk: our contract might stipulate that if we deliver the room early, we win a $5,000 bonus. If we deliver late, we lose the bonus. A quick trade-off analysis may show that the cleaning bill for a soiled carpet would not exceed $500, which means that in the worst-case scenario, we would gain $4,500 by doing the work in parallel in order to deliver the hotel room early. In this specific instance, the argument favoring parallel development is compelling.

SCHEDULING REALITIES

In the heat of a time-boxed scheduling effort, it is tempting to bypass formal scheduling discipline because scheduling takes time and the goal with time-boxed scheduling is to save time. However, circumventing formal scheduling procedures would be dangerous. In fact, use of a formal schedule in the form of a PERT/CPM network diagram may provide the information that is needed to identify which work can be carried out in parallel and which cannot. In addition, this network diagram can enable the project team to carry out a series of "what if" analyses to determine the scheduling implications of different configurations of work. What if task X were carried out in parallel with task Y—could that speed up work? What if extra resources were used on task Z—could that speed up work as well?

THE NEED FOR DISCIPLINE

Not only is there a need for scheduling discipline, but there is a need for discipline in two other areas as well: documentation and change control. Each of these will be discussed in turn.

Discipline of Documentation

It is important that projects scheduled with the time-boxed technique maintain good documentation in a variety of areas, including the technical, financial, resource utilization, requirements, and scheduling aspects. The documentation serves a number of functions. First, the documentation enables the team to trace the steps taken in carrying out the project—technical decisions that have been implemented, money that has been spent, people that have been employed, requirements that have been addressed, and milestones that have been achieved. In addition, the documentation identifies who authorized which actions, heightening decision-making accountability. In a sense, the documentation provides a history of the work effort. If any questions arise as to what has been accomplished or if disputes occur as to whether promises have been kept, the documentation can be used to resolve the questions authoritatively.

Second, a well-documented effort provides data to establish project baselines that can be used in the planning of future projects. Once project data have been recorded, the following types of questions can be raised and answered: How long does it actually take to conduct a certain type of test? How many employees are actually used to design a particular category of product? How much does it really cost to conduct a customer review? Thanks to the existence of baseline data, project planners can plan resource and time requirements more accurately.

Third, good documentation is necessary to provide operations and maintenance people with the information they need to run and maintain systems. If a ceiling light stops functioning and replacement light bulbs do not work, it is helpful to have access to a wiring diagram (documentation) to diagnose and fix the source of the problem.

Discipline of Change Control

One particularly appropriate form of documentation on all projects— time-boxed or conventional—is change control documentation. A predictable reality is that as a project is being carried out, changes to the authorized requirements will occur. (See Chapter Three for a detailed treatment of change control.) New features will be added, and others will be dropped. The driving forces behind the changes are legion. For example, key players may change (senior managers, technical team members, customers), and the new players will pursue an agenda that is different from that of their predecessors. Budgets change—money that was earmarked for project use might suddenly be withdrawn. Technology is continually changing—new technologies may be viewed as irresistible, and pressure to incorporate them into the deliverable may grow. The business environment experiences change—what was a compelling feature at the outset of the project is now regarded as a white elephant. People simply change their minds— at the outset of the project, the requirements they agreed to were abstractions written on paper, but when they see what they are actually getting, they may ask for additions or deletions.

The key point here is that change to requirements is inevitable. Given this reality, is the project operating under a regime of well-defined change control processes? Are change requests documented and systematically reviewed? Without a rigorous review process that challenges change requests, the project is likely to encounter scope creep. Are change requests entered into some sort of database so that the organization has an easily retrieved record of change actions implemented on the project? This information is crucial for future maintenance of the deliverable. It is also important to have in the event of legal disputes between customers and developers, when one party maintains that the other did not meet its contractual obligations.

Change control is needed on all projects. What makes it difficult on time-boxed projects is that owing to the hectic pace of work that is being carried out, it is tempting to bypass change control processes because they are regarded as bureaucratic impediments that retard progress. Although the concern that lies behind this sentiment is understandable, lack of systematic change control will ultimately haunt the time-boxed project. The team may produce a fantastic deliverable in record time, but the lack of documentation on how the deliverable was developed may lead to serious technical and legal problems later.

The trick is to create a change control process that is nonbureaucratic and easy to implement. Is it really necessary to have all change requests reported on a five-page form? Can't a one-page form do the trick? Do all change requests need to be reviewed by a formal change control board (CCB) comprised of senior managers? Can't a core group of three or four qualified people be tasked to review and judge change requests in a matter of minutes? As far as paperwork goes, it is important on time-boxed projects that administrative support be made available to handle this end of the business. It does not make sense to have project team members spending a third of their time dealing with administrative issues, particularly when they are operating under pressure to crank out deliverables as quickly as possible.

CRITICAL CHAIN SCHEDULING

Perhaps the single most famous tool in the project manager's tool box is the PERT/CPM network diagramming technique. The technique has undergone modifications over the years, and it is currently referred to as the *precedence diagram method* (PDM). The original PERT (program evaluation review technique) and CPM (critical path method) were developed in the late 1950s by the U.S. Navy and Du Pont Corporation, respectively. They reflected attempts by engineers engaged in project efforts to employ newly developed flowcharting techniques that were a spin-off of recent advances in systems engineering.

PERT/CPM became a valuable scheduling tool. Its value was rooted in a number of factors. First, to create a PERT/CPM network, a project team needed to engage in scheduling discipline. Tasks needed to be identified, durations estimated, and the relationships of the tasks to each other understood. One cannot create meaningful PERT/CPM networks in an ad hoc fashion. This scheduling discipline was salubrious because it required project workers to understand thoroughly the steps that needed to be taken to implement their projects.

Second, once a PERT/CPM network was created, it could serve as a mathematical model of the project because computerized PERT/CPM software routines linked cost and resource utilization data to the scheduling data. Consequently, the PERT/CPM network could be employed to address important "what if" questions. For example, what if I add five more resources to task A? What impact will this have on the project delivery date? What impact will it have on the project budget? What if the introduction of new government regulations requires us to slip task B by two weeks? Will this affect the final delivery date for the project? Will this require me to use more human resources to maintain my schedule? If so, how many new resources should I add to the project?

Third, the PERT/CPM approach was the principal approach estimators could employ to estimate the duration of projects. The duration could be derived by identifying the *critical path,* which is the longest path of linked tasks in the PERT/CPM network. By identifying the critical path, schedulers had a way of identifying which tasks needed to be monitored closely in order to avoid schedule slippages and which tasks needed to be adjusted in order to accelerate the project schedule.

The PERT/CPM approach served project managers well over a period of several decades. It remains the core scheduling technique used in project management today, and this turns out to cause a bit of a problem. To appreciate the nature of the problem, look at the simple PERT/CPM network diagram pictured in Figure 11.1. This chart shows a simple four-task project, where task B (a five-day effort)

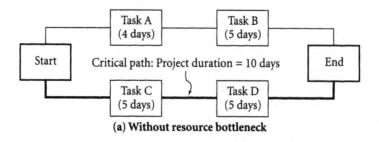

(a) Without resource bottleneck

Owing to resource constraints, the resource for Task B cannot
begin work on Task B until the beginning of Day 8.

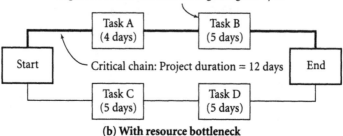

(b) With resource bottleneck

Figure 11.1. PERT/CPM and Resource Bottlenecks.

succeeds task A (a four-day effort) on the top path and task D (a five-
day effort) succeeds task C (a five-day effort) on the bottom path. A
quick review of the chart identifies the bottom path as the critical
path; the pictured project will therefore take ten days to carry out if
the plan is achieved.

To see the weakness of the PERT/CPM network, consider the most
basic information needed to create one. The creation of a PERT/CPM
network requires three basic pieces of information:

1. What tasks will be carried out?

2. What is the duration of each task?

3. How are these tasks linked?

Note that to create a PERT/CPM network, you do not need to address
resource issues directly. You deal with them indirectly (that is, you need
to have some sense of resource availability to estimate task durations),
but there is no express requirement that they be handled explicitly.

The reason why this is a serious problem is that project bottlenecks typically center on resources: Do we have the right skill sets assigned to the project? Do we have the right quantity of qualified resources? Are they available during the time we need them? Are the resources that are assigned to the project first-rate, or is the project stuck with deadwood?

Consider Figure 11.1 once again. Let's say that an investigation reveals that the resource scheduled to carry out task B will not be available to begin the job until the morning of day 8. However, the internal logic of the PERT/CPM chart suggests that this resource must be available no later than the start of day 6, or else the ten-day schedule will slip. Because of this resource constraint, the project cannot end earlier than the end of day 12, although the original PERT/CPM chart suggests that it will be finished at the end of day 10. If our contract is written on the basis of information supplied by the original PERT/CPM chart (Figure 11.1), we are contracted to do the job in ten days. Yet we have just seen that owing to a resource bottleneck, we will default on our contractual obligation by two days. The true critical path is not the ten-day bottom path but rather the twelve-day top path. A critical path that explicitly factors in bottlenecks (such as resource availability) is called a *critical chain*.

THE CRITICAL CHAIN AND THE THEORY OF CONSTRAINTS

The critical chain concept was developed by Eliyahu Goldratt. The name itself addresses two important notions. The word *critical* is taken from *critical path*, which defines the length of a project. The word *chain* is taken from the old adage that a chain is only as strong as its weakest link. It reflects the fact that project schedules must capture resource and other bottlenecks if they are going to be realistic. Taken together, *critical chain* suggests that we incorporate the realities of resource and other bottlenecks into our critical path reasoning. The critical chain concept does not discard the critical path idea. Rather, it enhances it by making it more realistic.

Goldratt came to project scheduling from the manufacturing arena. Manufacturing processes are well defined. To produce a manufactured good requires that the good pass through a number of clearly defined steps. For example, to build a metal box, a piece of sheet metal must be cut to the appropriate dimensions (station 1), then it must be bent (station 2), then the edges must be sealed (station 3), and then the resulting box must be conveyed to a storage bin where it can be accessed later. If the box is designed to have a handle, a bar of metal must be cut to the appropriate length (station 20), bent to the appropriate dimensions (station 21), and then brought together with the completed box so that it can be affixed to it (station 22).

The significance of bottlenecks is well understood in manufacturing. If supplies of sheet metal are delayed in arriving at station 1, the production of boxes will be delayed as well. If the handle-bending machine is producing defective handles one time out of every five, this will also lead to production delays. Goldratt and Jeff Cox summarized the effects of bottlenecks on manufacturing process in a best-selling book titled *The Goal* (1992). They gave their perspective the high-sounding name *theory of constraints* (TOC).

The chief message of TOC is that if you have a process that is troubled, you do not need to fix the whole system. Simply fix the bottlenecks, since they are the immediate cause of the system's suboptimal performance. For example, if delays in the production of metal boxes are triggered by the tardy arrival of pieces of sheet metal at station 1, you don't need to improve metal-bending processes. Instead, focus on getting the pieces of sheet metal to station 1 on time.

While this TOC message may appear self-evident, in the real world it is not, because the complexity of the processes we work with often hides the sources of bottlenecks. To get a system up to speed, it is tempting to fix everything in a shotgun fashion in the hope that through this approach the system's performance will improve. An obvious problem with the shotgun approach is that substantial amounts of money may be wasted fixing things that are not contributing to the problems. The key value of the TOC perspective is that it offers guidance on how to identify and deal with nonobvious bottlenecks.

In *Critical Chain* (1997), Goldratt extends the TOC view to project management. Goldratt contends that the problem with traditional project scheduling is that it does not address bottlenecks but is carried out mechanically through PERT/CPM-style networks, where attention focuses on identifying tasks, computing estimated task durations, and working out the dependence relationships among tasks. Invariably, Goldratt maintains, this approach produces results that lead to schedule slippages.

The following real-world example illustrates how bottlenecks must be identified and fixed to improve project performance.

THE EUROPHARM EXPERIENCE

EuroPharm is a European pharmaceutical company that has recently begun operations in the United States. It is attempting to introduce five drugs into the U.S. market. Before these drugs can be sold in the United States, however, they need to receive approval from the Food and Drug Administration (FDA). This means that the drugs need to go through several years of animal testing and clinical trials.

Dr. Maria Contini is the project director charged with getting the five drugs approved by the FDA. By the time EuroPharm had been operating in the United States for two years, senior management at headquarters in Europe was growing concerned that all of the projects were consistently missing key milestones that needed to be achieved before FDA approval could be granted. Senior management began pressuring Contini to start meeting milestone deadlines, because each day of delay in obtaining FDA approval was costing the company hundreds of thousands of dollars in lost income.

Contini met with her staff, and they concluded that they were missing deadlines because EuroPharm's U.S. employees lacked good planning and implementation skills. So all of EuroPharm's U.S. employees were put through a project management training program during a six-month period. Regrettably, this training had no impact in improving the delivery of project results. EuroPharm's U.S. operations continued to miss key milestones.

Contini was replaced by Eugenia Pascal, a marketing specialist. Upon arriving in the United States, she immediately reviewed the processes by which EuroPharm was carrying out its FDA approval projects. Within a week, she determined that project delays were tied to insufficient staffing of statisticians charged with reviewing data from the animal and clinical trials. Medical data were backing up in the statisticians' office. Meanwhile, clinical staff were underemployed as they awaited the results of the statistical reviews. The statisticians were the bottleneck. Pascal doubled the number of statisticians, the backlog disappeared, and schedule performance improved dramatically.

This case clearly illustrates the points made by TOC: to improve project performance, you need to identify and fix the bottlenecks.

THE CRITICAL CHAIN PERSPECTIVE AND THE PSYCHOLOGY OF ESTIMATING TASK DURATIONS

One of the most attractive features of the critical chain approach is that it deals with task scheduling from a psychological perspective. It raises a basic question: Why is it that project workers often take longer to do a job than they estimate, *even after they supply estimates that are heavily padded?* If they say it will take five days to do a job, they do it in six days. If for the exact same job they say it will take six days, they take seven days. What's going on here?

The critical chain perspective holds that a number of forces are at work here, most prominently the existence of Parkinson's Law. Parkinson's Law states that "work expands to fill the time available to carry it out." So if you allocate five days to do a job, it will take you *at least* five days, and if you had allocated six days for the job, it would take *at least six days.* The implications of Parkinson's Law for estimating task durations are profound: even though project workers pad their estimates of task duration so as to provide enough time to ensure that they can meet their deadlines, *they still will encounter schedule pressures and will often miss their deadlines!*

The critical chain perspective offers several explanations for the prevalence of Parkinson's Law in estimating task durations, including the following:

- *The student syndrome.* The term *student syndrome* refers to the tendency of students to hold off doing their assignments until the last minute. When they finally get to their assignments, they see that they have not allotted enough time to do the job right. So they stay up all night working on the assignments in order to meet their class deadlines. Many project workers suffer from the student syndrome.

- *Lack of pressure to perform.* When substantial padding has been added to an estimate of task duration, it seems as if there is plenty of time to do the job. Consequently, project workers do not approach the effort with much urgency. They are easily sidetracked or approach their work casually. However, the clock ticks on, and a point is often reached—a point of no return, as it were—when the project workers realize that not enough time remains to finish the job by the promised date. At this point, they panic and work at a frenetic pace. If they are fortunate, their last-minute forward surge enables them to meet the deadline. If they are not, they encounter schedule slippage. Notice that in both cases, they have used up all their allotted time to do the job, just as Parkinson's Law predicts.

- *The need to look busy.* The TOC perspective supports the view that in our jobs, the nature of the work effort dictates that we will be busier at some times than at others. For example, consider the lives of a crew of three men who are moving office furniture from one building to another, located five miles away. They arrive at the first site at

8:00 A.M. and immediately begin loading furniture onto dollies, transporting the furniture to the ground floor on a freight elevator, and loading the furniture into a large van. As they wait for the elevator, they are not occupied with work. There is nothing for them to do until the elevator finally arrives. Later, after the van is fully loaded, the workers climb into the cab of the truck for the trip to the second site, where the furniture will be unloaded. During the trip, which takes half an hour in traffic, only one worker—the driver—is actively engaged in work. The other two are idle. No one expects them to be busy because at this moment they have nothing to do. Once they arrive at the second site, they immediately commence unloading furniture from the van, and their work efforts resume.

The TOC perspective holds that project workers are expected to be continually busy, even if there is no work for them to do. If during the course of a day they have a short reprieve from chores (analogous to the movers riding in the van), they are not permitted to take a break but must look busy. This mentality pervades business life, with the result that in order to *look* busy, many workers stretch out their tasks so that they take longer to accomplish than truly necessary.

• *Lack of incentives for early completion of work.* Strange as it may seem, few organizations reward people for completing their assignments early. In fact, early completion of work may lead to hostile responses from coworkers because the recipients of the deliverable are unprepared to receive it. For example, if a shipment of goods is delivered to a loading dock early, it may be rejected because the receiving organization has nowhere to store the goods.

The bias against completing work early was reinforced with the advent of the just-in-time (JIT) philosophy in the 1980s. JIT holds that to minimize our need to carry inventory, we should insist that our suppliers provide us with the materials we need just moments before we need them. Early shipment is discouraged because it increases our inventory burden; late shipment is bad because it causes delays in producing our goods. Our supplies should arrive at precisely the moment we need them—not earlier, not later.

A little reflection suggests that the JIT perspective promotes last-minute behavior: we should finish our tasks at the last possible moment, supporting a scenario where work expands to fill the time available.

• *Multitasking.* While most the world views multitasking in a positive light, the critical chain perspective sees it as an evil. Multitasking refers to the situation that arises when project workers are trying to juggle a half-dozen balls at one time. When they arrive at work in the morning, they may be asked to attend a meeting about sexual harassment on the job. After the meeting, they begin work on their project chores, but this is interrupted by a request from a senior vice president to price out a series of activities that will be included in a bid to gain new contract work. Once this is completed two hours later, they are required to attend a luncheon in honor of an employee who is retiring. After lunch, they return to their project chores, but this effort is interrupted in an hour because they need to attend a kickoff meeting for another project that has recently been assigned to them. And so it goes.

According to the TOC perspective, multitasking hides a multitude of sins. For example, it is the haven of incompetent workers, providing them with excuses for not achieving their performance objectives. When criticized for their poor performance, they can always respond, "What do you expect? Look at how many things I am expected to do at one time!" Also note that when workers are operating in a multitasking environment, all of their chores get stretched out—because they are stretched so thin—with the consequence that the production of results is delayed across the board.

USING BUFFERS TO ACCELERATE PROJECT DELIVERY

As the critical chain perspective makes clear, people tend to pad their estimates of how long it takes to carry out a task in order to give themselves enough time to guarantee they will meet their promise dates. Unfortunately, they tend to consume all the allotted time and even face slippages, owing to Parkinson's Law.

The tendency to add padding task by task dramatically extends project duration beyond what is reasonable. To see this, consider part (a) of Figure 11.2. In this figure, we picture three tasks that are scheduled to be carried out sequentially. Experience shows that each of these tasks can be carried out in three days. However, the project worker adds a day of padding to each task to increase the likelihood that it can be achieved by the promised date. Consequently, the schedule calls for completing the three tasks in twelve days.

Let's say that Parkinson's Law affects each task. Thus the worker takes the full four days to work on each task, but because of the stu-

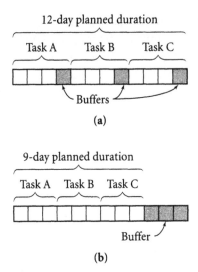

Figure 11.2. Using Buffers to Schedule Activities.

dent syndrome, he needs an extra half-day to complete each of them. So the twelve-day schedule now grows to a 13.5-day schedule. Remember, experience shows that each task can actually be carried out in three days, so in a perfect world, this project should have taken nine days to complete.

The critical chain perspective notes that the flaw in this traditional approach to scheduling is rooted in adding padding to each task. Parkinson's Law suggests that if you give people three days to do a job, they will take at least three days. If you give them four days to complete the same job, they will take at least four days. If you give them five days, they will take at least five days. Rather than add padding task by task, what project schedulers should do is the following: for each task, use reasonable unpadded estimates for task duration, and then add a buffer to deal with slippages at the end of the sequence of activities.

To see why this works, consider part (b) of Figure 11.2. In this case, we estimate that the duration of each task is three days. Since we know from experience that each task can in fact be carried out in three days, we hold our workers to achieving their work in this time frame. Now let's assume that Parkinson's Law is still with us and that each task experiences a half-day slippage. The total slippage is 1.5 days. We can add some buffer to accommodate slippage at the end of the sequence of tasks. This means that the three tasks will be completed in 10.5 days.

The same effort would take 13.5 days when we allow schedulers to add padding task by task. By simply removing a safety buffer from the individual tasks and adding one to the end of the task sequence, we have trimmed three days off the schedule duration!

The critical chain approach offers specific guidance on how to estimate task durations *and project buffers*. The best estimate of task duration is the median time it takes to do the job. The concept of median suggests that half the time the task will take longer than planned and half the time it will take less time than anticipated. Of course, in the real world, we generally do not have data to compute median durations, so what we need to do is estimate what we think is a reasonable, "average" amount of time it will take to do the job.

Project buffers (the buffers you add at the end of the critical chain) can be calculated by estimating how much buffer you would be using if you added padding task by task and then cutting that figure in half.

PROJECT BUFFERS, FEEDER BUFFERS, AND RESOURCE BUFFERS

The critical chain approach employs three sets of buffers. We have just examined the primary buffer, which is called the *project buffer*. As we have seen, the project buffer is used to absorb any slippages that occur on the critical chain.

A second type of buffer is the *feeder buffer*. Feeder buffers are used in conjunction with non–critical chain efforts that feed into the critical chain. Conceivably, a project can experience slippage on a noncritical path that is so pronounced that it causes delays to the critical chain. By introducing feeder buffers, we attempt to minimize on the critical chain the effect of slippages in noncritical streams of activities. These buffers are added at the end of a sequence of activities that feed into the critical chain, just at the point where the noncritical stream of tasks enters the critical chain. The rules for creating feeder buffers are identical to the rules for creating project buffers: estimate task duration as the median time it takes to do a job, and then add a buffer at the end of the sequence of activities.

A third category of buffer is the *resource buffer*. The need for resource buffers reflects the fact that owing to other obligations, people are often not available to do their project work at the time they are scheduled to do it. If they show up late, this may contribute to schedule slippages on the project overall. So with resource buffers, we add some padding to the estimated time of arrival for the resources. Consequently, even if they arrive on the job later than planned, this will not cause delays in the project—provided, of course, that the delays in their arrival are reasonable.

To learn more about the use of buffers and putting together critical chain schedules, see Newbold (1998).

CONCLUSIONS

The development of new approaches to scheduling project efforts demonstrates that we are moving beyond slavish adherence to the venerable PERT/CPM technique. A feature that distinguishes the new approaches from traditional ones is their consideration of psychological and other practical factors in scheduling. As we have seen, PERT/CPM takes a mechanical view of scheduling, requiring us only to identify tasks, their durations, and their linkages to each other. The new approaches go beyond this. For example, time-boxed scheduling has customers and developers sitting together, *negotiating* priorities with a view to accelerating the project's schedule. An important premise of critical chain scheduling is that Parkinson's Law—the propensity of people to consume whatever time is given them to do a job—must be factored into any intelligent estimation of work effort.

Ultimately, effective scheduling demands that we take a plethora of factors into account, ranging from the traditional factors incorporated in the PERT/CPM approach to psychological, risk, political, financial, production, and possibly marketing factors. We can anticipate that future advances in scheduling methodology will move away from the mechanical approaches we have been using to ones that incorporate the full range of life's realities, thereby providing us with richer, more realistic project schedules.

CHAPTER TWELVE

Outsourcing to Control Costs, Focus on Core Work, and Expand Resources

A n important trend in recent times has been the growing use of outsiders to carry out an organization's business. This employment of outsiders is called *outsourcing*. The underlying rationale for outsourcing is clearly economic. Companies have determined that they can do business more cheaply by working with outsiders than by relying on their internal workforce. This happens in various ways.

Offshore production allows companies to take advantage of the low cost of overseas labor. For example, in Asia or Mexico, they can find workers whose wages are a small fraction of what American workers demand (American hourly wages in 2000 were eight times higher than Mexican hourly wages). Initially, in the 1960s and 1970s, the shift to offshore producers occurred in low-skill areas, such as assembly. Increasingly, as the education level of the populations in poor and middle-income countries increased, work began to shift to higher value-added areas, including engineering and software development.

Outsourcing also occurs domestically. In the United States, domestic outsourcing is a response to cost-cutting pressures on American companies. By cutting back on employment and shifting the work to contractors, American companies reap enormous savings because they do not have to pay for such worker benefits as insurance and pension plans. Furthermore, in some environments, such as manufacturing, outsourcing shifts the burden of maintaining inventory and storage onto suppliers, thereby delivering substantial cost savings to the outsourcer.

An interesting phenomenon that is a spin-off of present-day outsourcing is that frequently the people doing the work on the outside are former employees of the outsourcing company. They may have been released from the company during a bout of downsizing, only to be rehired later as contractors. Not everyone is unhappy with this arrangement. The outsourcing company saves large sums by not paying fringe benefits to the employees, and the employees have a greater degree of independence than they did while working for the company. The price of this independence is, of course, reduced job security.

Outsourcing is driven by more than the desire to economize. It is also a tacit recognition that the old adage "bigger is better" no longer holds true for a whole range of activities. The "bigger is better" philosophy emerged from more than a century of industrial experience. In traditional manufacturing, larger efforts lead to economies of scale. The low-cost producer is the one who can produce large runs of widgets. In its extreme form, the drive to become large led companies to attempt to control the whole production process in order to achieve total self-sufficiency. A car company might get into the iron and coal business in order to obtain the steel needed to make cars. It might own rubber plantations in South Asia and plants that make tires. Of course, it would also develop capabilities in forging, machine tooling, metal cutting, and assembling. To sell cars, it would need advertising, distribution, and servicing capabilities. The achievement of total self-sufficiency is called *vertical integration.*

Today the "bigger is better" outlook is on the wane in most areas. For one thing, the financial and intellectual capital necessary to run a vertically integrated enterprise in today's complex and competitive environment is daunting. It is hard enough for a company to excel at its core business; to be a first-rate performer across a wide range of businesses borders on the impossible. Second, there is a feeling that the advantages of economies of scale may be offset by the cumbersomeness of running an enterprise that is so big and complex. Experience shows that large organizations are inordinately bureaucratic and incapable of responding quickly to market challenges. Third, when a company commits itself to operating self-sufficiently on a large scale, it is increasing its business risk. It invests capital and time to achieve a particular solution. If that solution fails in the marketplace, the company is a big-time loser because it has placed all its eggs in one basket.

The "bigger is better" outlook has been replaced by a "lean and mean" perspective. Large companies are consciously shrinking the size of their operations, thereby increasing their profitability. They focus on maintaining a core of activities and depend on outside sources to provide the auxiliary goods and services they need to conduct their business. In doing so, they are also shifting business risk to the outsiders. If an outsider's particular solution does not work, outsourcers need only turn to other solutions offered by other outsiders.

In this chapter, we examine different forms of outsourcing, explore its implications for project management, and investigate the principal mechanism for effecting it: the contract.

FORMS OF OUTSOURCING

Outsourcing can take different forms. At one end of the spectrum, it may involve nothing more than hiring someone temporarily to execute a task. At the other end, it may entail having outside contractors do the lion's share of the company's work. Let us look at some common outsourcing arrangements.

Consultants

Perhaps the simplest form of outsourcing is employment of a consultant to do needed work. This is done frequently in the broad areas of accounting, training, design, and software development, as well as in specialized technical and business areas.

Operating with consultants offers the outsourcing company a great deal of flexibility. In most areas of work, there is a fairly clearly defined market of consultants, so the company can pick and choose among a broad array of candidates. If this month we need an expert trainer conversant with the Oracle database language, we can hire one for a week of work. If next month we need training on project-scheduling software, we can hire someone else. Because of the ready availability of these capabilities on the outside, there is no need to develop them in-house.

Another advantage of hiring consultants is that they do not add to the burden of fringe benefit costs. The company's commitment to them is limited to paying their wages. When they have done their job, the company's commitment ends.

Yet another advantage of consultants is that if the company is unhappy with their performance, it simply ceases to employ them, without hassles involving unions or labor sensitivities.

The chief difficulties with consultants are problems that are common to all forms of outsourcing. For example, how well do the outsiders know the business? If it is important that they know the business well, a large fraction of the consultants' time may be dedicated to learning the business. Not only is the company paying them to educate them (thereby increasing their value in consulting with others), but it may find that the education effort disrupts ongoing activities as the consultants consume the valuable time of core personnel in their attempts to get up to speed.

A second problem focuses on the issue of commitment. Are the consultants fully committed to achieving the company's most important goals? In fact, do they even know what these goals are? Since consultants are often paid on a time-reimbursable basis, there is always the danger that their greatest commitment is to racking up the number of hours they put into the project. The more time they spend on the project, the more they get paid.

Finally, there is the problem of access to company secrets. Most companies have collections of confidential information that they do not want to fall into the hands of their competitors. Common examples include information on production costs, technical processes, market targets, operating procedures, technical data, growth strategies, and sources of internal problems. For outsiders to do their jobs effectively, they may need access to these secrets. Is the company really willing to provide them with such access? Generally, the secrecy issue is handled by having consultants sign nondisclosure agreements, but will they really abide by them? How will the company know if they do not?

Personal Services Contracts

Recently, I spent a week on-site at a facility of a Fortune 50 company. Because I had been working steadily with this group, I was issued a contractor's badge, complete with unflattering photo. As I walked through the corridors of this facility, ate lunch in the cafeteria, and visited clients in their offices, I became powerfully aware that about

20 percent of the people I encountered were, like me, wearing contractor badges. I asked my hosts who these people were. I was told that they represented a cross section of activities being conducted at the facility: secretaries, facilities maintenance personnel, systems developers, and so on.

Contract labor is a growing phenomenon in organizations. It is no longer uncommon to see a contracted secretary sitting at a desk adjacent to one occupied by a full-time corporate secretary. The motivations for hiring contract labor are the same as for other forms of outsourcing: to save money and maintain flexibility. In addition, I have encountered cases where professionals are hired initially as contract workers to test them out. If they are perceived to provide value to the organization, they may ultimately be offered a full-time job, complete with benefits. If not, they continue to work as contract workers or are released.

Two obvious problems stand out here. First, there is confusion as to where the contract workers fit into the existing organization. Are they second-class citizens? How seriously do full-time employees take them? Will full-time employees see them as a long-term threat to their jobs?

Second, individuals working on personal services contracts do not have much security. They often do not know whether they will still be employed by the company two or three months from now. They may have to cover the costs of essential services—such as insurance and retirement—out of their own pocket. (If their income is inadequate, they may decide that they cannot afford such services.) From society's point of view, a big question is whether we are willing to accept that an increasingly large portion of our fellow citizens are living lives of desperate uncertainty. From the company's point of view, there is a question of how effective workers can be when they feel insecure.

Organized Suppliers of Specialized Services

Employers of contract labor are not required to pay benefits, but these are often provided by companies that have been set up to provide specialized services to other companies. Take security services as an example: most businesses hire specialized companies to provide security services, including security guards, electronic monitoring capabilities, and alarm systems. Other examples include food service, printing services, and maintenance service. Higher-value-added services, such as training, design, marketing, and data processing services, are emerging as well. The employees of these specialized companies may be fully employed by them (although not always—consider the Kelly Services model) and may thereby be beneficiaries of a full range of fringe benefits.

Suppliers of Parts and Materials

Some of the most dramatic outsourcing involves having outsiders supply a company with the parts and materials it needs to produce its goods and services. Even previous champions of self-sufficiency, such as IBM, are increasingly turning to outsiders in this area.

Because it is vital that the parts and materials provided be of the highest quality, outsourcing arrangements are handled very carefully. In some cases, they are carried out through the formation of strategic alliances. For example, a large producer of computers may establish a joint venture with a chip manufacturer to supply the computer maker with needed semiconductor chips. Through the joint venture, the computer maker can exercise some measure of control over its supplier.

When dealing with an arm's-length supplier, producer and supplier must establish close relations to minimize misunderstandings and to build a joint commitment toward a successful venture. The producer must be assured of open and reliable access to quality parts and materials. The supplier must be confident that its customer is dependable in both the short and the long run. Today we call this kind of arrangement *partnering*.

THE MOTIVATION CHALLENGE

The focus on outsourcing leads to an interesting management dilemma. How do you motivate people when they do not work directly for you? Management practitioners and theorists have long recognized that organizational success is closely tied to motivation. Among the best-known management theories are those dealing with the motivation of employees, including Maslow's hierarchy of needs (1954), McGregor's Theory X and Theory Y (1960), and Herzberg's hygiene factors versus motivators (Herzberg, Mausner, and Snyderman, 1959).

Interest in motivation theory is based on the following proposition: a properly motivated employee will move mountains to get the job done. Business history is replete with stories of companies that made it to the top because their workforce was populated with workers who had a passion to be the best. A recent example of this has been the spectacular success of Wal-Mart.

The gist of most motivation theories is that the strongest motivator is opportunity for self-growth. (The preferred term among many management theorists is *self-actualization.*) But the presumption is that workers operate in a stable environment. Maslow (1954) stipulated this when he stated that a set of key needs—physiological, safety, group belonging, and self-respect—must be satisfied before self-actualization can take place. Similarly, Herzberg suggested that an environment of stability and consistency (his hygiene factors) must exist before self-actualization can be realized (Herzberg, Mausner, and Snyderman, 1959).

Outsourcing presents managers with a motivation challenge in at least two ways. First, the outsourcing environment is not particularly conducive to stability and loyalty. Outsourcing is driven primarily by unvarnished financial concerns. In recent times, we have seen massive layoffs of blue-collar and white-collar workers in the name of downsizing. The traditional moral contract between large corporations and their employees appears to have been broken. Motivating a workforce in an environment of fear and distrust is not easy to do.

Second, the resources that are hired through outsourcing arrangements are to a large extent borrowed resources. The customer who hires them is not their real boss. Their real boss—the person who decides their promotion prospects, their wage rates, and whether they can take a vacation in December—still resides at the home office. So the customer may find that he or she has little control over the hired resources. It is difficult to motivate these people through traditional means—bonuses, raises, promotions—because they are not really part of the customer's organization.

As managers find that more and more of their efforts are being carried out in outsourcing environments, a key challenge for them is to learn how to spur people to move mountains.

OUTSOURCING IN PROJECT MANAGEMENT

Outsourcing is not new to project management. In two lines of business, in fact, it has been the basic way project work has been carried out for decades. In construction, projects are often run by a general contractor, whose job is to select and manage a battery of contractors and subcontractors. To a large extent, the essence of the general contractor's job is simply contracting per se. This is the way large and small buildings, airports, dams, and other civil engineering products have been constructed for decades.

The second line of business that depends heavily on outsourcing is government business. The great share of government work is conducted through contracts. Governments seldom build weapon systems, highways, or computer systems using their own employees. The work is typically done by private outside contractors. Governments have been conducting their business this way for centuries.

What is new is that outsourcing is now being promoted in nontraditional areas. Nowadays, one can have software developed by outsiders; training conducted by contractors; reports edited, printed, and distributed by a modern, computer-based print shop; designs developed by outside engineering companies; and any number of other essential activities performed outside the organization.

Actually, most project personnel do not feel particularly awkward with this situation, probably because it is a natural extension of the matrix. In a classic matrix organization, data processing, training, printing, and design resided in functional departments within the organization. The acquisition of needed resources entailed a form of internal contracting in which the number of resources needed, individual job responsibilities, and time commitments had to be specified. What has happened in the era of outsourcing is that the internal contracting inherent in matrix organizations has been replaced by external contracting with outside performers. However, for the outsourcing approach to work, project staff must develop contracting skills. A violation of the terms and conditions of an internal contract might result in a slap on the hand; such a violation on an external contract could lead to a lawsuit.

CONTRACTING

The principal mechanism for outsourcing is the contract. Simply put, a contract is an agreement between buyer and seller stipulating the rights and responsibilities of each with respect to a specific transaction. The transaction may be something as simple as procuring ten thousand pencils, in which case the contract document may be less than a page long. Or it may be highly sophisticated, involving the construction of a space vehicle to be used on a mission to Mars. In this case, the contract document may be the size of the telephone book for a large city.

The contract process is broken into two phases: preaward and postaward. In the preaward phase, the buyer sets out to identify prospective sellers. Once a likely candidate has been found (perhaps through a competitive bidding process), the detailed terms and conditions of the contract are negotiated. Finally, the contract is signed by both parties, and an award is officially granted.

The postaward phase focuses on overseeing contract performance. Is the contractor performing its duties on time, within budget, and according to specifications? Close monitoring of the contract is particularly important for buyers on *cost-plus* (also called *cost-reimbursable*) contracts.

This last point highlights an important consideration in contracting: How has the contract been structured? There are many ways to structure contracts. We will focus on the two forms most commonly employed in project management here: fixed-price contracts and cost-plus contracts. The differences in these approaches is of more than academic interest to project managers. The type of contract employed has a major bearing on the management challenges they face.

Fixed-Price Contracts

In a fixed-price contract, both buyer and seller agree that the project deliverables will be produced for a price agreed in advance and expressly stated in the contract. For example, a contractor may be engaged to write a seventy-five-page user's guide describing how to use a new management information system. The contract stipulates that the contractor will be paid $10,000 for the document upon delivery on or before March 15. If the contractor's expenses are $6,000, he or she would realize a profit of $4,000 on the project. However, if the contractor's expenses mount to $11,000, he or she would experience a $1,000 loss. The key point here is that it makes no difference what the contractor's expenses are; the price of the product is "fixed" at $10,000.

The management implications of this form of contract are strong. The burden of project risk lies on the performer. The great risk is that expenses will outstrip the contract price. In such a situation, the contractor will suffer a loss. In theory, the buyer does not need to oversee execution of the project very attentively. Because the price is fixed, the issue of cost overruns is irrelevant to the buyer.

It should be noted that performers face good opportunities for gain under this type of contract. If they operate efficiently and realize cost savings, they can increase their profit margins dramatically. Every dollar saved translates to a dollar increase in profit.

Fixed-price contracts are most appropriate for routine implementation projects (for example, building the thirtieth house in a subdivision, installing telephone switching equipment in an office, conducting a credit check on a loan applicant). If a particular project has been carried out many times before, cost estimators have a good sense of what project costs will be, so they can estimate these costs with a high degree of precision. These cost estimates provide important insights into how to price the project. When bidders place their bids, they can be reasonably confident that their costs will be lower than the bid price, thus assuring them of a profit on the project.

Fixed-price contracts are generally not appropriate for high-risk development projects (for example, conducting research, designing new software, building a space station). With such projects, estimates of project costs are very speculative, owing to the unique nature of the work being carried out. If actual costs are much higher than the cost estimators anticipated, these costs may exceed the project price, putting contractors into a situation where they lose money. If the losses are great enough, the contractor may go bankrupt. Not surprisingly, competent contractors are reluctant to bid on high-risk projects if they are funded under a fixed-price contract.

It was suggested earlier that with fixed-price contracts, buyers typically need not monitor the project effort closely because the risk of overruns falls entirely on the contractor. There are occasions, however, when close scrutiny of the project effort is appropriate. In particular, if contractors begin having problems on their projects, their difficulties may translate into difficulties for the buyer. In extreme cases, cost overruns may force contractors to close down operations. Now buyers find that they have nothing to show for the money they have spent. A close monitoring of the project effort can give buyers advance warning of impending problems and allow them to prepare for unfortunate contingencies.

Cost-Plus Contracts

The dominant contract form employed on development projects is the cost-plus (or cost-reimbursable) contract. With this type of contract, contractors are reimbursed for their expenses. They are also awarded a profit above and beyond their expenses.

Obviously, the risk of cost overrun with this type of contract rests squarely with the buyer. If contractors' costs are covered, they have no worries about losing money. Without such worries, cost discipline may grow lax.

This high level of risk for buyers requires that they establish administrative mechanisms to monitor project progress closely. This drives up the administrative costs of the project because contractors now must spend a sizable portion of their time reporting on their progress.

Why do buyers award cost-plus contracts when these contracts pose such a great risk of cost overruns to them? The answer is simple: high-quality contractors will not bid on risky development projects that might drive them into bankruptcy. The only way to get them to bid on such projects is to underwrite the risk by covering project costs.

Cost-plus contracts can be structured in different ways to reduce incentives for contractors to engage in excessive spending. Three dominant types of cost-plus contracts have emerged: cost-plus-fixed-fee, cost-plus-incentive-fee, and cost-plus-award-fee contracts. Let's look at each in turn.

COST-PLUS-FIXED-FEE (CPFF) CONTRACTS. The CPFF contract removes incentives for excessive spending by limiting the contractor's profits to a fixed amount, regardless of project costs. The CPFF approach can be best understood through a simple numerical example.

Contractor A wins a contract award of $1 million to design a new product. During the contract negotiation process, the buyer agrees to pay contractor A a 10 percent fee of $100,000 for the work performed. Thus the contract price is $1.1 million. Because the fee is fixed at $100,000, contractor A will be paid that amount if it does the work for $900,000. Similarly, it will receive $100,000 even if project costs go beyond the $1 million target. There is no incentive here for the contractor to overspend.

The CPFF contract is very attractive to contractors engaged in high-risk development work. With this form of contract, the buyer effectively becomes a risk capitalist, underwriting the risks associated with a new, speculative venture. Developers undertake work that would otherwise be too risky to engage in. Through this process they acquire new skills that help them grow.

To a large extent, California's Silicon Valley and Route 128 outside Boston were built with U.S. Defense Department CPFF contracts (Bylinsky, 1976). After World War II, many scientists and engineers involved in the war effort returned to their jobs in academia. Having worked with the military for a number of years, they were now wise to the ways of defense procurement. Back home, many of them set up small independent business operations to continue their relationships with the military.

Let's assume that one particular group of engineers invests $5,000 to establish a storefront operation on Route 128 (prices were low in 1947). They then discuss an idea for a new radar component with their former colleagues in the army. They submit a proposal for a $1 million CPFF contract to support them in their development work. During the negotiation phase, it is agreed that they will be paid a fixed fee of $50,000.

Consider what the contracting engineers have gained here. They have received what amounts to $1 million in risk-free capital to put toward the development of new capabilities. Later, they can use these new capabilities to increase their business opportunities. Furthermore, they have a locked-in profit of $50,000. They will receive this profit even if the product does not pan out. In view of the fact that their initial investment was $5,000, this translates into a 1,000 percent rate of return on their investment!

COST-PLUS-INCENTIVE-FEE (CPIF) CONTRACTS. Although the CPFF does nothing to encourage cost overruns, neither does it actively attempt to save money. The CPIF contract, in contrast, provides carrots and sticks to encourage cost-effective project performance. It has rewards built into it for saving money and punishments for profligacy.

Here is how the CPIF contract works: before the contract is issued, buyer and contractor negotiate target cost, target price, and target profit for the project. If contractors do the work for less than the target cost, they will share the cost savings with the buyer. Thus the actual price of the contract decreases—saving the buyer money—while the contractors' profit increases.

If the contractor exceeds target costs, this decreases profits. For the contractor, this is less risky than the situation with a fixed-price contract, since project costs will be covered by the buyer. However, as with the fixed-price contract, poor performance is punished—in this case, profit margins are reduced.

COST-PLUS-AWARD-FEE (CPAF) CONTRACTS. An increasingly popular form of contracting among buyers is the CPAF contract. It offers them more flexibility in dealing with contractors than a CPIF contract. Under the CPIF contract, rewards and punishments are effectively determined by formulas. With CPAF contracts, subjective judgments can be included in determining rewards.

At the outset of a CPAF contract, an award pool is created. The funds that are set aside can be used to reward contractors for good performance. The level of award is determined by an award committee, which reviews contractor performance. Awards are not made only according to objective criteria (as they are with CPIF contracts); they can also take into account subjective factors (such as the attitude of the contractor).

CONTRACTING: PREAWARD

As the name implies, the preaward phase is concerned with events leading up to the issuance of a contract award. Two key issues must be resolved here: source selection and contract negotiation. Let's examine each of these issues in turn.

Source Selection

The principal objective of source selection is to identify who will carry out the contracted work. Obviously, many factors must be taken into consideration before this issue can be resolved. The size of the project, the complexity of the work to be done, risk, and procurement rules help determine what sources we select. For example, on most government projects, the rules require that contractors be selected through a competitive bidding process. However, competitive bidding procedures can be waived in special cases. An example of this is the sole-source contract, which is issued to a contractor who has unique capabilities for conducting the needed work.

In general, for small, simple efforts, informal source selection procedures are followed. A list of possible performers can be quickly generated through some exploratory phone calls to people who know the business. Typically, the search procedure ends when the list contains three to five prospects. One by one, the prospects may be contacted to find out what they charge and whether they would be interested in doing the work. Follow-up discussions may be held to define the buyer's requirements more carefully and to identify what the potential contractors propose to do. Finally, the prospects are asked to submit short proposals that outline their work plans, describe their capabilities, and provide cost and schedule estimates. The final selection decision is made by reviewing the proposals. In addition, impressions of the competence of the bidders gained through discussions with them may play an important role in the final decision.

Requests for Proposals (RFPs)

For large awards and complex work efforts, formal source selection procedures are carried out. Too much is at stake to depend on an informal approach. The process may begin with the buyer developing and issuing a *request for proposal* (RFP). The RFP provides bidders with the guidelines they need to prepare a proposal. Some of these are procedural, describing the format the bidders' proposals should take (for example, how many pages long it should be or how it should be structured), identifying points of contact in the buyer's organization, and describing the buyer's policies regarding such things as equal employment opportunity.

Others are substantive. A work statement is issued to explain the nature of the proposed work to potential bidders. The bidders are expected to build the substance of their proposals around this work statement. In addition, guidelines are offered regarding the amount of work the project should entail (for example, "It is anticipated that the project will consume 22 person-years of effort"). Bidders scrutinize this section carefully, since it gives them insights into how much the buyer is willing to spend on the project (for example, if a person-year of effort typically costs $120,000, the labor costs associated with a 22-person-year project lies in the neighborhood of $2,640,000). Finally, a deadline for proposal submissions is given, and criteria for evaluating the proposals are provided (for example, "In evaluating bids, cost will be given a weight of 50 percent, personnel qualifications a weight of 20 percent, technical solution a weight of 15 percent, management plan a weight of 10 percent, and facilities a weight of 5 percent").

A well-formulated RFP is a vital first step in managing a successful contracted project. Its work statement provides bidders with the cues necessary for them to put together detailed proposals. A poorly fashioned work statement will lead bidders astray and will result in unsatisfactory solutions to the buyer's problems. Later on, in the event of contract disputes, the contractor may point to the original poorly formulated work statement as a leading cause of project problems.

If the proposed effort is truly large and complex, development of the RFP may become a major undertaking in its own right. It may, in fact, become a stand-alone project. Consider how much precise and detailed information must be contained in an RFP associated with a project to build a next-generation fighter aircraft or a nuclear power plant. Development of such an RFP can take years to carry out and entail millions of dollars' worth of efforts.

Advertising the Tender

It is generally in the buyer's best interest to have as many qualified bidders as possible become aware of the proposed project. Generally, the more bidders the better. (This is not always true: if too many responses are received, who will have the time to evaluate all of them?)

For potential bidders to become aware of the proposed project, the project must be advertised as a tender. The specific mechanism for doing this depends on the particular circumstances of the project. All openly bid U.S. government contracts, for example, must be advertised in a publication called *Commerce Business Daily*. Typically, the advertisement describes the proposed contract in a few sentences and then gives possible bidders a phone number or postal address that they can contact to get more detailed information. Municipalities often advertise their upcoming contracts in a special section of the local newspaper. Data processing contracts to be issued by companies might be advertised in DP trade journals. Small Third World countries often advertise capital construction projects in the international magazine called *The Economist*. Basically, buyers advertise where they think they will get results.

Evaluating the Bids

Once the bids have been submitted, they are opened and reviewed. On large, complex projects, this process can be time-consuming because there is so much material to look over. Evaluations of proposals proceed according to evaluation criteria that have been established in advance. For each bid, the qualifications of the proposer's personnel must be assessed and noted. Similarly, evaluations must be made of work plans, management capabilities, proposed solutions, proposed costs, and many other factors.

During the evaluation effort, a winnowing process takes place. Some bids may be completely off target from a cost point of view and can be rejected out of hand. Others may display marginal capabilities and receive a low score. Still others may be viewed as competent and fairly priced and may be put on a short list of possible candidates.

At this point, when several real contenders have been identified, the buyer may contact each contender to clarify various points. Some pre-offer negotiation may occur at this time. Occasionally, the buyer may have the short-listed bidders submit a *best and final offer* (BAFO); this allows bidders to make one more pitch to sell their projects.

Ultimately, a decision is made to accept the offer submitted by one bidder. Then a detailed contract, based on the offer contained in the proposal, must be negotiated, drafted, and signed.

Contract Negotiations

Note the iterative nature of the process described so far. First, buyers specify their needs for goods and services in an RFP. The substance of the need is described in the work statement. Then bidders react to the RFP by crafting proposals, which they submit to the buyers for review. During the review process, the buyers have an opportunity to adjust the bidders' approaches through discussions and requests for clarification. Finally, a decision is made to accept one bidder's proposal, and this serves as the basis of a contract.

Many important details must be worked out and included in the contract. Common items for negotiation include the following:

• *Data rights.* Nowadays, information is often an organization's most valuable asset. Who has rights to the data generated through the project, the buyer or the contractor?

• *Penalties.* The contract will surely have clauses that cover actions to be taken in the event that things do not go according to plan. These are usually described as penalties. For example, what penalties will contractors pay if they do not deliver their products on time? What penalties will be instituted if they walk away from the contract? How much extra will buyers be charged if they make late payments?

• *Payment schedules.* The contract needs to specify how payments will be made. Common approaches include progress payments, made in conjunction with the reaching of prespecified milestones; monthly cost reimbursement for time expended on the project and materials purchased; pro rata payments issued evenly over the life of the project (for example, four payments of $25,000 every two months on an eight-month, $100,000 project); start-up payments; and closeout payments.

• *Fee structure.* On cost-plus contracts, as discussed earlier, buyer and performer negotiate the details of fee structure. *Fee* refers to the profit that is built into the project. On cost-plus-fixed-fee contracts, the negotiations focus on a specific fee amount that will be paid, regardless of the cost of actually executing the project. On cost-plus-incentive-fee contracts, a fee schedule is laid out, showing how the fee will increase if the performer does a better job than planned and how it will decrease in the event of schedule slippage or budget overruns.

• *Schedule of deliveries.* Buyers are invariably impatient to receive the goods and services covered in the project as soon as possible. During contract negotiations, they may press to accelerate the proposed schedule of deliverables offered by the performer. Performers often resist this pressure out of fear that they will be committing themselves to unachievable targets. Ultimately, a compromise is reached, and hard-and-fast delivery dates are stipulated in the contract.

When the negotiations end, all the agreed terms and conditions are written into the contract, and both parties sign it. It now becomes the basis of project activities.

Invitation for Bid (IFB)

The RFP tendering process is geared to a bidding process where terms can be negotiated after the bids have been opened. Another approach to tendering is the invitation for bid (IFB) process, where proposals are submitted by bidders as sealed bids. On a defined date, all the proposals are opened publicly. The award is then given to the lowest bidder who is qualified to do the job.

With this process, there is no opportunity to engage in buyer-bidder negotiations once the proposals have been opened. Thus in writing its proposal, a bidder is also making its best and final offer.

IFBs are most appropriate for well-defined work. If we know exactly what must be done on a project, there is no need to compare the proposed features described by different bidders. Our principal concern will be price. The IFB tendering process puts pressure on bidders to bid as low as they can, since there is no leeway for negotiation.

Proposal Development Teams

Bidders must organize themselves to respond to RFPs. First, they must review the RFP to see whether it is worth bidding on. If the proposed work lies outside their domain, if they sense that the contract is "wired" to a predetermined contractor, or if they believe that many companies will submit a bid, they may decide not to write a proposal.

If they choose to respond to the RFP, they must organize a proposal-writing team. In many companies, the proposal development effort is guided by people from the marketing and sales department. They create a team that can work together to write a responsive proposal. Typically, key team members are technical people who can provide credible technical insights into how the proposed project might be carried out. In addition, pricing specialists may work on the team in order to price the effort. Functional experts from areas such as manufacturing, quality assurance, and data processing are consulted when needed. Physical production of the proposal is put into the hands of professional editors, who may also write large segments of it.

A major problem in writing proposals is the tendency of the proposal-writing team to stray from a focused view of what will satisfy the customer. In their brainstorming sessions, they may grow excited about exercising new capabilities and "pushing the envelope." Gradually, what they propose to do may no longer have a bearing on what the customer needs and wants.

In order to keep the proposal properly focused, many companies subject the evolving document to "sanity checks." For example, when a tight outline of the proposal is first drawn up, it may be required to pass through a *pink team* review. The pink team is a group of people outside the proposal team who are asked to review the proposal outline from the perspective of the buyer. They identify flaws in the presentation in the early stages of the proposal development. The hope is that their comments will keep the proposal on track. Their suggestions can be adopted at a time when it is still easy to make adjustments to the presentation.

Later on, after a draft of a fully developed proposal has been written, the document might be subjected to a *red team* review. Like pink team members, red team members view the proposal from the perspective of the buyer. Their function is to see whether the proposal is still responsive to customer needs and wants. If it has weaknesses, they suggest changes that can be made to it before it is finally issued.

CONTRACTING: POSTAWARD

Once a contract has been signed, energy is concentrated on executing the project. The big question now is, is the work being carried out on time, within budget, and according to specifications? Postaward contract management efforts are directed primarily at addressing this question. They do this through contract monitoring.

There are two principal components to the monitoring effort. One entails regular reviews of progress—say, monthly reviews of status reports. On cost-plus contracts, these monthly reports enable buyers to track cost and schedule performance in detail. It is important that buyers do this, since they are paying for the work directly. In the reviews, attention focuses on examining cost and schedule variances, where *variance* is defined as planned performance minus actual performance. It is important to examine cost and schedule variances concurrently. By itself, a cost underrun for a given month may be interpreted as a cost savings. However, when viewed in conjunction with schedule data, it may become evident that costs were underrun because work was not being done and that the project is in fact behind schedule.

A second component of the monitoring effort entails looking at whether the contractor is achieving predetermined milestones effectively. Over the years, various standard checkpoints have emerged over the project life cycle. For example, on development projects, preliminary design reviews (PDRs) and critical design reviews (CDRs) are often built into the monitoring process. However, most of the milestones to be reviewed are project-specific: Was phase 1 completed on June 4, as planned? Was a particular component tested by August 10, as planned? Was the first draft of user documentation edited and submitted for approval by March 31, as planned?

As the project is carried out, it is likely that pressure will be brought to bear to change the project's original scope. Perhaps an unanticipated technical glitch requires a different approach to solving problems. Perhaps a new player decides to change the specifications on a whim. Perhaps delays demand that more people be put on the project to get it back on track.

The problem with change is that it typically leads to cost overruns. Obviously, when additional work is being done, costs will rise. But even when there is no additional work, change can have negative cost consequences—there is often a cost associated with abandoning old commitments and making new plans.

To deal with change, change control procedures must be implemented during the postaward phase. These procedures have important contractual implications. With well-established procedures, distinctions can be made between authorized and unauthorized changes. Clearly, customers do not want to pay for unauthorized changes made by contractors. By the same token, contractors do not want to implement unauthorized changes for which they will not be paid. A common dispute on contracts revolves around whether specific changes were authorized and who pays for them. Change control is discussed in more detail in Chapter Three.

CUSTOMER ACCEPTANCE AND THE HANDOVER

If one point in the course of a typical contract can be called the "moment of truth," it would be customer acceptance. *Customer acceptance* is a term employed in project management to indicate the point in the contract life cycle when the customer determines whether the deliverable meets the terms and conditions of the contract. This determination frequently occurs in conjunction with tests of the deliverable (for example, a first article test) to see whether it meets specifications, as well as a customer walk-through in which the contractor reviews different features of the deliverable with the customer, step by step. If the customer accepts the deliverable, the contractor's obligations have been met. The project is over, and the contractor can move on to other projects.

Problems often arise at the customer acceptance stage. Disputes typically stem from different interpretations of the contract's terms and conditions. Customers may complain that the deliverable does not satisfy all their needs and wants, as set forth in the statement of work. Contractors may counter this argument by showing test results that prove that the work statement has been satisfied. When the situation is viewed objectively, it frequently becomes apparent that both parties are correct—the differences in opinion are rooted in interpretation, not in willful misconduct on the part of any player.

The consequences of a dispute at this point can be dramatic for both buyers and contractors. If buyers refuse acceptance, they do not get the deliverable they need. As the dispute lingers on, the lack of the deliverable may have adverse effects on their operations. At the same time, contractors do not receive final payment for their work. Furthermore, as long as the contract is still on the books, both parties must expend energy and resources to deal with it. If final contract sign-off is delayed indefinitely, this can become both costly and tiresome.

Problems at the customer acceptance phase stem from a number of causes. Some problems are tied to the fact that buyers and contractors did not come to grips with their different perspectives earlier in the project. For example, as the deliverable becomes more tangible, it may be clear to buyers that what is emerging is not what they reckoned on. However, both parties want to avoid conflict, so they put off making hard decisions, hoping that somehow the problems will take care of themselves. Of course, they seldom do. It is generally a good idea to deal with problems early on when they are small and can be handled with relatively low-cost solutions.

Other problems are rooted in the dynamic nature of projects. Throughout their lives, they may be subjected to a barrage of change: players, budgets, technology, and the environment are in constant flux. A technical requirement written into the work statement at the outset of the project may take on a different meaning six months later owing to a change of context. This sort of situation is typical of all but the shortest and most trivial projects. Both buyers and contractors must recognize this fact and be prepared to deal with it. They should build in periodic reviews of project requirements to make certain that perspectives on them do not begin to diverge. They should also implement tight change management procedures to avoid scope creep.

Still other problems arise because of mismanagement on the part of contractors. For example, to get an award, they may submit a bid at an unrealistically low price. As the money runs out and it becomes clear that there are not enough funds to finish the project, they may grow churlish and cut corners. Another example: because of poor management, project documentation may be treated as an afterthought. As the project approaches its end, it is difficult to bring things together coherently, owing to a lack of good documentation. Chaos ensues. The customer loses confidence in the contractor and questions the quality of the deliverable.

CONCLUSIONS

Outsourcing has grown into a dominant business practice. Today we find many companies trying to cut back on their operations even as they attempt to grow their businesses. They do this by farming out large portions of their operations to outsiders. A key slogan of the opening years of the twenty-first century is that companies are destined to be "lean and mean." This stands in marked contrast to the traditional view of "bigger is better."

Outsourcing has a long tradition in project management, particularly in the construction industry and on government contracts, where it has been the principal mode of operation for decades. But even in project management, the degree of outsourcing has hit new highs as more activities are being outsourced across a broader range of organizations. Today, outsourcing should be in the tool boxes of all effective project managers. Contracting skills in particular have become a sine qua non of project management.

CHAPTER THIRTEEN

Integrating Cost and Schedule Control to Measure Work Performance

A well-known joke in project management circles states that the last 10 percent of a project typically takes 50 percent of the effort. We often encounter projects that are stuck at the 90 percent mark for months. It happens so frequently that I have given it a special name: the 90 percent hang-up. The problem is not that project staff are suddenly encountering insurmountable obstacles; rather, it is that the reporting on the amount of work achieved has been incorrect. On most projects, staff do not know how to measure work performance effectively.

Perhaps the most important control information project managers have is data on the amount of work that has been done. If they do not know how much work they have accomplished, they cannot really know whether they are overspending or underspending or whether they are near to meeting their schedule objectives. Effective project control requires that project organizations generate accurate measures of work performance.

Traditionally, work performance data are collected by having project staff report on "percentage of task completed" month by month. Staff are usually left to interpret what this means. Most estimate the percentage completed on the basis of gut feeling. I call this the "dartboard school" of work performance measurement, since one has the sense that the data are chosen by throwing darts at a board. Their reliability is low. It is likely that five people reporting on the percentage of work completed will offer five different assessments.

Occasionally, staff may review their budget expenditures and report the percentage of budget spent as their estimate of work completed. Unfortunately, in the real world of project management, the correlation between money spent and work done is weak, so this is not a good measure. Furthermore, with this approach, project staff are not providing new insights to the organization, since the accounting department already knows how much of the budget has been spent.

So how does one measure work performance? This question is the key concern of this chapter. As we shall see, the answer centers on the concepts of earned value and integrated cost and schedule control.

A GRAPHICAL APPROACH TO INTEGRATED COST AND SCHEDULE CONTROL

The interpretation of cost and schedule variance data must be undertaken cautiously. If the project accounts show that we have a positive cost variance of 10 percent in March, we should not jump to the conclusion that we have saved money. Perhaps the positive variance reflects the fact that we have not done much work. If we have not done the job, we have not spent our money. Similarly, a negative variance of 10 percent does not necessarily mean that we have overspent. It may reflect the fact that we did more work than planned in March.

Common sense suggests that to have an accurate perception of project status, we should look at cost and schedule variances concurrently. A 10 percent positive cost variance actually reflects a true savings if we are on or ahead of schedule. A negative 10 percent cost variance indicates overspending if we are slipping our schedule or even if we are on schedule.

An effective way to examine cost and schedule variance is to use cumulative cost curves (also called S-curves) and Gantt charts. Employment of these control tools allows staff and managers to assess overall project status at a glance. This is seen in Figure 13.1, which employs Gantt charts and cumulative cost curves to illustrate three different scenarios. The Gantt chart in part (a) of the figure shows that

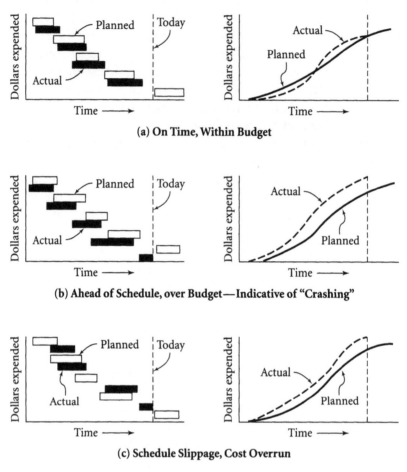

Figure 13.1. Integrated Cost and Schedule Reporting.

the project is fundamentally on schedule, and the cumulative cost curve shows that money is being spent in conformance with the budget. This reflects a situation where progress appears to be going according to the plan.

Part (b) of the figure shows that tasks are being accomplished earlier than planned. At the same time, more money is being spent than budgeted in the time period under review. This reflects a situation of "crashing," in which extra resources are thrown into a project to either maintain or accelerate schedule.

Part (c) of the figure shows the worst possible situation. The project is experiencing both schedule slippage and a cost overrun.

The beauty of the simultaneous use of Gantt charts and cumulative cost curves is that managers can determine at a glance what their project status is. Furthermore, integrated cost and schedule control portrayed through graphical means is an effective communication tool. As such, it can be employed to report project status both to upper management and project staff in a way that is easy to understand. Another advantage of the graphical approach is that today's project scheduling packages typically generate good-looking cost and schedule charts so that producing the graphics is no problem.

The principal deficiency of the graphical approach is that it is cumbersome from an analytical perspective. The graphs provide a visual impression of project status. By themselves, they do not offer other important information, such as the rate at which the budget is being spent vis-à-vis the amount of work being accomplished, the contribution of individual tasks to budget and schedule performance, or the percentage of the work that has been carried out. In addition, on projects of moderate or substantial size, the number of Gantt and cost curves that must be generated can be overwhelming.

Next we will examine an analytical approach to reviewing budget and schedule status called the *earned value management* (EVM) method. It is one of the cleverest techniques developed in the arena of management. Although it originated in the late 1960s, its early use was exclusively in large defense programs. Today, project managers have discovered that it can be usefully employed in small projects as well as large ones, and its popularity on projects of all sizes is growing rapidly.

THE 50-50 RULE FOR MEASURING WORK PERFORMANCE

Here we introduce the earned value approach by examining one method cost accountants have developed to measure work performance, the 50-50 rule.

Using the 50-50 rule is quite straightforward. At the moment a task begins, we assume we have achieved half its value, where value is measured by the budgeted cost of the task. Thus for a $1,000 budgeted task, we assume that $500 in work has been accomplished the moment the task begins. We do not assume that the full value of the work has been achieved until the task actually ends. Thus once our hypothetical $1,000 task has been completed—whether it is completed early, late, or on time—we say we have achieved $1,000 worth of work.

The utility of the 50-50 rule in measuring work performance can be seen in Figure 13.2, which presents the Gantt chart for a very simple four-task project. To keep the arithmetic simple, each task has a budgeted value of $100.

Task A begins on time, and when it begins, we assume that we have accomplished $50 in work. Task 1 finishes on schedule, and upon its completion, we note that the full $100 value of the task has been achieved.

Task B begins on time, so we assume that we have done $50 of work. At the time of its scheduled finish, work remains to be done, so we do not close the books on it. We note that the task has achieved its full $100 value only when it has been completed.

Task C begins late. We do not indicate the accomplishment of any work until the task actually begins. At that time, we note the achievement of $50 in work. The task slips its deadline. Not until it actually finishes do we state that it has achieved its full $100 value.

Finally, we see that task D begins late and that it is still incomplete. Consequently, we report that it has achieved only half its $100 value, or $50.

In making a status report, we compute that as of today, we have achieved $350 worth of work out of a planned $400 of effort. The measure of the $350 of work performed is called *earned value*. The

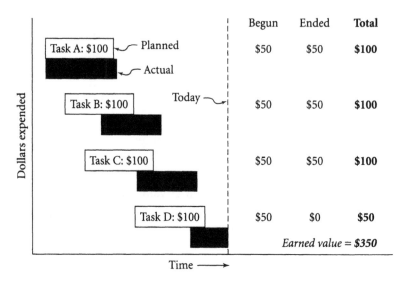

Figure 13.2. The 50-50 Rule in Action.

fact that $350 of work out of a planned $400 of work has been achieved suggests that we have reached 87.5 percent of our target.

Note that we have said nothing about how much it cost us to accomplish our work. Let's assume that a tally of time sheets and invoices tells us that we spent $700 to achieve $350 of work. Thus for each dollar actually spent, we attained 50 cents of value. If this project has a $10,000 total budget and if we continue to get 50 cents of value for each dollar spent, the final cost of this project will reach $20,000!

This simple example demonstrates the power of the earned value approach. It gives us a method for calculating the percentage of the job that has been achieved. It also lets us measure the "burn rate" of our expenditures, thus allowing us to calculate the budget impact of our performance. Earned value computations can be carried out at any level of the work breakdown structure (WBS): we can examine project performance from the perspective of the whole project down to the level of individual work packages (that is, the lowest level of the WBS). In other words, the earned value approach allows us to conduct integrated cost and schedule control analyses analytically, in contrast to the graphical approach discussed earlier.

OTHER WAYS TO CALCULATE EARNED VALUE

There are several ways to calculate earned value beyond the 50-50 rule. Data processing personnel tend to be very conservative. To them, the 50-50 rule is recklessly optimistic because it is based on the premise that the work is half-finished the moment it is begun. Anyone who has written software code realizes that half-finished software has no value. Consequently, they employ the 0-100 rule in calculating earned value. When a task begins, it is not assumed that anything has been accomplished. Only when the task has been completed is it given its full value. In the example shown in Figure 13.2, the total earned value as of today using the 0-100 rule is $300. This means that the project has achieved only 75 percent of its target.

The favored way to calculate earned value is to make computations based on historical experience. I will illustrate this with a simplified example of a company that assembles computers. The assembly process involves five steps. First, auxiliary memory chips are installed on the motherboard. Experience suggests that when this step is complete, the assembly process has reached the 25 percent mark. Then the motherboard is installed in the chassis (the 30 percent mark). After this, a hard drive is installed in the hard drive slot (the 70 percent mark). All cables are linked to their appropriate connectors (the 85 percent mark), and then the chassis is slipped into the computer housing (the 100 percent mark).

To calculate earned value status each month, a tabulation is made of the number of computers found at each stage of the assembly process, and a weighted average is computed estimating the total value of work achieved during the month. For example, suppose that the work value of a complete assembly operation is $100. If during the review of work in progress it is found that five computers have had auxiliary memory installed (the 25 percent mark), the value of work achieved for these computers is $100 times 5 times 0.25, or $125. If another two computers have just had the motherboards installed in the chassis (the 30 percent mark), the value of work achieved for these computers is $100 times 2 times 0.30, or $60. The value of work completed for all seven computers is $125 plus $60, or $185.

Calculating earned value based on gut feeling is not forbidden but is the least preferred approach. In this case, a task leader might guess that she has achieved 85 percent of her $1,000 assigned effort, indicating that she has accomplished an earned value of $850 worth of work.

A NEW LOOK AT COST
AND SCHEDULE VARIANCE

The traditional approach to measuring cost variance has been to subtract actual costs from planned costs. A negative variance suggests that more has been spent than planned; a positive variance indicates that less has been spent than planned. For example, suppose that for the month of March, we planned to spend $1,000 but actually spent $900. This would yield a positive cost variance of $100. As we saw earlier, this cost variance cannot be interpreted meaningfully by itself. It must be examined in conjunction with information on schedule status.

With the earned value approach, we take a different tack to calculating cost variance. It is computed by subtracting actual costs from earned value. Staying with the example in the preceding paragraph, if earned value is computed to be $850, cost variance will be $850 minus $900, or −$50. This means that we paid $900 to do $850 in work. For the work we have done, we have overspent by $50. Note that cost variance here is being assessed *against the value of the work that has been performed.* In this case, it is not necessary to look at the Gantt chart to determine that we have overspent our money. By itself, the cost variance data indicate that we have spent too much. Any negative cost variance figure suggests overspending, and positive cost variance indicates cost saving.

Schedule variance is defined as earned value minus planned cost. In our example, this is $850 minus $1,000, or –$150. In words, this says that although we were supposed to have achieved $1,000 in work, we accomplished only $850, resulting in a work shortfall valued at $150.

Note that schedule variance is being measured in monetary units, not time units. This may seem peculiar at first because people normally think of schedules in the context of time. However, the logic of the approach takes on meaning when we realize that *earned value measures work performance* and that when less work is performed than planned, schedule slippages ensue.

The viability of earned value in measuring schedule variance is seen clearly when earned value schedule variance is mapped to the Gantt chart. This is illustrated in Figure 13.3.

The Gantt chart in part (a) of Figure 13.3 shows a two-task project that is experiencing schedule slippage. The first task (valued at $700) is complete, but the second task (valued at $300) is only half complete. Although the planned amount of effort to be accomplished is $1,000, earned value is only $850. Schedule slippage is thus $850 minus $1,000, or –$150. In general, a negative schedule variance figure indicates schedule slippage and reflects a Gantt chart that shows such slippage, whether the Gantt chart has two tasks, twenty tasks, or two hundred tasks!

Part (b) of the figure shows a project on which the planned work has been achieved. As of today, $1,000 in work was supposed to have been accomplished, and $1,000 in work has actually been finished. Schedule variance is $1,000 minus $1,000, or 0. In general, a zero variance indicates that the planned effort has been accomplished.

Part (c) of the figure shows a project on which work has been accelerated so that more work has been accomplished as of today than originally planned. The first task (valued at $700) is finished early, so work on the second task begins. This second task (valued at $300) is also finished early, so work on the third task (valued at $200) begins early. As of today, $1,000 of work was supposed to have been accomplished, whereas $1,200 has actually been achieved. Schedule variance is $1,200 minus $1,000, or $200. In general, a positive schedule

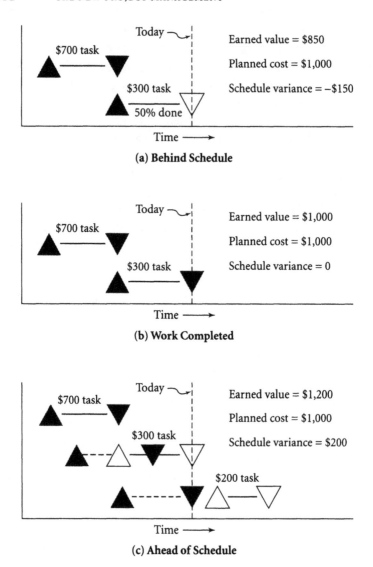

Figure 13.3. Earned Value: Examining Schedule Variance.

variance indicates that more work has been accomplished than planned.

Integrated cost and schedule control occurs when cost and schedule variances are examined concurrently. This is done in Table 13.1, which shows seven different cost and schedule variance scenarios that might be encountered. On project A, cost and schedule targets have been achieved, yielding zero cost and schedule variances. On project

	Planned Cost	Actual Costs	Earned Value	Cost Variance	Schedule Variance
Project A	$800	$800	$800	0	0
Project B	800	800	600	−200	−200
Project C	800	600	1000	200	200
Project D	800	1000	1000	0	200
Project E	800	600	800	200	0
Project F	800	1200	1000	−200	200
Project G	800	400	600	200	−200

Table 13.1. Cost and Schedule Variance Scenarios.

B, the value of work performed ($600) is less than what was planned ($800). In addition, the actual cost of this work ($800) was greater than the value achieved. Thus project B has experienced a cost overrun and a schedule slippage. The other projects can be examined in like fashion.

A NEW VOCABULARY

One of the confusing features of the fully developed earned value approach is that it has its own terminology that does not reflect the commonsense understanding of words. I find when teaching the earned value approach that students spend more energy trying to master the vocabulary than they do mastering the concepts.

In the earned value approach, planned cost is called *budgeted cost of work scheduled* (BCWS). Actual cost is called *actual cost of work performed* (ACWP). Both BCWS and ACWP correspond exactly to traditional understandings of the meanings of planned and actual cost, respectively. Earned value itself is called *budgeted cost of work performed* (BCWP).

Using this new vocabulary, we define schedule variance (SV) as

$$SV = BCWP - BCWS$$

We define cost variance (CV) as

$$CV = BCWP - ACWP$$

The portion of a job achieved, which is called the *schedule perfor-mance index* (SPI), is computed as

$$SPI = \frac{BCWP}{BCWS}$$

The "burn rate" at which we are spending money—it can also be interpreted as an efficiency rate—is called the *cost performance index* (CPI) and is computed as

$$CPI = \frac{BCWP}{ACWP}$$

The estimate of final project cost is called *estimate at completion* (EAC) and is computed as

$$EAC = \frac{BAC}{CPI}$$

where BAC stands for *budgeted at completion,* which is the total bud-geted value of the project. EAC allows us to forecast final project costs on the basis of the efficiency with which work performance is achieved for each dollar actually spent. If a project is budgeted to cost $500,000 (that is, BAC = $500,000) and 80 cents of work is being generated for each dollar spent (that is, CPI = 0.8), the final estimated cost of the project will be $500,000 divided by 0.8, or $625,000 (that is, EAC = $625,000).

CASE STUDY:
THE BORA BORA OFFICERS' CLUB

The power of the earned value approach as an analytical tool is best seen through an example. The example employed here is a project to build the hypothetical Bora Bora Officers' Club. Data on progress to date are provided in Table 13.2. The bottom line of this table shows that as of today, three phases of the construction project should have been com-pleted, for a budgeted cost of $96,300 (BCWS). As of today, $87,100 has actually been spent (ACWP). The value of the work achieved is only $78,650 (BCWP). The data on schedule and cost variance tell us that

	Planned Costs	Actual Costs	Estimated Percentage Completed	Earned Value	Schedule Variance	Cost Variance
Phase 1						
Clear ¼-acre site	$1,500	$1,500	100	$1,500	0	0
Excavate site	2,500	2,600	100	2,500	0	(100)
Pour concrete foundation	3,500	3,600	100	3,500	0	(100)
Emplace basic plumbing	1,000	1,200	100	1,000	0	(200)
Erect cinderblock foundation	2,500	2,500	100	2,500	0	0
Waterproof foundation	800	900	100	800	0	(100)
Total, phase 1	$11,800	$12,300		$11,800	0	(500)
Phase 2						
Frame house	$35,000	$41,000	100	$35,000	0	(6,000)
Finish roof	6,500	7,300	95	6,175	(325)	(1,125)
Insulate house	3,500	3,200	100	3,500	0	300
Install electrical wiring	3,000	3,000	100	3,000	0	0
Install plumbing	3,500	3,100	90	3,150	(350)	50
Attach siding	4,500	4,000	80	3,600	(900)	(400)
Total, phase 2	$56,000	$61,600		$54,425	(1,575)	(7,175)
Phase 3						
Put up dry wall	$12,000	$6,000	50	$6,000	(6,000)	0
Finish floor	6,000	5,200	80	4,800	(1,200)	(400)
Finish interior woodwork	6,500	2,000	25	1,625	(4,875)	(375)
Paint interior	3,000	0	0	0	(3,000)	0
Paint exterior	1,000	0	0	0	(1,000)	0
Total, phase 3	$28,500	$13,200		$12,425	(16,075)	(775)
Total project to date	$96,300	$87,100		$78,650	(17,650)	(8,450)
Total budget (BAC): $115,000.						

Table 13.2. Subcontractor's Report on Progress to Date: Bora Bora Officers' Club Project.

Note: All tasks were to have been completed by the time of this report.

this project is behind schedule and over cost. Schedule variance (BCWP – BCWS) is –$17,650, and cost variance (BCWP – ACWP) is –$8,450. The project has achieved 81.7 percent of the planned effort (SPI = 78,650/96,300). The burn rate (CPI) for the expenditure of funds is 0.903 (that is, 78,650/87,100)—in other words, for every dollar spent, the project is achieving 90.3 cents of value. Given this burn rate, the final project cost (EAC) of this $115,000 budgeted project could be $127,353 (that is, 115,000/0.903).

The analysis of the bottom line gives us a good sense of progress on this project. The verdict is that it is not doing very well. It has a substantial schedule variance, and its final cost will be greater than what has been budgeted.

A strength of the earned value approach is that we are not restricted to an aggregate overview of the project. Budget and schedule analysis can occur at any level of the work breakdown structure. To see this, consider the data on phase 1 of the Bora Bora Officers' Club project. The schedule variances of zero for individual tasks shows that work on this phase is complete. At the end of the work, a small cost overrun of $500 exists.

The phase 2 data suggest some problems. Three tasks have negative schedule variances (finish roof, install plumbing, and attach siding), indicating that more work must be done before the phase is complete. The overall cost overrun for the phase is $7,175. The lion's share of the cost overrun is tied to problems in framing the house (a $6,000 overrun).

Phase 3 is in even greater trouble. Schedule variance data reveal that a whopping $16,075 of work remains undone. Although the cost variance appears small (–$775), the project is so far behind schedule that it is likely that it will incur substantial cost overruns before it is completed.

COLLECTING DATA

On very large and complex projects, data collection on work performed can become quite complicated. The way companies handle data collection is by assigning cost account managers (CAMs) the responsibility for gathering data. On large projects, an individual CAM may have responsibility for millions of dollars of effort.

The principal data CAMs focus on are figures that will enable them to estimate the amount of work performed (that is, earned value). They do this by walking around the organization asking task leaders how much of their work they have achieved. The CAMs know what the milestones are, so their inquiries focus largely on the reaching of planned milestones.

CAMs are also responsible for taking the raw data and fashioning them into earned value reports. These reports are the first line of defense in identifying deficiencies in meeting the plan. Each month, they highlight these deficiencies, alerting management to their existence.

On smaller projects, it is not cost-effective to hire CAMs to track data. Work performance can be tracked in a number of ways without incurring major administrative costs. By employing something like the 50-50 rule or the 0-100 rule, all that needs to be tracked is whether a task has begun and whether it has ended. The clever use of milestones can also facilitate measurement of work performance (for example, "We have achieved twenty out of thirty milestones, where each milestone represents 100 person-hours of work. Thus we have achieved two-thirds of our target"). As a last resort, work performance can be measured by guesswork (for example, "Experience tells me we have done about 85 percent of our planned effort").

TREND ANALYSIS USING THE EARNED VALUE APPROACH

Earned value analysis can be employed to determine general trends in work performance. This is illustrated in Figure 13.4, which shows trends in actual costs (ACWP), earned value (BCWP), and planned costs (BCWS). If everything is going exactly according to plan, the lines reflecting these three measures should be collinear (represented

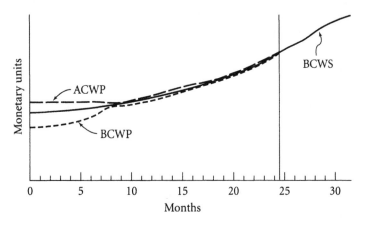

Figure 13.4. Earned Value Analysis over Time.

by a single line). Deviations of the ACWP line from the earned value line indicate cost variance. Deviations of the BCWS line from the earned value line indicate schedule variance.

Figure 13.4 shows that in the early months of this project, there are abundant cost and schedule variances. Both ACWP and BCWS are substantially larger than BCWP, indicating negative variances. However, as time goes on, the size of these variances shrinks, and by month 8 the variances have virtually disappeared, indicating that the project is under control.

Use of a chart such as this can offer managers a high-level view of project status at a glance. If the chart indicates that the project is generally faring well, there is no need to burden managers with detailed tables of numerical data. If the chart indicates problems, this might suggest a review of more detailed data.

WHEN IS THE EARNED VALUE APPROACH APPROPRIATE?

The earned value approach was originally devised to provide government contractors and government program managers with guidance on how to track progress on large, complex projects. Because the fully developed earned value system is governed by detailed instructions that create a substantial administrative burden, the assumption has been that this approach is appropriate only on projects in the range of $100 million or larger. Using it on smaller projects would be like trying to kill a mosquito with a shotgun.

The Bora Bora Officers' Club case demonstrates that stripped of unnecessary administrative requirements, the earned value approach can give project managers valuable insights into project progress even on small projects. If a project has information on planned costs and if actual cost data are being reported accurately and promptly, the earned value approach can be employed usefully. It offers a numerical substitute for the use of Gantt charts and cumulative cost curves. Although these graphical tools serve the purpose of communicating project progress visually, the earned value approach is far more powerful analytically.

With well-maintained data, an earned value system can provide precise measures of work performed, the proportion of effort achieved, and the burn rate for the expenditures of project funds. It can even offer rough forecasting capabilities through the computation of the EAC. Note that these analyses can be carried out at any level of the WBS.

Use of the earned value approach has two key limitations. One is the availability of accurate and timely cost data. Unfortunately, the majority of the organizations with which I work have not established systems to collect such data. I suspect that these organizations are not the exception but the rule. It is difficult to fathom how an organization expects to manage its projects effectively without such data.

A second limitation is educational. For the earned value approach to work properly, everyone in the organization who touches the project management function should have an understanding of its mechanics. For example, they should be able to read and understand status reports based on earned value. This includes upper management. If they do not study this approach and learn how it can yield improved insights into project performance, much of its impact is lost.

A HISTORICAL NOTE

The earned value approach was developed in the United States in the 1960s to help manage very large defense projects. Most of the effort in its development was driven by the U.S. Air Force. During the heyday of defense contracting in the 1950s and 1960s, it became apparent to the Defense Department that as projects get larger and more complex, it becomes increasingly difficult to track what is happening on them. This problem is compounded by the fact that these large projects are being carried out in multiple contractor organizations, each of which employs its own peculiar planning and control system.

By the early 1960s, it was obvious that the Defense Department was no longer able to track the efforts of its contractors with accuracy. It decided that contractors on large, complex projects should be required to report their project efforts in a consistent fashion. It worked to develop rules for reporting project progress and in 1967 issued Department of Defense Instruction (DODI) 7000.2, known also as the *Cost/Schedule Control System Criteria* (C/SCSC). In 1972, the Defense Department issued its *Joint Implementation Guide,* which gave practical advice on how to implement DODI 7000.2.

The focus of the earned value system was the development of consistency and management discipline in contractor organizations in five areas:

- *Organization.* Instructions are provided on the development of work breakdown structures and organizational breakdown structures.

- *Planning.* Key planning requirements are highlighted—for example, the establishment of performance baselines.

- *Accounting.* Requirements are specified for the collection and maintenance of cost accounting data.

- *Analysis.* Guidance is offered on use of earned value techniques for reporting budget variance, schedule variance, and EAC.

- *Reporting.* Instructions are given on reporting project status through cost performance reports (CPRs), which are required on very large projects, or cost and schedule status reports (C/SSRs), which are less burdensome to generate than CPRs and are required on smaller projects.

In the 1990s, the earned value approach as promulgated by the Defense Department underwent a number of modifications. In 1991, DODI 7000.2 was superseded by DODI 5000.2, which was in turn was superseded by DOD Regulation (DODR) 5000.2-R in 1996. The *Joint Implementation Guide* was revised and replaced by a document titled *Earned Value Management Implementation Guide* in 1997. The current version of the earned value management system is designed to be less bureaucratic than its predecessors. It focuses less on mandating certain actions and more on providing guidelines.

Because of the big-project focus of the Defense Department's approach to earned value management, coupled with its arcane nature, organizations outside of the defense community were unaware of its potential usefulness on nondefense projects. This situation began to change in the late 1980s. As the Bora Bora Officers' Club example demonstrates, the earned value approach can be used effectively on small projects when bureaucratic requirements—such as those found in DODI 7000.2, DODI 5000.2, and DODR 5000.2-R—are stripped away. Today, most project management leaders in high-performing organizations acknowledge the great contribution the earned value method can offer them in planning, executing, and controlling their projects.

CONCLUSIONS

There cannot be much accountability on projects if no one is sure how much work has been done. If project staff's rigor in reporting progress is restricted to "I think we're basically on target," they are not likely to know they are in trouble until it is too late.

A special effort must be made to measure work performance. Knowing how much work has been done is one of the most important pieces of information a project manager can have. The good news is that well-tested methods exist for measuring work performed. These methods focus on what is called *integrated cost and schedule control*. They can entail something as simple as generating and comparing Gantt charts and cumulative cost curves. Or they may involve following the detailed guidelines of DODR 5000.2-R in order to track the world's largest, most complex projects. In any case, measuring work performed is vital if project staff desire to spot problems when they are little and can be fixed with few resources. The alternative is to be ignorant of problems until they are large and damaging.

CHAPTER FOURTEEN

Evaluating Projects to Maintain Goals, Strengthen Accountability, and Achieve Objectives

~~~

G ood management requires accountability. Accountability means that people are answerable for their decisions and actions. To the extent that accountability is diffuse, we can expect to find things falling through the cracks, inadequate levels of follow-through, and finger-pointing when things go wrong.

The issue of accountability is particularly acute in project management, for at least two reasons. First, projects are typically carried out with borrowed resources whose loyalties lie with their functional areas. Computer programmers are loyal to the data processing department, engineers to the engineering department, designers to the design shop, and so on. These resources drift in and out of projects on an as-needed basis. They do their jobs; then they are gone. Their functional bosses typically have little or no idea of what they do when they are farmed out to projects. Their project managers, who have little direct control over them, usually lack the technical knowledge to assess their efforts. In a sense, these borrowed resources are accountable to no one.

Second, as projects are carried out, the players change, and continuity in outlook is often lost. Requirements tend to drift according to the interpretation of the latest project players. Decisions are made whose rationale is almost immediately lost when a new set of players come on board. In the end, no one is quite sure who authorized or built what. No one is answerable for either good or bad decisions and actions.

This chapter explores one way to strengthen accountability in project organizations. Accountability can be bolstered by implementing fair, systematic, and rigorous evaluation procedures. With effective evaluation, people will find it difficult to sweep problems under the rug or to shrug off important decisions. They are answerable for their decisions and actions.

The value of evaluation extends beyond its contribution to accountability. Through evaluation, we are able to measure our progress according to some preestablished criteria. Evaluation is an integral part of management by objectives (MBO). MBO is a management technique that emerged in the 1950s. It operates on the principle that the best way to get people in an organization functioning in harmony is to have them focus their work efforts on achieving well-defined objectives. To make sure the objectives are being achieved in the desired fashion, evaluations are undertaken periodically to review the progress that has been made on their attainment.

If evaluation is carried out regularly, we can identify problems when they are still small. We can act on them immediately, before they become big problems. It is much cheaper to fix a problem in the design phase than in the prototype phase, and it is cheaper to fix it in the prototype phase than in the production phase. Evaluation provides us with a mechanism to fix problems relatively cheaply.

Unfortunately, a major constraint to effective evaluations is that they can be scary. They entail scrutiny of performance. Sometimes the scrutiny involves a detailed inspection of how things are going. Furthermore, a key goal of this scrutiny is to uncover problems. Even the friendliest evaluations can be painful when they unearth difficulties in planning, design, or execution. Nobody enjoys being inspected for flaws. Sadly, many evaluations are not friendly.

Early in my career, I spent six years as a professional evaluator. I became familiar with various methodologies, conducted numerous evaluations, read evaluation journals, wrote articles on evaluation techniques, and attended symposia with other evaluators. Through this in-depth exposure to evaluation activities, I became convinced that the key to success has little to do with the specific techniques employed. Rather, successful evaluation hinges on creating a non-threatening environment so that people are willing—perhaps even eager—to share with others the details of some of the problems they are encountering in their work. Consequently, this chapter is more concerned with understanding the nature and purposes of evaluation than with detailing evaluative techniques.

WHAT IS EVALUATION?

Evaluation involves periodic stock taking. When we evaluate, we step back and ask whether we are achieving a set of criteria we have established. They may be schedule, budget, technical, or some other kind of criteria. Evaluation is thus a mechanism to build follow-through into project management. It is not enough simply to establish targets; staff must conduct tests to see whether the targets are being met.

Evaluations are ubiquitous. They are being carried out all around us, although we may not recognize them as evaluations per se. To illustrate this point, I have had students in my management seminars list some of the activities they experience in their organizations that could be construed as evaluations. These lists can grow to be quite long. Following is a scaled-down version that highlights the most common kinds of evaluations my students have experienced.

Bid Versus No-Bid Evaluation

For projects undertaken in a contractual environment, companies cannot spend precious resources bidding on every contract opportunity that comes their way. They must husband their resources and bid only on projects that are winnable and promise outstanding rewards. A decision on whether to bid or not can be made after studying a number of factors associated with a particular project. For example, if technical criteria are important, you might want to address such key questions as Will this project strengthen our technical capabilities? and Will it enable us to use existing capabilities in the best way?

Business Case Evaluation

A significant portion of making bid or no-bid decisions may depend on the business case that can be advanced for pursuing a project. As the name suggests, a business case review focuses on the business implications of a project. A *competitive analysis* may be undertaken to identify strategies, goals, market presence, and capabilities of key competitors. Careful cost and revenue projections may be developed (these may be part of a *cost-pricing evaluation*). From these projections, insights into profitability can be inferred.

Feasibility Studies

The term *feasibility study* is used in many ways. Generally, it denotes undertaking a technical, economic, and commercial review of a project concept. In the international arena, it has a more focused meaning. It is associated with the financing of projects by public or private lenders. These lenders (for example, the World Bank, commercial banks, and government development agencies) use the results of the feasibility study to determine whether they will support a project financially.

Technical Evaluation

Over the life of a project, the deliverable that is being developed and produced will undergo many technical reviews. In the development stage, for example, two critical technical reviews that are often undertaken are the *preliminary design review* (PDR) and the *critical design review* (CDR).

The purpose of the PDR and CDR is to add an element of stability to the design process. In the earliest stages, the design will be very dynamic as project staff explore different design alternatives. At some point, however, the design team must settle on a particular design so that the project is not bogged down in an endless loop of design changes. With the PDR, a particular design choice is reviewed and approved. Since this is still early in the development process, the design will likely undergo substantial modification. Ultimately, to prevent endless modification, the design is subject to a CDR. The result of the CDR is an approved design that will serve as the basis for building the physical deliverable.

Technical evaluation is closely associated with testing. For example, a piece of software may be tested to see whether it meets defined throughput standards, or an O-ring may be tested to see whether it performs effectively at low temperatures.

One clever technical evaluation approach that will be examined later in this chapter is the *structured walk-through*.

Proposal Evaluation

Companies that bid on large contracts often subject their proposals to evaluations to see whether or not they are credible. One way this is done is through the establishment of teams whose job is to tear the evolving proposal apart. In the early stages, a proposal may be put through a *pink team* review. This review is analogous to a PDR. Its purpose is to offer guidance on future directions the proposal should take before too much effort has gone into its development. Later, after the proposal is more fully developed, it may be put through a *red team* review. This review is analogous to a CDR. Its purpose is to make last-minute adjustments to the proposal before it is submitted.

Acceptance Testing

Throughout its life, the project may be punctuated with acceptance test milestones. Generally, customers review the results of these tests to see whether the deliverable is making acceptable progress as it evolves. The most crucial of these tests is the final *customer acceptance test*. This last test will determine whether the customer is satisfied that the deliverable meets the specifications. This last test is often the basis of determining whether final payments should be made to the developer.

Root Cause Analysis

When projects get hopelessly bogged down, management may initiate a root cause analysis to identify the origins of the difficulties. If these can be perceived, attention can be focused on fixing the sources of the problems rather than the symptoms. The root cause analysis may show management that things are so bad that the best course of action might be to shut the project down.

Postmortems

After a project has ended, many companies undertake postmortems to see what went right and what went wrong. The postmortem can be a valuable exercise, particularly if the lessons learned are documented and incorporated into revisions of project methods and procedures. In this way, the organization can learn from its experiences and avoid making the same mistakes twice.

Unfortunately, the circumstances surrounding most projects often lead to ineffectual postmortems. For example, because of discontinuities typical of most projects, where new players continually replace old players, it may be difficult to reconstruct the project experience with any cogency. Who was working on the project during the design phase? Do these people remember what went right and what went wrong? (Do they even care?) What were the specific circumstances under which the project was selected? Is any one around who remembers?

These problems are not insurmountable. However, to deal with them requires a major commitment by management and the project team to document decisions and actions throughout the project's life and to minimize staff turnover.

Performance Appraisals

All the evaluations mentioned to this point focus on project performance. Performance appraisal focuses on the achievements of individual players. The chief problem with performance appraisal on projects is rooted in matrix management. Typically, project workers are borrowed resources who come from a functional area, do their job on the project, and then return to their functional homes.

The big question is, how do you evaluate their efforts? Their functional bosses are too far removed from the project to understand what they have done on it. Their project supervisors usually do not contribute to their performance appraisal reviews, and even when supervisors do contribute, their observations are called into doubt for a variety of reasons (for example, they are deemed incapable of evaluating the technical contribution of the borrowed resource, or they do not understand the career development targets of the functional group).

The question of how to conduct performance appraisals of matrixed employees is one of the most significant questions project management faces today. Each of the three key players in the matrix has a great deal at stake in this matter. Project workers want to know how they will be evaluated. Their future in the organization depends on the outcome of their evaluations. They are nervous about being evaluated by functional managers who do not see them at work on projects. By the same token, they may be uneasy about being evaluated by project managers who are unaware of their career objectives and who lack the technical insights to assess their work.

Functional managers may be distressed that they are evaluating employees in a vacuum since they may not have firsthand exposure to the efforts of their workers. They may also be bothered by the fact that project managers are giving the functional workers guidance that runs contrary to accepted procedures in the functional department.

Because they typically have little or no role in the performance appraisal of project workers, project managers find themselves lacking the carrots and sticks needed to motivate their borrowed staff.

Unfortunately, there are no easy fixes on how to carry out performance appraisals in matrixed organizations.

Audits

A commonly encountered form of evaluation is the financial audit, carried out by outside auditors whose job is to review project accounts to check their accuracy. Scheduled audits are not particularly frightening because they can be planned for in advance. Surprise audits can be scary because they suggest a lack of trust in day-to-day budget management procedures.

Quality Assurance

People may not realize it, but quality assurance is fundamentally an exercise in evaluation. Targets are set (for example, acceptable defect rates may be established), and then a process is periodically examined to see whether the targets are being achieved.

EVALUATIONS AND THE PROJECT LIFE CYCLE

A review of the different kinds of evaluation commonly encountered on projects suggests a tie between the type of evaluation and the stage of the project life cycle. Evaluations that occur in the preproject phase are typically conducted to see whether the project is worth pursuing. Included here are approaches such as feasibility studies, bid versus no-bid evaluations, and business case evaluations.

Evaluations that occur during the project phase are concerned with measuring performance. Is the project achieving its targets? Many of these evaluation efforts are technical and are associated with technical tests. If the project is in serious trouble, an evaluation may provide the rationale for making major course corrections or even for killing the project. Toward the end of the project phase, one evaluation stands out over all others: customer acceptance. Without customer acceptance, the project can lumber on endlessly.

Evaluations carried out in the postproject phase focus on lessons learned. Although they will not affect the outcome of the current project, if the lessons are captured and incorporated into project methods and procedures, they can affect how future projects are executed.

PROBLEMS WITH EVALUATION

As I mentioned at the outset of this chapter, I spent six years developing evaluation systems for high-technology organizations. Through this experience, I gained firsthand insights into how evaluations are carried out in the real world. I was fortunate because the evaluation offices I worked with at places like the National Institutes of Health (NIH) and National Science Foundation (NSF) were staffed with professional evaluation experts who were well acquainted with evaluation's pitfalls. Still, even when approached intelligently, evaluation caused its share of pain.

Over the years, I have reflected on why evaluations are so painful. Having been part of dozens of evaluation efforts and having witnessed scores more, I have noticed a number of common problems. Many of these are rooted in distortions of the purpose of various evaluations. Others are tied to specific characteristics of evaluation, such as its disruptive nature and the threat inherent in it.

Distortions of the Purpose of Evaluation

Few individuals in organizations understand what evaluation is about. Unfortunately, this is as true of upper-level managers as of the rank and file.

One common misunderstanding is that evaluation is a tool to identify poor performers. By this reckoning, it is designed primarily to separate the chaff from the wheat. It is something to be feared. This perception arises from evaluation's focus on identifying problems when they are minor so that they do not grow into large problems. There is no question that when we conduct evaluations, we are looking for problems. However, this is not to say that we are looking for troublemakers.

Along these same lines, some managers see evaluation as a mechanism to keep staff on their toes, regarding it as something akin to a surprise audit. I once had a manager say to me, "I like to conduct surprise evaluations. This way I can see how my staff function at any given time, when they don't have the opportunity to prepare for an audit. It keeps them sharp because they never know when they will be scrutinized."

Actually, effective evaluation requires that surprises be kept to a minimum. Evaluation criteria should be clearly laid out. They should be reviewed according to a well-established schedule and clearly defined rules. In this way, project staff know what is expected of them. They can work to meet those expectations. This outlook on evaluation lies at the heart of management by objectives.

A third and highly destructive distortion is the use of evaluation to serve political ends. Certain individuals use evaluation to further their political objectives. If it confirms their position, they employ it to strengthen themselves. If it contradicts their position, they ignore it. Evaluation in this case is simply an instrument of convenience. When used politically, its credibility as a management tool is destroyed. Project staff justifiably see it as a dangerous weapon.

Inherent Characteristics of Evaluation

Much of the pain of evaluation is tied to some of its inherent characteristics. The people being evaluated often do not see its value as a feedback mechanism designed to keep the project on track. At worst, they feel threatened by it; at best, they see it as a nuisance.

Perhaps the most negative feature of evaluation is its inherent threat. As mentioned earlier, evaluations look for problems. They are exercises in criticism. The people being evaluated are put into a defensive posture. Their natural tendency is to resist attacks. For evaluations to succeed, project staff must be made to realize that this criticism is not designed to hurt them. Management must convey a sense that it recognizes that problems occur naturally and for everyone. The existence of problems does not indicate incompetence. If the need for evaluation is properly conveyed to staff and its level of threat is lessened, staff are more likely to participate fully and honestly.

Another problem with evaluation is that it is disruptive. Frequently, evaluations are carried out by teams of outsiders. The theory here is that we do not want conflicts of interest to arise—we do not want foxes guarding the chicken coop. Unfortunately, when outsiders come in to review project work, enormous amounts of time must often be dedicated to educating them about the project, its goals, its history, the composition of the team, and so forth. Project staff may find themselves pulled off project work to help in this effort. The act of evaluation may actually contribute to schedule and cost overruns.

A final problem with evaluation is that it can easily be carried out in an arbitrary and capricious fashion. Project staff are painfully aware that if the evaluation team arrives on a Monday rather than a Thursday, their conclusions might be different. They are also aware that evaluation team A will likely come up with different conclusions than team B or C. The problem is excessive subjectivity and a lack of consistency. If indeed the process is carried out in an arbitrary and capricious fashion, the results of the evaluation effort lack value. We might as well determine our conclusions by throwing dice.

Incidentally, evaluations do not have to be highly subjective. Effective evaluation attempts to make the process as objective as possible. One way to do this is to specify the evaluation criteria long before the evaluation is carried out, so that the project team knows what is expected of it. Another way is to make the criteria objectively verifiable. For example, a criterion might read: "The team should finish all tasks associated with phases 1 and 2 by March 15" (determining whether or not the tasks are complete should be relatively straightforward), or "Data entry errors should be no more than one error per five hundred keystrokes."

Clearly, significant problems are often associated with the attempt to evaluate project work. To the extent that project staff perceive the evaluation to be dangerous to their future or a waste of time, they are unlikely to supply information needed to make it meaningful.

How can you reduce the level of threat inherent in evaluation? And how can you eliminate the sense that it is carried out in an arbitrary and capricious fashion? There are various ways that evaluations can be conducted effectively. One example will be presented here. This approach, called the *structured walk-through*, has been employed a great deal since the late 1960s. People who have experienced it generally perceive it to be a useful exercise and do not see it as threatening. Consequently, they openly participate in the evaluation effort, greatly increasing the likelihood that it will result in meaningful conclusions.

THE STRUCTURED WALK-THROUGH

The structured walk-through technique was developed by IBM in the late 1960s as a relatively friendly approach to evaluating project efforts. It demonstrates that with a bit of creative thinking, management techniques can be developed to deal with seemingly intractable problems. In the case of evaluation, the intractable problem is that the negative aspects of evaluation discourage project staff from partaking forthrightly and readily in the evaluation process. The structured walk-through approach deals with this problem by giving the people who are being evaluated control over the evaluation process.

Following are the key rules for conducting a structured walk-through. These rules reflect the original rules created by IBM, as well as modifications that have evolved over the years. The following discussion also incorporates observations gleaned from interviews I conducted with project staff associated with some thirty structured walk-throughs.

Rule 1: The Group Being Evaluated Chooses Its Judge and Jury

This rule reduces the sense of threat felt by the people being evaluated. If they choose the evaluators, they cannot complain that the evaluation team was selected in an arbitrary fashion. They also can be assured that the team was not chosen in accordance with some hidden political agenda. Finally, they can select an evaluation team that is made up of people who are already educated as to how the organization functions and what is being developed. By doing so, they reduce the amount of time they must dedicate to bringing the evaluation team up to speed.

Obviously, there is a danger that the group being evaluated will rig the jury. That is, they can choose evaluation team members who are their close associates and who would be reluctant to criticize them too harshly. In practice, this potential abuse of privilege does not appear to be a serious problem. None of the people I interviewed suggested that they worked with a rigged jury. The structured walk-through approach creates a sense of trust, and the people being evaluated are reluctant to violate this trust. They recognize that it is a greater crime to distort the walk-through process than to experience difficulties on the project.

In addition, in many organizations, the team being evaluated is not given full latitude in choosing its evaluators. Rather, it is given the opportunity to select its evaluators from a list of candidates preapproved by the organization's evaluation office.

Rule 2: The Group Being Evaluated Determines the Rules of the Evaluation Effort

The people being evaluated continue to control the process by establishing the rules of the game. They identify the evaluation criteria. They send the evaluation packages with instructions to the evaluation team members. They set the agenda for the evaluation sessions.

As with rule 1, there is the possibility that this rule can be abused. Specifically, the group being evaluated can create rules that steer the evaluation team away from problem areas. Once again, this does not seem to be a real problem in practice. Group members realize that by avoiding problems, they are defeating the whole point of the evaluation.

In addition, in many organizations, the rules the team can establish are governed by a set of guidelines established by the evaluation office.

Rule 3: The Group Being Evaluated Runs the Evaluation Meetings

The evaluation review occurs through one or more meetings. This constitutes the actual walk-through. The people being evaluated actually run the meetings. They determine which people talk, when they talk, and how long they talk.

Interestingly, in my interviews, the greatest complaints about the structured walk-through focused on how the meetings were conducted. Typical complaints include "The people running the meetings are not experienced facilitators—they conduct the meetings in an amateurish fashion"; "The meetings do not stick to the agenda—for example, technical evaluators tend to go off on a technical tangent"; "Discussion is not effectively limited—some participants drone on endlessly"; and "The evaluation meetings can provide a forum for different groups to grind their political axes—in selecting outside evaluators, it is important that people are chosen who get along with each other." These complaints are not directed at the structured walk-through process itself. Rather, they are directed at the lack of skills many of us have in running a meeting.

Rule 4: No Upper-Level Managers
Should Be Present at the Evaluation Sessions

The whole point of the structured walk-through process is to create an environment that engenders honesty. How honest will employees be if they are asked to discuss serious problems in their work in the presence of individuals who rate their performance? A substantial minority of the people I interviewed reported that higher-level managers would occasionally sit in on their structured walk-throughs. Most indicated that they were not pleased with this management presence and said they found that it stifled the free flow of ideas.

Rule 5: Customers Should Not
Be Present at the Evaluation Sessions

This fifth rule never appeared in the original IBM guidelines on conducting a structured walk-through. But people who have experienced the presence of customers during a walk-through session strongly recommend that customers be excluded. Their rationale is identical to the rationale underlying rule 4. How honest will people be in uncovering problems when the customer is present? Furthermore, there is the danger that the customer may actively join in the criticism process and use the occasion to change project requirements.

This rule may sound anticustomer, but it is not. Customer satisfaction remains a key objective of project management. However, there are many other avenues through which we can obtain customer inputs—for example, through customer walk-throughs.

One class of projects in which we cannot exclude customers from the structured walk-throughs emerged during the 1990s: projects that involve close partnering between customers and project staff. In these cases, the customers are already aware of the inevitable difficulties that arise on projects, so their presence during evaluation sessions will not be disruptive.

Rule 6: Maintain Good Documentation
Throughout the Evaluation Process

Virtually everyone I interviewed believed strongly that a structured walk-through will not be effective unless the whole process is documented carefully. In particular, notes should be taken of comments and decisions made during the evaluation meetings, and action items should be created from these notes. These action items should detail what actions should be undertaken by what time and by whom. Follow-up reviews should be made to ensure that the action items have been adequately addressed.

Organizations that employ the structured walk-through approach to evaluation are highly satisfied with the results they achieve. It is not a panacea and can be a bit painful to carry out. However, most employees are aware that the alternative is to bring in outsiders whom they may not trust, and consequently they much prefer the structured walk-through approach.

CONCLUSIONS

Projects are cybernetic systems—feedback and control are essential to their proper execution. A major source of feedback information comes from evaluations. As we have seen, these evaluations cover a broad range of topics, from performance appraisals to technical reviews to selection appraisals to postmortems. This reflects the fact that projects are driven by forces coming from a variety of sources, and feedback from each of these sources is needed to keep the project on track.

Without systematic evaluation procedures, the project will lose its way. It's like trying to drive a car in a severe rainstorm when the windshield wipers aren't functioning. The view of the road is so distorted by the raindrops that one cannot drive effectively. The driver can slow down to a crawling pace, but this may mean that he misses his appointments. He can continue driving at a speedy rate, but this makes it more likely that he will have an accident.

Evaluation systems must be developed with great care. Their purpose is to generate honest, timely, and accurate insights on project progress. If they are perceived to be threatening, the probability of obtaining honest information is diminished. If they are conducted in a disorganized, haphazard way, they won't generate timely results. And if the instruments for measuring performance are no good—for example, if they depend on excessive use of subjective judgment—the conclusions will lack accuracy.

Evaluation serves a function beyond providing feedback to keep the project on track: it is an instrument to heighten accountability. Too many projects fail because accountability is diffuse. With properly conducted evaluations, people are answerable for their actions and decisions. They have no choice but to adopt a "buck stops here" outlook on their efforts.

CHAPTER FIFTEEN

Understanding and Using Performance Metrics

Measuring the Right Stuff

I magine driving an automobile with a nonfunctioning speedometer. You would probably feel very uncomfortable. As you passed posted speed limit signs, you would not know whether you were exceeding the limit, thus risking a speeding ticket. On the highway, you might decide to travel the same speed as the other cars on the road, but when you saw the police pulling over cars in your group, you might decide this was not a wise policy. Without the speedometer, you would have high levels of uncertainty about your driving performance.

Our lives are filled with measurement. Upon awakening in the morning, we check our weight by standing on a scale. We then go into the kitchen where we measure out two scoops of ground coffee, which we put into our coffee brewer. We set the brewer for "extra-strong" coffee. The newspaper delivery boy drops by, and we pay him for two months of newspaper deliveries. We look at our watch and realize with horror that we have only fifteen minutes left before we should leave for the office. The office is located ten miles away. Given an average commuting speed of thirty miles per hour, we estimate that it should take us twenty minutes to reach the office.

Clearly, using measures is an important part of our daily lives. Lord Kelvin emphasized this importance in a famous statement when he said that if something in science cannot be measured, it has little value. Kelvin was a renowned scientist. The role of measurement in science and engineering is obvious. Less obvious is the role of measurement in management.

Measurement is extremely important for effective management. Imagine a for-profit company trying to manage its affairs without cost and income data. Or imagine it trying to plan its affairs without any knowledge of the time it takes to carry out its activities. Nevertheless, many organizations seem to be content to fly blind without the measures they need to track their efforts and to make reasonable decisions.

Occasionally, one encounters stiff resistance to attempts to measure work effort. Frequently cited as grounds for this resistance is the belief that "there are some things that are just not amenable to measurement." I suspect that this resistance to measurement is largely rooted in what John Allen Paulos calls the innumeracy—numerical illiteracy—of management and the workforce. In his insightful and entertaining book *Innumeracy* (1988), Paulos convincingly demonstrates that Americans often lack the most basic grasp of what measurement is about. They simply do not understand numbers and what they can do. Consequently, they have little appreciation of the power of measurement to help them function more effectively—or they accept numerical results too readily because they lack the competence to assess the genuine pitfalls of measurement.

Some of the key topics discussed in this book—estimation, risk management, evaluation, integrated cost and schedule control, accountability—have a strong measurement component. If one is to get a firm grasp of estimating time and cost performance, evaluating work performance, or determining the range of risk associated with a decision, one must have some sense of how measurement plays a role in each of these areas. What makes for a good measure as opposed to a bad one? How are measurement data collected? What measures can we employ when "hard" measures are lacking? What are the pitfalls of measurement?

This chapter should be viewed as a primer on measurement in project management. Anyone who has taken a doctoral-level research methodology course will be comfortable with the topics covered here, for they are standard fare in such courses. The approach I employ is commonsensical rather than formal and rigorous. The objective is to heighten awareness among project managers and staff of the role that measurement does and should play on their projects.

THE ROLE OF MEASUREMENT IN MANAGING PROJECTS

Measures serve a variety of functions in project management. Their uses range from the establishment of unambiguous targets to the tracking of accomplishments to modeling project processes. The common thread running through these different uses is *accountability*. When something is measured, its fundamental features are laid bare. Measurement implies clarity, replicability, and verifiability. With proper measurement, vagueness and obfuscation are no longer viable recourses for the inept manager. Accountability reigns!

Let us look at some of the key uses of measurement in projects.

Establishing Clear Targets

An important feature of management by objectives is the creation of unambiguous goals. A goal is ambiguous when five people reviewing it come up with multiple interpretations of its meaning. When a goal is clear, the five people hold a single view of its meaning.

A good way to establish an unambiguous goal is to build verifiable measures into it. The goal "to arrive at Grandma's house as fast as possible" is considerably strengthened when phrased "to arrive at Grandma's house within half an hour." Similarly, the goal "to carry a lot of grocery bags into the house from the car" is less ambiguous when stated "to carry into the house a minimum of four grocery bags taken from the car."

By establishing measurable goals, we create more clearly defined targets toward which we can direct our efforts. With clear targets, there is less chance of misinterpreting what should be done.

Tracking Performance

Without clearly defined targets and well-defined performance measures, it is impossible to track performance accurately. How does one determine whether the vague goal "to do the job as quickly as possible" is actually being achieved?

By allowing people to track performance more precisely, measures provide feedback about the achievement of specified goals. This feedback gives people a sense of what they have accomplished and what it will take to complete the job. To see this, consider the following simple example.

George is told that he has two weeks to write Chapter Three of a user's manual for a software system his organization is developing. The specified length of the chapter is thirty pages, including eight drawings. By the end of week 1, he finds that he has written only ten pages of manuscript and has completed two drawings. When the project manager contacts him to determine what progress he is making, how should he report his progress?

He could say, "I'm slipping a bit, but with a little more effort I might be able to meet the deadline." The problem with this answer is that it provides little insight into the actual status of George's effort. Furthermore, it offers no real insight into what will be needed to complete the job on time.

By phrasing his response in terms of work measurement, George can provide the project manager with a better sense of the project's status. For example, he may estimate that for this chapter, it is taking him one person-week of effort to produce ten manuscript pages and two or three drawings. If he continues to work alone at this rate, he calculates that he will miss his deadline date by one week, since the job entails producing thirty pages of text and eight drawings in two weeks and he will actually have completed only twenty pages and five or six drawings in this time. His computation of his actual work performance rate suggests how he can meet the two-week deadline: if an additional person can be assigned to the effort, the job can be finished on time.

George's analysis can be extended to compute the cost implications of his schedule slippage—for example, he can compare the additional costs of adding a new person to the project and contrast that to the costs associated with extending the project one week. The point is that by examining the quantitative implications of George's work performance, the project manager now has key data to allow for rational decisions.

Rewarding and Punishing Behavior

The achievement or nonachievement of defined measurable goals often serves as the basis of individual performance appraisals. For this approach to be viable, the people being appraised should play a role in defining the measurable goals. If they do not play such a role, they may feel they are being measured against an unrealistic yardstick. They are not likely to feel a personal commitment to achieving the goals. They may even distort their reporting of data because they do not want to be punished for failing to achieve unrealistic goals. The dictum that workers be part of the goal-setting process is a fundamental precept of MBO.

With individual performance appraisal, qualitative factors clearly play an important role. Such hard-to-measure things as attitude, energy, and employees' team orientation are important evaluation criteria. However, these subjective judgments should be reinforced with objective measures. A subjectively determined criterion such as energy level or a good attitude is not by itself useful if the evaluated worker is consistently deficient in meeting his or her defined goals. Without the use of measurable performance indicators, we run the risk of rewarding substandard behavior on the basis of "feel good" sentiments or punishing basically good behavior because of "bad" feelings.

There is nothing new in the use of measurable performance indicators to reward good behavior. The best-known example of this is the commission paid to sales personnel. The more sales made, the greater the commission. To encourage superperformance, commission rates may be accelerated for a sales volume above a threshold.

Modeling and Predicting Project Performance

With the creation and employment of performance measurements, it becomes possible to develop quantitative models of project activities. The advantage of modeling the project process is that it allows project staff to generate "what if" scenarios associated with different situations. Through modeling, a change in the value of such things as the number of human resources available or the estimated duration of a task can provide staff with important information about the cost, schedule, or quality implications of specific changes.

The models created need not be elaborate. A simple budget maintained on an electronic spreadsheet is an example of a rudimentary but useful computerized model. By changing wage rates on the spreadsheet, the analyst has instant data on what project costs will be with the new rates.

A commonly employed modeling tool in project management is the PERT/CPM network. Such networks can be built using a wide variety of PERT/CPM software packages. Today's packages integrate budget, schedule, and human resource data, thus creating a truly robust overview of project performance. Some of these packages are easy to learn, requiring only a morning of instructional effort. Of course, the more sophisticated packages require more time to master.

Of recent interest to project managers are analytical approaches that allow them to model risk. A variety of software packages have emerged in recent years that permit even mathematically naïve managers to estimate the range of possible budget, schedule, and human resource outcomes they face under conditions of uncertainty. This topic is discussed in more detail in Chapter Four.

THE NATURE OF MEASUREMENT

Not all measures are good. If the instrument that records data is defective, this will lead to the generation of bad measures. For example, a miscalibrated thermometer will consistently yield incorrect temperature readings. If a measure is used inappropriately, it will also provide bad results. For example, using blood pressure measures as an indicator of anxiety will yield poor results because high blood pressure has other causes beyond intense anxiety.

To use measures effectively, we should have some appreciation of their fundamental nature. In this section, we explore some basic features of measures, an understanding of which can allow us to use them more effectively.

"Strength" of Measurement

Numerical data that serve as the basis of measurement can be viewed as possessing varying degrees of "strength." The "softest" data are *nominal scale* data. These are nothing more than labels. The numbers on the shirts of athletes are nominal data. Basically, nominal data are useful in categorizing phenomena. Counts of boys versus girls in a room, counts of steak dinners versus chicken dinners at a reception, and counts of blue dresses versus green dresses versus yellow dresses in a dress factory all exemplify the use of nominal data.

Ordinal scale data are more powerful than nominal data. They allow us to rank things in some order. When we say that ice is colder than tap water, we are making an ordinal comparison. Similarly, when we say that Jackie ranks first in her class, Myron ranks second, and Marsha ranks third, we are engaging in ordinal measurement. These measures are commonly employed in performance appraisal and often take the form of classification into categories such as "greatly exceeds standards," "exceeds standards," "meets standards," and "falls short of standards." They are also frequently encountered on evaluation questionnaires when we are asked to rank something on a scale of 1 to 5.

One thing to keep in mind when dealing with ordinal data is that they are not additive or subject to the full range of arithmetic manipulation. You cannot add first place to fourth place to tally fifth place. Neither does it make sense to subtract, multiply, or divide ordinal measures.

Interval scale data are numbers that can be employed fully in arithmetic manipulations. The price of a piece of pie, the temperature on a winter day, and the number of days it takes to carry out a task are examples of interval scale data. These data can be added and subtracted meaningfully ($2.00 + $3.00 + $4.00 = $9.00; $5.00 − $2.00 = $3.00), multiplied and divided (2 × $5.00 = $10.00; $10.00/2 = $5.00), and manipulated in every conceivable way. Because of this versatility in their employment, they are considered the most powerful of the three scales of data discussed here.

Most attempts at gathering work performance measures on projects focus on collecting interval scale data. Task durations, budget expenditures, number of resources available, fraction of effort achieved, efficiency measures, and technical performance data are among the measures commonly employed on projects, and they all provide interval scale data.

When such measures are not readily available, project staff often shrug their shoulders and give up trying to collect data, arguing that what they are looking at is fundamentally unmeasurable. Before they give up, they should attempt to see whether the thing they are trying to assay can be measured ordinally. I may not be able to say that customer satisfaction with feature A of my software system is twice as high as with feature B, but I can make the ordinal statement that "satisfaction with feature A far exceeds satisfaction with feature B." This may not be a precise insight, but at least it gives us a sense of what is happening in reality.

If something appears to be difficult to measure ordinally, an attempt to measure it nominally might be undertaken. The mere classification of something is a form of measurement and can provide project staff with valuable insights. For example, categorizing activities by risk factor is a form of nominal measurement that is valuable on projects.

Subjective Versus Objective Measures

A great drive to quantify human behavior arose in the 1960s. At that time, the social sciences were titillated by the possibility that social science could be carried out with the same degree of precision as the physical sciences. The prevailing view was that the chief difference between human behavior and physical action is one of degree rather than kind. That is, human behavior is sloppier than physical behavior because it is more complex, made up of a myriad of variables that affect outcomes. Although in the physical sciences we actually encounter parsimonious relationships such as $e = mc^2$, the complexity of human activity makes such relationships unlikely in the social sciences. However, the advent of the computer made the handling of complex relationships easier. From the computer's perspective, manipulating fifty variables is only marginally more burdensome than manipulating three. The power of the computer to harness massive quantities of data that allow for social engineering was captured in the pop culture of the time in Michael Crichton's science fiction thriller *The Andromeda Strain* (1969), which portrayed computers as capable of measuring all aspects of human activity.

In their attempts to quantify human behavior, social scientists focused on developing measures that were as objective as possible. Objectivity was regarded as "scientific" because of its association with replicability. It also implied the absence of human judgment in making the measure; this detachment in arriving at judgments was also seen as "scientific."

The following simple example illustrates the objective-versus-subjective dichotomy: determining temperature by employing a well-calibrated thermometer is viewed as objective, whereas asking someone to describe it based on personal sensations is considered subjective. Objective measures tend to give consistent results, whereas subjective ones do not.

In management, the drive toward objectivity reached an extreme form in the Delphi process that emerged in the 1960s. Delphi is a forecasting tool that attempts to convert subjective judgments into objective data. To see how the Delphi process works, consider the problem of estimating how long it will take before the United States has operational factories in place. Let us suppose that a panel of fifteen experts on the economics and technology of space commercialization and manufacturing is identified. With Delphi, the views of each panelist are collected independently, typically by means of a questionnaire. The panelists are not permitted to interact with each other directly. Their views are statistically analyzed and summarized. The statistical summary is then returned to the panelists, who are instructed to study the results. In view of the summary—which in effect reflects the collective judgment of all the panelists—the individual panelists are asked to reconsider all original estimates and adjust them accordingly. The panelists' revised views are then analyzed and summarized, and the latest results are sent back out to them. This procedure continues in this iterative fashion until some preestablished degree of convergence of views is achieved.

The striking feature of the Delphi approach is that in the interest of maintaining objectivity, direct interaction of the panelists with each other is proscribed. The rationale for such a "sanitary" procedure is to avoid "contamination" of judgments that might arise if the panelists were permitted to interact directly and thereby be influenced by personality factors.

The obsession with objectivity characteristic of the 1960s appears a bit quaint from today's perspective. For one thing, viewing human judgment and interaction as a contaminant seems rather shortsighted. Today, we tend to feel strongly that new insights are achieved through human interaction. Ideas are less likely to grow stale because they are continually challenged. Interestingly, one of the most popular contemporary tools for converting subjective judgments into objective data is the analytical hierarchy process (AHP), a fairly sophisticated mathematical approach that requires the heavy interaction of people in a face-to-face forum.

For another thing, the whole concept of what is objective and what is not has turned out to be harder to define than people thought back in the 1960s. Even the most seemingly objective judgment is ultimately based on premises that are rooted in human biases. This is seen clearly in the public debates on standardized examinations of human capabilities, such as IQ tests and the SATs. Several decades ago, the objectivity of such exams was widely accepted. Today, however, these and other similar examinations are under severe attack for being culturally biased. It has reached the point where the Educational Testing Service (the developer of the SAT) has agreed to include a subjective essay component in future editions of the examination in order to make the examinations less biased. In this case, subjectivity is seen to be more scientifically valid than objectivity.

Reliability

The measurement of anything but the most trivial objects often results in some measurement error. If I ask five people to count the number of bricks visible on the front elevation of a brick house, I will likely get five separate numbers. Some of the variance might be attributable to definitional problems. For example, what constitutes a "brick" for counting purposes? At the corners of the house or along window frames, many bricks are cut in half to fit properly into the structure. Should these be counted as whole bricks or half bricks? Some of the variance is simply a result of counting error. A number of bricks might be double-counted, and others might be skipped entirely.

The big issue here is not whether everyone comes up with the same count. Chances are they don't. The issue really is how much variance there is in their counts. If one individual reports that the house has 3,500 bricks, another 6,200 bricks, and still another 8,200 bricks, there is a large variance in the counts. In this case, we say the measures have low reliability. On the other hand, if the reported number of bricks coming from three estimates are 6,150, 6,200, and 6,225, there is a high degree of consistency in the counts, and we say the measures are highly reliable.

A measure is reliable, then, if after repeated samplings, the results we achieve are close to each other. A measure with low reliability is of little use. Wild "guesstimates," common on projects, typically have low reliability. They often exemplify the old data processing adage "garbage in, garbage out."

Reliability can be enhanced by developing careful methods and procedures for collecting data. Substantial attention should focus on defining carefully what should be counted. In the example of the brick facade, data collection procedures might specify that bricks that have been split in half should be counted as half bricks. If data gatherers are allowed to make up their own rules as they do their jobs, there will be inconsistency in the measures.

Validity

Validity addresses the question, Are we really measuring what we think we are measuring? For example, temperature is not a valid measure of humidity (although it may be correlated with humidity). It *is* a valid measure of the hotness or coldness of a body or environment. Gross domestic product is not a valid measure of national economic well-being because a country can have a high GDP but its wealth may be concentrated in the hands of an elite, leaving the majority of the population in poverty. GDP *is* a valid measure of the market value of goods and services produced in a country.

The issue of validity is particularly relevant in our attempts to develop measures for performance appraisal. Is absenteeism a valid measure of a worker's commitment to doing a good job? Is the worker's consistent achievement of objectives a measure of effectiveness? Is the frequency of complaints directed at a worker a valid measure of his or her concern for customer satisfaction?

The validity of a measure must be determined in the context in which it is used. Consider the three measures mentioned in the preceding paragraph. In general, absenteeism reasonably reflects worker commitment to doing a good job. The hotel clerk who repeatedly calls in sick in order to take time off to go to the beach is not heavily committed to doing a good job. However, during flu season, absenteeism may reflect nothing more than the fact that some workers had the misfortune to be exposed to the flu virus. In this case, its validity is suspect.

The consistent achievement of objectives *can* accurately reflect an employee's effectiveness, particularly if he or she played a role in defining them. But if unrealistic objectives are imposed on the employee, failure to achieve them may be more strongly rooted in the fact that they are poorly specified than in the employee's lack of effectiveness.

Frequent complaints directed at an employee *might* indicate that he or she lacks a commitment to customer satisfaction. They might also indicate that the organization in which the employee works is not adequately supporting its workers to do a good job. For example, if only one employee is assigned to deal with a multitude of complaints and this results in slow responses to individual complaints, it is likely that customers will focus their anger on that employee.

One way to test for the validity of a measure is to see whether it correlates positively with other closely related measures. For example, if we find that measures of absenteeism do not correspond at all to other measures of employee commitment (for example, hours of unpaid overtime worked or employee attitude), they are probably not valid measures of commitment.

Another way to deal with the manner of validity is to constantly scrutinize the measures we employ and ask if they are really measuring what we say they are measuring. This scrutiny should be carried out by a wide array of people, including different members of the management team, the individuals being evaluated, and disinterested outsiders.

GENERATING MEASURES

Most organizations are sitting on a gold mine of useful measures, but they do not realize it. Quite frequently, when I ask a project manager, "How long does it take you to test the XYZ component on your products?" I get the answer, "I'm not sure. We don't have those data." I know for a fact that in this organization, a dozen projects have been carried out that have tested the XYZ component, yet basic data on its duration, resource requirements, and costs are not handy. In actuality, the organization *does* have the basic data, but they are buried in a morass of other facts and figures. The problem is that no one has taken the effort to retrieve the data and put them into a useful form.

When I suggest to people that they begin collecting data that can serve them well on their projects, they often look at me in wonder.

"We've never done that," they say.

"Why not begin now?" I respond.

The greatest obstacle to the effective generation of measures is ignorance. The vast majority of people I encounter do not have a clue as to how they should begin the data generation process. They see it as a highly complex undertaking requiring specialized skills that they simply lack. They are overwhelmed by the effort involved, so they deal with it in the most convenient way possible: they avoid it.

In this section, we shall examine a number of ways that people can generate useful measures on their projects. There is nothing magical about developing good measures. They are all around us. Our job is first to identify them and then to put them into a usable form. In developing good measures, we should take some guidance from the great French cubist painter Georges Braque. When asked how he came up with his vision for his pictures, he responded, "It's easy. With my paintbrush, I brush away the white surface of the canvas, and the painting emerges from beneath."

We will look at two broad approaches for generating measures: using existing data and creating new data.

Generating Measures from Existing Data

The file cabinets and mass storage media of most organizations are filled with data that can lead to improved project management if employed productively. It is merely a question of identifying which data can be used effectively and then massaging them to make them useful. Following is a list of untapped data sources that can be found in most project organizations.

TIME SHEETS. Well-constructed time sheets provide valuable information on how project staff allocate their time. They show the variations in the usage of different categories of personnel. Technical support personnel (such as testers, maintenance personnel, statisticians, and editors) will be allocated across several projects. Core personnel (such as designers and developers) will commit their time to fewer projects. Drawing on past patterns of personnel usage that emerge from a review of time sheets, project planners can predict future allocations of people to tasks.

Other valuable information can be extracted from time sheets. For example, they might indicate which workers and categories of work have high levels of administrative overhead associated with them. By examining overtime allocations, they can provide information on how realistic the organization has been in estimating work requirements for tasks. They also show work cycles, alerting management that there are predictable times when staff might be underemployed or overemployed. All this information can be used to help organizations make better resource allocation decisions on projects.

The key problem with time sheets is reliability. In many organizations, the rules on how to fill out a time sheet are very loose. For example, if administrative time is not carefully defined by the organization, one employee may count a half-hour conversation with the accounting department as administrative time while another may deem it a legitimate charge against a project. For time sheets to be a valuable source of project data, organizations must carefully define how they should be used and should apply the rules consistently across all employees and projects.

BUDGETS. Like time sheets, budgets contain valuable information nuggets that can help us manage our projects more effectively. For example, a careful review of past project budgets may allow cost estimators to establish cost standards for carrying out various tasks, such as report production, testing, and data analysis. These standards permit more consistent cost estimating in the future. Instead of creating brand-new estimates of how much it should cost for data entry tasks each time a new project is conceived, estimators can review standards generated from past experience and adjust them according to the specific characteristics of the new project in question. Incidentally, these new standards should not be cast in concrete. They should be updated constantly to reflect recent project experiences.

In collecting data from budget forms, analysts should pay special attention to what it actually cost to do work and contrast that with what was initially budgeted. The actual expenses will play an important role in formulating our cost standards. They also provide us with insights into the adequacy of previous estimates. If we find that in our budget projections we consistently understate project costs by 15 percent, we should take this information into account in future projections.

PREVIOUS SCHEDULES. Most organizations have voluminous project reports stashed away in their file cabinets, and a good number of these contain schedules for previous projects. With the advent of microcomputer-based scheduling software, we increasingly find that historical data on schedules are archived electronically. These old schedules contain valuable information that can be employed on future projects. At a minimum, they list activities and milestones that crop up on multiple organization projects. These activities and milestones can be scanned across a broad range of previous projects and used to create punch lists of things to consider in scheduling future projects.

The old schedules may also contain estimates of task durations. These estimates can be checked against actual performance (gleaned from old status reports) and can lead to the establishment of estimating baselines.

Organizations interested in employing good project metrics should establish consistent procedures for reporting schedules so that scheduling data can be readily fed into a historical database for projects.

STATUS REPORTS. Status reports come in a variety of shapes and sizes. A well-configured status report clearly establishes actual performance against planned performance. If this information is readily accessible in the status report, it becomes a treasure trove of valuable project measures. For example, planned versus actual cost and schedule data can be derived from twelve months of status reports and plotted graphically. The plots show visually the extent to which previous plans were met. If we find that previous plans consistently understated costs by 20 percent, this information should be reviewed, and future plans might be adjusted accordingly. Furthermore, the "actuals" data can be collected task by task and can serve as the basis for cost and scheduling standards against which future performance can be assessed.

POSTMORTEMS. Postmortems are conducted after projects have concluded and serve a "lessons learned" function. Well-executed postmortems often contain thoughtful insights as to what worked well and what did not work on projects. In addition, the insights are typically backed up with tabular and graphical data. Postmortem reports should be scanned for useful measures they contain.

Generating New Measures

Project staff should not feel constrained to work only with existing measures garnered from time sheets, schedules, status reports, and the like. In certain situations, they may find it useful to generate wholly new measures. We will examine two approaches to generating such measures.

QUESTIONNAIRES AND INTERVIEWS. A common way to collect data about human activity is through questionnaires and interviews. These are ubiquitous in modern societies. At home, pollsters phone at inconvenient hours—usually at dinnertime—to determine the opinions of homeowners regarding a new tax initiative. In the supermarket, customers are queried in the aisles about their buying preferences. In the mail, people receive all manner of questionnaires soliciting their views on everything from their satisfaction with the service they received at the auto repair shop to their opinions on candidates for the presidency.

Questionnaires and interviews also have their place on projects. One obvious way to determine how project staff spend their time is to ask them directly: How long does it typically take you to review client needs? How much time do you spend filling out forms? How many hours a week do you spend on project work? (This can also serve as a check on data gathered from time sheets.) Questionnaires and interviews can also be used to assess the risk of a set of activities, to identify when a set of resources will be freed up, to determine satisfaction with project management procedures, and many other things.

Questionnaires and interviews generally fall into one of two categories. Some are open-ended and are designed to generate information in an unstructured fashion. Questions associated with this approach permit any and all answers: What do you think are the three most significant quality problems the design department faces? How can response time to customer queries be shortened? Who are the individuals in your department who have the greatest impact on generating effective project procedures?

A second type of questionnaires and interviews are structured and are geared toward generating information that can be analyzed objectively. Examples of questions associated with this approach give quantifiable results in a predictable format: On a scale of 1 to 5 (where 1 represents "poor" and 5 represents "excellent"), how would you rank the probability of technical success for this project? Given the following five options, which most accurately describes the factors that result in better-formulated documentation? How many years have you been a project manager?

With structured data, it becomes possible to conduct sophisticated inquiries into important issues. Results can be reported as percentages ("Seventy-two percent of the respondents stated that work conditions have not improved in the department"), reported as cross-tabulations ("Of the 72 percent who stated that work conditions have not improved in the department, three-quarters had been with the company less than two years"), or analyzed according to any of a large number of sophisticated statistical methodologies (analysis of variance, regression analysis, factor analysis, discriminant analysis).

Individuals employing questionnaires and interviews should be aware of a number of potential pitfalls. Some of these are dependent on questionnaire design. Are the questions unambiguous? Are they biased? Do they really measure what they set out to measure? On a structured questionnaire, are the structured responses clearly written? Do they reflect the broad universe of potential responses? Is the questionnaire or interview too long? If so, respondents may be reluctant to cooperate with the query. Is it too superficial?

Other pitfalls stem from the environment in which the query is carried out. Are people willing to "go on record"? Will confidentiality be maintained? Has an attempt been made to query a random sample of respondents, or is the sample biased?

DIRECT MEASURES. Modern management owes a large debt to the scientific management principles of Frederick Taylor. Taylor was obsessed with measuring work performance. He invented the concept of time and motion studies, during which trained observers systematically scrutinized people's work efforts. The tools of the trade were the clipboard, a pad of paper, a pencil, and a stopwatch. Work would be broken down into its most elemental steps and then measured.

Direct measures of work effort are often appropriate on projects. Consider the situation facing the designer of a new information system. One important design consideration is the usability of the new system. To test for usability, a number of experiments might be set up. One experiment might test to see which of several data entry forms best facilitates data entry. The performance of data entry clerks on the different forms might be measured on a number of criteria: Which form has the least number of data entry errors associated with it? How quickly can a standard set of data be entered into each of the forms? Which forms allow for the speediest correction of errors?

Project staff should be trained to see how they can generate direct measures when appropriate. This training need not be elaborate. It can include simple exercises in measurement. For example, staff might be required to track in a diary how they use their time over the course of a week. Or they might count the pieces of mail they receive, sorting letters into appropriate categories (for example, project-related, department-related, messages requiring a response, junk mail). Or they can tabulate the durations of everyday tasks (How long does it take to brush my teeth? To prepare breakfast? To travel between stations on the subway? On the average, how long is the queue at the sandwich stand in the cafeteria at 12:15 P.M.? On the average, how long does it take before the fourth person in the queue is fully served?).

THE SHADOW SIDE OF MEASURES

Numbers seldom speak for themselves. In an amusing book titled *How to Lie with Statistics* (1954), Darrell Huff shows how a given set of numbers can be employed in countless self-serving ways. When manipulated skillfully, statistics can be used to make practically any desired argument. When used carelessly, well-intentioned analyses can produce erroneous results that lead to disaster. Clearly, metrics have their shadow side. Let us look at some common problems.

Unintended Consequences of Measurable Performance Targets

Earlier in this chapter, I noted that an important use of metrics in projects is to establish performance targets. A pharmaceutical company may set a target to enroll forty new patients a month in its clinical trials. A telecommunications company may set a target to spend no more than two days per site to install its low-end telephone switches. Sales staff are given quarterly sales targets to achieve. When used effectively, these targets greatly strengthen the project management process. However, experience shows that great care must be taken in establishing them, since poorly formulated targets can lead to unintended consequences. This point is illustrated in the following examples.

CASE 1: SORRY, WRONG NUMBER. In keeping with the new focus on customer satisfaction, ABC Electronics Company established a telephone hot line to field customer complaints and queries. Some concern was expressed that operators might linger in their chats with customers, so the number of calls handled was computed, and rewards were offered to those operators who handled the most calls. To give visibility to the superlative performers, a Top Operator was identified quarterly. Anna Smith won the first Top Operator award. Everyone was amazed at her performance: she handled 25 percent more calls in the quarter than the runner-up. Anna also won the second Top Operator award. This time she topped the runner-up by 30 percent.

Management became suspicious of Anna's performance. In a horse race, horses typically win by a nose or a horse length. Anna was consistently winning by the equivalent of ten horse lengths, an incredible performance. The top managers did some investigating and determined how their star operator achieved her prize-winning performance: each time Anna received a phone call from a caller with a foreign accent, she would hang up. She reasoned (correctly) that talking to someone who was struggling with English would be time-consuming and would reduce her call-handling performance. In her drive to satisfy the metrics, she was unwittingly defeating the whole purpose of the telephone hot line, which was to increase customer satisfaction.

CASE 2: KILLING THE MESSENGER. Otto Stuttgart was a district manager at a Fortune 50 company. He was a firm believer in the efficacy of management training. He was generous in offering his employees training opportunities, and he took advantage of such opportunities himself. Early in his career, he made a rule that whenever he attended a training session, he would return to work with at least one lesson that he would apply. In this way, he assured himself that he got something useful out of the training effort.

In the early 2000s, Otto attended a one-week course on total quality management (TQM). He enjoyed the course enormously. He was particularly impressed with the instructor's discussion of zero-defects programs. Otto's understanding of this concept was that organizations should constantly strive to reduce defects, no matter how low the defect level is. The ultimate goal is to have no defects.

Otto resolved to apply the zero-defects concept to his district. The only problem was that zero-defects programs were implemented in manufacturing environments, where defects in products are obvious, whereas he worked in services. Suddenly it hit him what he could do: he would implement a zero-complaints program. He could hardly wait to return to the office to launch this initiative.

The day he returned to the office, Otto announced to his staff that they would undertake a zero-complaints program. All staff members would work consciously to reduce customer complaints to zero. To give the program some teeth, individual performance evaluations would be tied in part to complaint levels.

The program was seemingly an astounding success. Within a month, complaints dried up almost completely. Otto was very pleased with the initiative. His faith in the conscious application of management training was reaffirmed.

Of course, complaints did not magically stop. Otto's employees were not about to report complaints if doing so would jeopardize their careers. Otto had resurrected the ancient practice of killing the messenger who conveyed bad news. (One can surmise that in ancient times only extremely stupid messengers actually wound up dead. The survivors would lie through their teeth.)

What his staff did was creatively redefine the concept of "complaint." Were they being dishonest? In a sense, yes; they were misrepresenting data. However, this dishonesty was forced on them when Otto tied complaints to their performance appraisals. While Otto returned to his office with the concept of zero defects, he neglected to bring home another key lesson in quality management: recognition that 85 percent of quality problems lie beyond the control of workers. They are systemic. Only upper management has the power to correct them. If this is true, then 85 percent of the complaints arising in Otto's district were associated with problems beyond the control of his employees. By themselves, they could not correct most of these problems. Realizing this, they refused to play Otto's game in the way he intended. Otto's scheme might have worked had he established a process for distinguishing system-induced complaints from those tied directly to employee actions.

Garbage In, Garbage Out

Clearly, the effective use of measures in project management requires good data. If the data are not good, the analysis of the measures will yield erroneous conclusions. We have already explored earlier in this chapter two criteria of goodness of data. One is that the data should be reliable—that is, repeated measures of the same phenomenon should give consistent results. Another is that the data should be valid—it should be demonstrated that the measures do indeed measure what they purport to measure. In particular, we should guard against biased measures that tilt our conclusions in a particular direction.

Every attempt should be made to collect reliable and valid data. This requires the establishment of clear data collection methods and procedures. It also requires constant quality checks on the data to make sure they are good.

Problems of Misspecified Models

Even when we have good measures, we may derive false conclusions from them if they are employed in models that poorly reflect reality. In statistics, this difficulty is called the *specification problem*. One common source of the specification problem is the assumption that we can predict future events by extrapolating from the past in a straight line. The technical name for this is the *assumption of linearity.* Forecasters and statisticians have traditionally assumed that the variables they deal with are linearly related because it has been convenient to do so. It has been much easier to deal with a linear relationship such as $y = mx + b$ than with relationships filled with square roots, trigonometric functions, power functions, and the like. Today, much of the problem of nonlinearity has disappeared since modern computer algorithms make it as simple to work with nonlinear relationships as linear ones.

Another variant of the specification problem is employment of the wrong variables in the model. Key variables may be left out. Irrelevant variables may be included. In both cases, the model will provide a poor reflection of reality.

CONCLUSIONS

Innumerate managers are at a disadvantage. Because they do not understand the nature of measurement, they do not know how to use measures to help them function more effectively. They also do not know how to assess whether the numbers being presented to them by others are meaningful. A common strategy they employ to deal with their innumeracy is to deny the value of measures for management. "We are dealing with people," they say, "and people are unpredictable and defy attempts to tag them with numbers." The implication is that they are humanists struggling against the exertions of technocrats to digitize humans.

The real issue is not one of humanism versus technocracy. The discussion offered in this chapter is not designed to deny people their humanity. The real issue is, do we have *effective* information on which we can make informed judgments? Is it objective? Is it replicable? Does it allow us to determine whether we are doing our jobs properly? Can it clarify accountability on the project?

As we have seen, projects contain plenty of information that meet the criteria of effectiveness. Much of this information is in the form of measures. The challenge is to collect data and present it in a usable manner. The innumerate manager can do neither.

Establishing and Maintaining a Project Support Office to Strengthen Project Management Capabilities

A s project management has assumed growing importance in the management of enterprises, managers have come to realize that project management processes need to be formalized. Without some measure of discipline and formalization, the benefits of project management are lost, swamped by the chaos that ad hoc management generates. For example, if each team in a company takes a unique approach to building work breakdown structures, employs different scheduling software, and sponsors different change control processes, the company will find itself mired in messiness.

New-style project offices first surfaced in the 1980s. Their sponsorship was driven largely by the perceived need to establish and maintain project management standards in a variety of areas (including scheduling, budgeting, and change control) so that project managers and project workers in the organization were all reading from the same song sheet. Most of these early initiatives failed, however, because in their enthusiasm to introduce standards, the project office missionaries bureaucratized the project management process and increased the burden of implementing projects. "We are in charge, and we will save the day!" they seemed to be saying. "Follow our rules, and things will go splendidly well!" Recognizing that the ukases flowing out of the project offices were making their lives more difficult, project workers were able to sabotage these initiatives and kill off the offending project offices easily.

Project offices were resurrected in the 1990s, and many carried the title "project support office" to emphasize that their mission was to help project workers do their jobs more effectively, not to make their lives more miserable. Once project workers gained trust in these initiatives and recognized that these offices made their lives easier, project support offices became wildly successful.

This chapter examines what it takes to establish and maintain successful project support offices.

TRADITIONAL PROGRAM AND PROJECT OFFICES

Traditional program and project offices have been around for decades. Major military projects are always managed through a program office. For example, the Ballistic Missile Defense Program was managed through the Ballistic Missile Defense Program Office, the F-16 fighter aircraft project was managed through the F-16 Program Office, and the U.S. Department of Energy's Superconducting Super Collider Program was managed by its own program office.

The construction industry also uses project offices. For example, the construction of a new skyscraper, airport, or water treatment plant is generally coordinated by means of a project office.

Following are the characteristics of a traditional project office:

- It is oriented toward the implementation of a single, well-defined project, such as the construction of an office building.

- Its job is to direct and oversee the project effort.

- It controls the resources that enable the project to be carried out (for example, it manages budgets and has contract authority over contractors and subcontractors).

- A substantial portion of its effort is geared toward dealing with contractors and suppliers (acquisition management).

The military program office has additional features:

- It has cradle-to-grave life cycle oversight over the project, from design to implementation to operations and maintenance.

- Because of its life cycle orientation, it exists over many years—for example, the Navy's A-6 Intruder program office was established in the early 1950s, when the Intruder was first designed, and endured through the mid-1990s, when the Intruder was decommissioned.

- Because it deals with major acquisitions, comprising multiple projects, it usually coordinates the efforts of multiple projects with a view of bringing them together to achieve ultimate program goals.

WHAT PROJECT SUPPORT OFFICES DO

The relatively new project support office is quite different from traditional project and program offices. As its title indicates, its primary job is to support the project efforts carried out by the organization, not to direct project efforts proactively. It is not charged with running projects but rather to back up project management activities throughout the organization. This means that it is not focused on a single project but rather on a range of projects being carried out within the organization.

Project support offices come in a wide variety of shapes and sizes and perform different functions. What they have in common is that they are designed to make project teams' lives easier.

In terms of size, project support offices may be minuscule, offering the part-time services of one person in one or two areas. Or they may be substantial, full-service operations, as in the case of Electronic Data Systems (EDS), with more than two hundred employees offering the organization a wide range of project management support in multiple countries.

In terms of services provided, they may do nothing more than assist the organization in establishing basic project management standards or may offer a full range of management services. Following is a description of key services that can be provided by project support offices.

Provide Administrative Support

For better or for worse, project efforts often entail substantial amounts of paperwork. Time sheets need to be filled out weekly, status reports must be submitted, schedules and budgets should be developed and maintained, and so on. To the extent that a project support office can assume a substantial portion of the administrative burden associated with doing project work, project team members will be freed to do directly productive work to achieve project goals.

The administrative support function, when carried out properly, is strongly appreciated by project team members. To see why, consider one administrative function that some project support offices provide: maintaining status sheets for project workers. Back in the old days, project workers were asked to submit regular progress reports on the work they achieved in a defined time frame—say, once a month. Typically, these reports were generated at the last minute by resentful project team members who viewed them as waste-of-time obstacles to doing their jobs. To fill them out, project workers would have to dig out old files to identify what they promised to do during the month. As they listed accomplishments on tasks, they needed to make sure that they were consistent in the nomenclature they employed. If two months earlier they promised to complete a task titled "Gather functional requirements," then in reporting progress they would need to employ this exact terminology, otherwise their progress reports would lead to confusion. Because they saw these progress reports as bureaucratic impediments, they were not likely to take them seriously. The best way to deal with them was to handle them in a perfunctory fashion. The key point was to make sure the information reported was more or less on target.

When project support offices take on the function of helping team members to fill out their status reports, they remove a great burden from the shoulders of these people. It now becomes the offices' job to be sure that pertinent tasks are included in the reports, that promised delivery dates are identified, and that the task nomenclature is consistent. They supply project team members with a filled-out form that requires project workers simply to check a number of boxes reporting status on each task. What may have been a one- or two-hour bureaucratic effort in a traditional status reporting environment now becomes a ten-minute chore.

Provide Consulting and Mentoring Services

Inexperienced workers need substantial amounts of hand-holding to carry out the work they have been asked to do. For example, almost no recent graduates from universities—even the most prestigious universities—have been given guidance on how to plan a work effort.

Planning is not a subject covered in the curricula of liberal arts programs. Engineering programs may pay lip service to planning schedules and budgets, but their planning exercises are too abstract to be useful to students. Consequently, college grads hired by companies and government agencies generally have no idea of what it takes to plan any sort of effort. They learn planning on the job.

Project support offices can supply organizations with the internal project consulting expertise they need—including expertise on the fundamentals of planning. When new teams are assembled to carry out project work, these internal consultants can work with the teams to develop preliminary plans. In doing so, they are offering just-in-time training to team members on planning basics, and they are also increasing the likelihood that the project being planned will be implemented successfully.

The project consulting services that project support offices can provide are not limited to planning services. They can address any topic: how to undertake a needs assessment, how to convert business needs into technical requirements, how to conduct an effective risk assessment, how to maneuver through the thickets of project politics, and so on.

With project mentoring, professionals in the project office can sit side by side with project workers and offer them guidance as they carry out their work on a day-by-day basis. The mentoring approach is especially effective in educating senior managers on the value and use of project management in the workplace. For example, a mentor can be assigned to work with a senior manager for one week, during which the mentor can explain how project management can be employed to improve the organization's general effectiveness and can show the senior manager how it may even help in the more efficient conduct of his or her own affairs.

Develop and Maintain Project Management Standards

A key function of many project support offices is to establish and maintain project management standards for the organization. Typically, at the time a project support office is created, many project teams carry out their efforts according to their own singular standards. As a result, the overall project management effort in the organization is characterized by chaos. To create a harmonious environment, the project support office needs to identify, establish, and maintain enterprisewide standards.

These standards apply in a variety of areas, including these:

- *Project selection standards:* What methods should be employed to prioritize project alternatives?

- *Status reporting standards:* How frequently should status reports be issued? What subjects should they cover?

- *Cost, schedule, and resource tracking standards:* What cost, schedule, and resource data should be tracked? In what format should they be presented and stored?

- *Change control standards:* What approach should be adopted to manage changes to project requirements?

- *Project closeout standards:* What steps should be taken to hand over the deliverable to clients? What documentation needs to be employed to close out the project? What kind of postimplementation review should be carried out?

- *Project software standards:* Should the organization employ a single project software product? What features should this product contain?

To a large extent, the development of standards entails the creation of forms and templates that can be used by project workers to guide them in their project efforts and to document steps that have been undertaken. The challenge is to create uniform processes without becoming excessively bureaucratic and rigid. In general, the standards should follow the principle that simple and flexible is best.

Provide Guidance on Pertinent Project Management Training

As organizations adopt project management principles and practices, they need to take steps to increase the project management competencies of their employees, customers, and contractors. To a large extent, this can be accomplished through management training. Consequently, a function that project support offices can serve is to provide their organizations with the guidance needed to promote effective project management training programs.

Following are some of the training related activities that project offices can engage in.

ESTABLISH A PROJECT MANAGEMENT TRAINING CURRICULUM. Organizational competencies in project management will not be handled effectively simply by importing a trainer who offers a three-day course on project management fundamentals. A solid training effort should focus on training in a number of areas. Courses provided through training might include the following:

- *Project management basics:* An introduction to the project management approach and its basic tools and techniques
- *Scheduling and cost control:* An in-depth treatment of the key issues and tools associated with managing time and costs on projects
- *Contracting and procurement basics:* An introduction to contracting fundamentals that will enable project workers to be more effective in managing contracted projects and in dealing with subcontractors and vendors
- *Project management soft skills:* An examination of soft skills that effective project workers should possess, including negotiation, political influence, conflict resolution, and team-building skills
- *Hands-on project management:* A practical course that enables students to gain hands-on experience dealing with the principal tools and techniques needed to manage projects effectively
- *Project risk management:* An overview of the risk management process, looking at risk identification, risk quantification, risk response planning, and risk response control
- *Project management processes at a particular organization:* A practical introduction to the organization's project management processes, including a review of the project life cycle adopted by the organization, an introduction to forms and templates, and a review of pertinent documents and procedures.

IDENTIFY TRAINING PROVIDERS. All organizations that support employee training wrestle with the question of who should supply the needed training. In view of their expertise on the practice of project management, the professionals working in the project support office should play a central role in identifying training providers. Issues that need to be addressed include the following:

- Should the training be supplied principally by internal resources or outside vendors? For a variety of practical reasons—such as lack of qualified internal resources or the desire to employ best-practice training—most organizations are opting to fill their project management training needs by using outside vendors.
- If an outside vendor is to be used, how should it be identified? Some issues that need to be resolved are course pricing, vendor willingness to customized offerings, availability of top-notch instructors, and use of in-house versus public seminars.

HELP DEVELOP COURSE MATERIAL. Increasingly, training clients insist that the management training programs offered to their employees contain a strong dose of course customization. Although general project management principles can be taught with generic off-the-shelf courses, this material should be adapted to the special circumstances the client organization faces. Typically, the customization requirement can be satisfied simply by creating short case studies that reflect the client organization's operating environment and by including material that illustrates the key features of the client's project management methodology. Clearly, professionals in the project support office should play a leading role in this customization effort.

Maintain a Stable of Project Managers

In most organizations, project managers are employees associated with specific functional responsibilities. For example, project managers who develop Internet products work in the networking department, while those who engage in facilities management work in the facilities department, and those who roll out new products report to the marketing department. In this instance, it doesn't make sense to house these people in a central project support office. If they are removed from their functional turf, they may lose touch with the people and skills associated with that turf. The governing principle, then, is let them reside where they work.

There are occasions, however, where it may make sense to house project managers in a central project support office. For example, if the project support office is "owned" by the information technology division, and this division follows a well-defined system development life cycle (SDLC) methodology that applies to all of its projects, then having all information technology project managers work out of a single project support office may be salubrious. They will be familiar with a common set of project management tools and standards. They will rub shoulders frequently with other IT project managers with whom they will be dealing on their project efforts. From a human resource development perspective, they can be formed into a cadre of professionals who follow a well-established career track. Certainly, if they are housed under a single roof, salaries, bonuses, and other forms of compensation can be allocated to the employees in a fair and consistent way.

If project managers are housed in a project support office, the office must develop solid capabilities in two areas. First, it must develop processes to serve as an employment agency of sorts. To the extent that office staff are managing a stable of project managers, they must be able to field requests for project managers who have specific abilities. This means that they must know who has what skills and when they are available for assignment. Then they must make the job assignments and follow up to be sure that the right people have been assigned to the right jobs.

Second, the project support office must develop a career development path for project managers. The office will have responsibility for the care and feeding of project managers. Following are two capabilities the project support office should have if it is going to fill this role effectively:

• *Establishment and maintenance of a performance appraisal review system.* Project managers working through the project support office will need to have their work reviewed periodically by means of a performance appraisal review system. The results of performance appraisal reviews will provide senior management with a good idea of the effectiveness of its project managers and will provide the project managers themselves with feedback on their work.

• *Establishment and maintenance of a project management career track.* Increasingly, organizations committed to developing a cadre of qualified and experienced project managers are creating a special career track for these people that will enable them to become "black belt" project managers. These initiatives are commonly implemented by project support offices. The career path has candidates pass through a number of gateways that reflect their professional advancement. For example, they may be required to take a series of courses leading to an Executive Certificate in Project Management. The next gate may be tied to passing the Project Management Institute's project management certification examination. Those who pass the PMI certification process are designated Certified Project Management Professionals (PMPs). Beyond this, as the project managers gain management experience, they may be assigned to increasingly large and complex projects.

WHERE SHOULD THE PROJECT SUPPORT OFFICE RESIDE?

Today's project support offices are located in a number of places within organizations. Because so much project activity is being driven by information technology, it should not be surprising that at the start of the twenty-first century, half of the project support offices identified in a survey reported being housed in the IT department. To some extent, this heavy weighting toward IT departments is an artifact of the Y2K problem. Toward the end of the 1990s, as organizations prepared to deal with Y2K glitches, large teams of people were assembled to handle Y2K issues, and their efforts were typically carried out under the auspices of a Y2K project support office. Nonetheless, it seems likely that in the foreseeable future, project support offices will continue to gravitate toward IT departments because the content of so much business activity today is rooted in handling information.

What is likely to occur over time is that a central project office will be established in one department, and satellite offices will be established in different business units. This configuration is pictured in Figure 16.1. It is being adopted increasingly in knowledge-based organizations in the financial, pharmaceutical, telecommunications, and IT fields. With this configuration, the role of the central project support office is to maintain uniform standards for conducting project work within the organization. For example, this office may establish a common standard for processing project change requests. It will create this standard after conferring with players in the satellite project support offices, to make sure that the emerging standards have the support of the different business units, as well as to ensure that the standards are relevant to local conditions.

There are two attractive features associated with the central-satellite configuration. One is that this configuration promotes uniform project

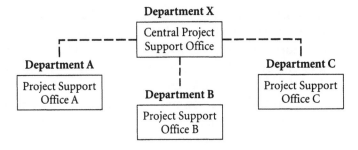

Figure 16.1. A. Typical Project Support Office Configuration.

management standards while allowing the standards to be implemented according to local requirements. This is certainly more appealing than having a single project management czar dictate standards to folks in the field without having much sense of what is happening there.

A second attractive feature of the central-satellite configuration is that it is more likely to be acceptable in a political sense than a single-office configuration. For example, in one major American financial services company, the central project support office is located in the financial controller's department. However, most projects are carried out in other departments, such as IT, equity, fixed income, and operations. Because of various turf issues, it would be unlikely that any of these departments would passively follow directives coming out of the controller's department. However, because the central-satellite configuration establishes a partnership between the central project support office and its counterparts in the other departments, it engenders an environment of cooperation.

When considering the evolution of centralized project support offices, an interesting question arises: In view of the growing role of project management in organizational operations, will project support offices ultimately become functional stovepipes, analogous to sales, finance, and IT departments? Will we soon encounter senior managers with the title "vice president of project management"? Answer: probably not. Even as the project management function becomes more important in organizations, the organizations themselves are growing more fluid and resistant to stovepipe structures. What may occur is that a chief project management officer position may be created in some organizations, to be filled by the organization's project management guru. This individual's role would not be that of a czar but rather of a visionary who would attempt to set the general direction of project management affairs within the organization.

To a certain extent, this role was originally created to help the U.S. Department of Energy (DOE) gain a handhold over its many out-of-control projects. In response to a congressional directive, the DOE established the Office of Engineering and Construction Management (OECM) in 1999, headed by a director whose job is to provide agencywide guidance on project management practices. OECM has only ten staffers trying to influence DOE projects whose value amounts to tens of billions of dollars!

STAFFING THE PROJECT SUPPORT OFFICE

In staffing a project support office, we should recognize that the typical full-service office will have a number of job classifications to fill. It will have a director, administrative support, junior project professionals, and senior project professionals. Each of these job classifications will be discussed in turn.

Director of the Project Support Office

As with the directorship of any office, the director of the project support office should have good administrative skills. One obvious area of strength should be the possession of good budgetary skills, since the director needs to gain budgetary support from senior management and then manage the budget effectively once it is provided. Other standard administrative skills include dealing with personnel matters, such as hiring staff, providing career guidance, conducting performance appraisal reviews, and establishing salary levels and bonuses; managing the paper flow typical of any bureaucratic enterprise, including submission of progress reports, checking invoices for big expense items, and supplying senior management with budget reports; and attending meetings to coordinate with other managers in the organization.

The director should have project management work experience if he or she is to gain credibility with the employees who work in the office, as well as with colleagues and senior management. This experience is also needed to enable to director to understand substantive matters that the office must deal with.

The single most important skill needed by an effective director of a project support office is the ability to communicate the office's needs and activities to senior management and colleagues, in order to gain backing for the office's efforts. To a large extent, the director is a salesperson, constantly selling the value of the project support office to the organization. More will be said about this important function later in this chapter.

Administrative Staff

A large portion of the value that the project support office provides to project workers is tied to its administrative support function. To the extent that administrative staff in the office can take care of basic scheduling, budgeting, time sheet, and related chores, they free project workers to do their jobs.

Administrative staff should have a solid grasp of today's office technology. They should be able to use spreadsheets, word processors, and graphics packages and should be able to learn to work with project-specific software, particularly scheduling software. Their formal education achievements are less important than their reliability and capacity to learn quickly on the job.

Junior Project Professionals

Junior project professionals are men and women with college degrees who are new to the project management discipline. Their job will focus primarily on carrying out project-related technical chores, such as helping project teams in the organization develop schedules and budgets and plan resource allocations. They should become proficient in the use of project management tools—a substantial portion of their value is their help in enabling project teams to create plans at the outset of the project and then to track progress once the project is under way. They will need to fill this junior role for three to five years before they are sufficiently experienced to take on a more senior role.

Senior Project Professionals

Senior project professionals should have substantial hands-on project management experience. The most senior professionals are men and women with ten to fifteen years of experience in leading projects of increasing size and complexity. These people can say, "Been there, seen it, done that." There is little they encounter on projects that they have not encountered before. Their principal contribution lies in their ability to provide project teams with periodic "sanity checks." They have a good idea of what works and what does not work. They can review a project effort and in a matter of minutes identify the project's strengths and weaknesses and can suggest steps to strengthen the project effort.

Less experienced senior professionals are men and women who have served an apprenticeship of five or more years on projects. They can play a valuable role in facilitating the planning and control efforts of less experienced project teams. Ideally, at this point in their development, they have achieved a strong mastery of key tools and techniques so that they can serve as an information source, offering project teams answers to questions regarding use of project management tools and techniques.

Senior project managers usually hold a university degree, and many even hold a master's. Increasingly, they are expected to gain project management certification from the Project Management Institute to demonstrate their mastery of the core knowledge-based competencies of project management.

SELLING THE PROJECT SUPPORT OFFICE

Establishing and maintaining an effective project support office is not an easy undertaking. A number of forces conspire against the successful implementation of the office. The project support office champions should be aware of these forces and should be prepared to deal with them. They must recognize that project support offices do not spring out of the ground magically, like an iris in April, but are the result of hard work and a good sales job. Following are some of the negative forces that project support office champions must contend with.

• *The view that the project support office is an unnecessary cost.* Back in the 1960s, when a handful of people were preaching the value of effective quality management to manufacturing organizations, one of the major obstacles they had to overcome was the sense that investment in good quality control processes would be too expensive. This led Philip Crosby (1985), an early guru of quality management, to declare that "quality is free." His point was that by reducing rework and increasing customer satisfaction, quality programs would pay for themselves quickly. He challenged opponents of the quality movement to respond to the following question: Can your organizations afford *not* to have good quality programs?

Proponents of project support offices face a similar issue. Management, which is expected to foot the bill to establish and run these offices, is concerned that they are unnecessary expenses that add little value to operations. In an era of reengineering, streamlining, and downsizing, the creation of new structures goes against the grain. Consequently, the project support office champion must be prepared to make convincing arguments to senior managers demonstrating that these offices will dramatically improve the organization's bottom-line performance.

• *Suspicion among the rank and file that project offices will make their lives more difficult.* Rank-and-file workers are justifiably suspicious of management initiatives that claim that they will make the workers' lives easier. Past experience shows that many of these initiatives do nothing but make life more difficult. Regrettably, some of the early rollouts of project offices in the 1980s confirmed the workers' jaded views. These efforts imposed tremendous paperwork burdens on project workers, as project office staff insisted that they create sophisticated schedules for their projects, fill out detailed weekly status reports, employ sophisticated time-tracking systems, and so on. Project team members resisted the heavy-handed initiatives of the project offices, with the result that these offices soon disappeared.

Today's champions of project support offices must strive to overcome the natural suspicions of project workers in the organization. They must demonstrate that the project support office will, in fact, make team members' lives easier by reducing the paperwork burden, not adding to it. Experience shows that once the rank and file see the value of project support offices, they become fervent boosters of these offices.

• *Concern that the project support office initiatives encroach on the territorial prerogatives of other offices.* If the project support office is established in the finance department, it is reasonable to expect that the managers of other departments that carry out project work will express concern about the finance department's right to "own" project management in the overall organization. Turf issues are common in organizations, and the champions of project offices should be prepared to deal with them. This matter was discussed earlier when we addressed where project support offices should be housed. As we saw, a good way to deal with turf issues is to have a central project support office housed in one department with satellite offices in other departments. The central-satellite structure is a partnering arrangement that entails a measure of power-sharing. Consequently, it can mitigate turf problems to some degree.

• *Struggling against the "fad du jour" phenomenon.* I have conducted interviews with senior managers in several companies in which I attempted to gauge their level of support for the project management initiative in their organization. In general, most of these people stated that they believed project management to be a good thing. However, a number of them issued a warning that is summarized in the following statement:

> Although today we believe that project management is worth supporting, you have to understand that we senior managers have a tendency to get caught up in the fad *du jour.* We can easily bounce from TQM to self-managed teams to 360-degree reviews to business process reengineering to project management. I suppose this means we have a limited attention span. So if the project support office initiative is going to succeed, its champions must keep the initiative continually on our radar screen. When management begins to lose interest in project management, the champions must beat the kettledrums to capture our interest. Without the sustained interest of senior management in the initiative, it will die.

The project offices that are most likely to succeed are those whose champions communicate project management developments regularly with senior management. They arrange to showcase their achievements to senior management periodically. They conduct dog-and-pony shows that demonstrate that the organization is carrying out its efforts faster, cheaper, and better since the project management initiative was implemented.

CONCLUSIONS

Increasingly, the work of enterprises is being carried out by means of projects. New product development, business process reengineering, training, installing a supply chain management system, research and development—each of these efforts is a project effort. It has reached the point where a wide range of companies in finance, manufacturing, pharmaceuticals, information technology, and other business areas have declared themselves "project-based enterprises." It is understandable, then, that they are establishing project support offices to help them execute their project efforts effectively.

Project support offices can certainly help organizations deliver project solutions faster, better, and cheaper. However, the mere establishment of a project support office will not achieve desired results automatically. Experience shows that if a project support office is to succeed, it must enable project workers to do their jobs better. The operative word is *support*. If these offices are perceived to make the lives of project workers more difficult through increased bureaucracy, they will fail. So in developing and nurturing project support offices, their champions must relentlessly strive to provide a service that people in their organizations will clamor to receive. The sign of a successful project support office is its being inundated with requests for its services from the organization's cadre of project workers.

CHAPTER SEVENTEEN

Carpe Diem
Seize the Day!

In *Dead Poets Society,* a fine motion picture released in 1989, a teacher in a private boy's school admonishes his students to follow the Latin dictum *carpe diem,* "seize the day." His point is that they should avoid being overly restricted by the old rules. Those who travel down a familiar path may have a comfortable, safe journey, but they miss seizing the astonishing opportunities that exist off the beaten path.

People working in project management today are positioned to "seize the day," to take advantage of the central role project management has taken in the management of organizations. A review of some of our most perceptive management thinkers—Charles Handy, Peter Drucker, Tom Peters, Peter Vaill, Robert Reich—shows that the capabilities they have identified as necessary to survive and thrive in today's chaotic world are the very competencies that have long been associated with effective project managers. For decades, these men and women have had to function in environments where chains of command are fragmented or nonexistent, where they have had large amounts of responsibility without commensurate authority, and where flexibility is a requirement for effective action. The project manager's world has long been governed by Murphy's Law.

The central position of project management today is largely a consequence of historical accident. So long as the world of commerce was governed by regularity and standardization, project management's position was on the periphery. This was the state of affairs from the beginnings of the Industrial Revolution in the early nineteenth century. But with the explosive intrusions of global competition that occurred in the 1980s, regularity and standardization became artifacts of a bygone age. *Customization* and *chaos* are the new watchwords.

So today's project professionals are in a position to seize the day. However, they won't be able to do this unless they redefine their roles. If they see themselves in the traditional way, as mere implementers of other people's initiatives, nothing will change. They must see themselves with new eyes. They must recognize that their skills and insights have great value in today's chaotic business climate.

They must be eager to play the role of initiator rather than reactor. For example, if their customers expect the project team to help them develop business solutions, they must be prepared to fill this new role. Certainly, when challenged to help the customer, they should not respond, "Our job is to provide technical solutions, not business solutions."

A central theme of this book has been that for project professionals to function effectively in their new roles, they must develop new skills. Traditionally, the key skills they were expected to possess lay in the areas of scheduling, budgeting, and allocating human and material resources. Basically, if they knew how to create Gantt charts, PERT/CPM networks, cumulative cost curves, and responsibility matrixes, they were judged to possess the core skills needed to fulfill their role as mere implementers.

The new project management has far more challenging skill requirements. Necessary scheduling and budgeting proficiency now extends to integrated cost and schedule control. More than ever, project professionals need to develop people skills to deal effectively with their customers, their staff, and their managers. Similarly, the new project managers should develop capabilities in the areas of risk analysis, decision making, basic financial analysis, and requirements analysis.

If today's project professionals invest in learning and mastering the new skills, they will find that their efforts pay off handsomely. However, as this book has suggested, project success depends on more than simple mastery of tools. One attitudinal holdover from traditional project management that they should keep is a can-do attitude. The traditional project management obsession with getting the job done must persist in this new era. The marriage of the results-oriented, can-do attitude and the new skills set make for a valuable project professional.

What does the future hold? Is project management simply a passing fad? Will project professionals gain recognition in their organizations for their special capabilities?

Project management assuredly is not a passing fad. As I stated at the outset of this book, humans have been carrying out sophisticated projects for millennia. There is no sign that projects will fade away. If anything, we are seeing a growth in the number of projects being undertaken. As we move away from standardization to customization, the volume of projects organizations try to manage will continue to grow explosively. Consequently, the need for men and women possessing the skills to handle projects effectively will also increase.

As project management becomes more important to organizations, we are witnessing pressures to professionalize it. Much of this pressure comes from major organizations desperately attempting to develop cadres of effective project professionals. It was in response to this pressure that the Project Management Institute initiated a project management certification examination in 1984. It started slowly, but by 1990, the number of people sitting for the exam began to grow exponentially, and by now more than 35,000 people have become certified Project Management Professionals. Interest in certification continues go grow dramatically.

A predictable side effect has accompanied the growing demand for the most capable project professionals: their salaries are climbing. I know quite a few senior project managers who are receiving compensation greater than that of their vice presidents.

What are these highly paid project managers doing to justify their generous incomes? Interestingly, many of them are operating like independent entrepreneurs running their own businesses. Many have profit-and-loss responsibilities. All are charged to work closely with their customers. Most are given impossible deadlines to achieve—and somehow they achieve them. All are practitioners of the new project management. They certainly do not see themselves as mere implementers of other people's initiatives. They have defined their roles broadly in order to serve their organizations and customers well.

The future looks bright for project management and project professionals. The individuals who will fare best in these exciting, chaotic times will be those who follow the old Latin dictum, *carpe diem*. So seize the day!

‑‑‑ References

Abernathy, W. J., Clark, K. B., and Kantrow, A. M. *Industrial Renaissance.* New York: Basic Books, 1983.

American Heritage Dictionary of the English Language. Boston: Houghton Mifflin, 1978.

Block, R. *The Politics of Projects.* New York: Yourdon Press, 1983.

Boehm, B. "Industrial Software Metrics Top Ten List." *IEEE Software,* Sept. 1987, pp. 264–271.

Bolles, R. N. *What Color Is Your Parachute? A Practical Manual for Job-Hunters and Career-Changers.* (2001 ed.) Berkeley, Calif.: Ten Speed Press, 2000.

Buss, M.D.J. "How to Rank Computer Projects." *Harvard Business Review,* 1983, *61,* 118–125.

Bylinsky, G. *The Innovation Millionaires.* New York: Scribner, 1976.

Cohen, A. R., and Bradford, D. L. *Influence Without Authority.* New York: Wiley, 1990.

Crichton, M. *The Andromeda Strain.* New York: Knopf, 1969.

Crosby, P. B. *Quality Is Free: The Art of Making Quality Certain.* New York: Dutton, 1985.

Devlin, K. *Goodbye, Descartes.* New York: Wiley, 1997.

Drucker, P. F. *Managing in Turbulent Times.* New York: HarperCollins, 1980.

Frame, J. D. *Managing Projects in Organizations: How to Make the Best Use of Time, Techniques, and People.* (2nd ed.) San Francisco: Jossey-Bass, 1995.

Frame, J. D. *Project Management Competence: Building Key Skills for Individuals, Teams, and Organizations.* San Francisco: Jossey-Bass, 1999.

Gleick, J. *Chaos: Making a New Science.* New York: Viking Penguin, 1987.

Goldratt, E. M. *Critical Chain.* Great Barrington, Mass.: North River Press, 1997.

Goldratt, E. M., and Cox, J. *The Goal: A Process of Ongoing Improvement.* (2nd ed.) Great Barrington, Mass.: North River Press, 1992.

Handy, C. B. *The Age of Unreason.* Boston: Harvard Business School Press, 1989.

Hanon, M., Cribbin, J. J., and Heiser, H. C. *Consultative Selling.* New York: American Management Association, 1970.

Herzberg, F., Mausner, B., and Snyderman, B. B. *The Motivation to Work.* (2nd ed.) New York: Wiley, 1959.

Huff, D. *How to Lie with Statistics.* New York: Norton, 1954.

Jewkes, J., Sawers, D., and Stillerman, R. *The Sources of Invention.* (2nd ed.) New York: Norton, 1969.

Johnson, S. *Who Moved My Cheese? An Amazing Way to Deal with Change in Your Work and in Your Life.* New York: Putnam, 1998.

Kanter, R. M. *Change Masters: Innovation for Productivity in the American Corporation.* New York: Simon & Schuster, 1983.

Keirsey, D., and Bates, M. *Please Understand Me: Character and Temperament Types.* Del Mar, Calif.: Prometheus Nemesis Books, 1978.

Maslow, A. H. *Motivation and Personality.* New York: HarperCollins, 1954.

McGregor, D. *The Human Side of Management.* New York: McGraw-Hill, 1960.

Nadler, D. A., Gerstein, M. S., Shaw, R. B., and Associates. *Organizational Architecture: Designs for Changing Organizations.* San Francisco: Jossey-Bass, 1992.

Newbold, R. C. *Project Management in the Fast Lane: Applying the Theory of Constraints.* Delray Beach, Fla.: St. Lucie Press, 1998.

O'Connell, P. M. "An Analysis of DOD Requirement Handling Procedures and Major Program Overruns." Unpublished doctoral dissertation, George Washington University, 1990.

Paulos, J. A. *Innumeracy.* New York: Hill & Wang, 1988.

Peters, T. J. *Thriving on Chaos.* New York: Knopf, 1987.

Peters, T. J. *Liberation Management: Necessary Disorganization for the Nanosecond Nineties.* New York: Knopf, 1992.

Petroski, H. *To Engineer Is Human: The Role of Failure in Successful Design.* New York: St. Martin's Press, 1985.

Price, D. D. *Little Science, Big Science.* New York: Columbia University Press, 1963.

Project Management Institute. *A Guide to the Project Management Body of Knowledge.* Newton Square, Pa.: Project Management Institute, 2000.

Reich, R. B. *The Work of Nations: Preparing Ourselves for 21st-Century Capitalism.* New York: Knopf, 1991.

Saaty, T. L. *Decision Making for Leaders: The Analytical Hierarchy Process for Decisions in a Complex World.* (3rd rev. ed.) San Francisco: RWS, 1999.

Senge, P. *The Fifth Discipline.* New York: Doubleday, 1990.

Solomon, J. *The Signs of Our Time.* Los Angeles: Tarcher, 1988.

Tyler, P. *Running Critical: The Silent War, Rickover, and General Dynamics.* New York: HarperCollins, 1986.

U.S. General Accounting Office. *Automated Information Systems: Schedule Delays and Cost Overruns Plague DOD Systems.* Report to the Chairman, Legislation and National Security Subcommittee, Committee on Government Operations, House of Representatives. May 1989. (GAO/IMTEC-89-36)

Vaill, P. B. *Managing as a Performing Art: New Ideas for a World of Chaotic Change.* San Francisco: Jossey-Bass, 1989.

Weber, M. *The Theory of Social and Economic Organization.* New York: Free Press, 1964.

Webster's New World Dictionary of the American Language. Cleveland: World, 1964.

Weinberg, G. M. *The Psychology of Computer Programming.* New York: Van Nostrand Reinhold, 1971.

—ᴡᴡ— Index